Managing Debt For Dummies®

What to Do (And Not to Do) When a Debt Collector Calls

Being contacted by a debt collector can be unnerving, to say the least. The following advice can help you stay calm and avoid saying anything that could create more problems. Keep it close to your phone so you can refer to it when a debt collector calls. And for more advice on dealing with a debt collector, see Chapter 9.

- **Never engage in casual conversation with a debt collector.** You may give the debt collector information that could be used against you.

- **Don't answer any questions that you don't want to answer, and *never* share personal or financial information.** Don't give a debt collector your Social Security number, the name of your bank, or your bank account number.

- **Ask the debt collector to send you a written accounting of exactly how much you owe.** Ask that the accounting itemize the original amount of the debt plus all interest, fees, and collection costs.

- **If you think that the amount the debt collector says you owe is incorrect, or if you do not agree that you owe any money, dispute it.** However, don't expect to win this argument on the phone. Put your dispute in writing and send it to the debt collector no later than 30 days after the collector contacts you for the first time.

- **If you don't have the money to pay the debt, just say so, and tell the debt collector not to call you again.** Send a certified letter making the same request as a follow-up. Your debt won't go away, but the debt collector should stop hassling you.

- **If you agree that you owe a debt, but you can't afford to pay it in a lump sum, try working out an affordable payment plan.** This process can start on the phone, but be sure to get the terms of any agreement you reach in writing before you make your first payment. Another option is to settle the debt for less than what you owe on it. Don't ever agree to pay more than you can afford!

- **If a debt collector threatens you, is verbally abusive, uses profane language, or calls you repeatedly during one day or day after day, take notes.** The debt collector is violating federal law with these actions. Write down each violation, including the date and time it happens, the name of the debt collector or debt collection agency, and the specific debt you are contacted about. If things get really bad, share your information with a consumer law attorney: You may have grounds for a lawsuit.

For Dummies: Bestselling Book Series for Beginners

Managing Debt For Dummies®

Cheat Sheet

Finding a Credit Counseling Agency

A credit counseling agency can be a godsend when you are over-whelmed with debt. However, some agencies are not all they say they are. Use any of the following resources to find a credit counseling agency you can count on:

- ✔ **The National Foundation for Credit Counseling:** www.nfcc.org or 800-388-2227.
- ✔ **The Association of Independent Consumer Credit Counseling Agencies:** www.aiccca.org or 800-450-1794.
- ✔ **U.S. Bankruptcy Trustee:** The Web site www.usdoj.gov/ust/eo/bapcpa/ccde/cc_approved lists credit counseling agencies that have been federally approved.

Preparing to Meet with a Credit Counselor

You may want to ask a credit counselor to help you negotiate concessions from your creditors. Before you meet with a credit counselor, you've got some homework to do. Arrive at your initial meeting with the following things in hand:

- ☐ **A list of all your debts.** Include the amount of your current monthly payments, the interest rate on each debt, whether a certain debt is secured or unsecured (see Chapter 4), and whether you have fallen behind on a debt (and by how much).

- ☐ **Debt-related paperwork.** This includes loan agreements, credit card statements, and any threatening notices you may have received recently from creditors.

- ☐ **Your budget.** Take a stab at figuring out how much you can realistically afford to pay on your debts, starting with the highest-priority ones. See Chapter 4 for help.

- ☐ **A list of what you want from each of your creditors.** You may need a temporary or permanent reduction in your interest rate, to make interest-only payments for a while, or a temporary or permanent reduction in the amount of your monthly payments.

- ☐ **A list of what you are willing to give up to get what you want.** Here are some ideas: You'll stop using your credit card until your debt is paid off; you'll allow the creditor to put a lien on an asset you own; you'll pay more on your debt than what you offered at the start of your negotiations (if you're certain you can afford it); or after you've made a certain number of reduced payments, you'll give the creditor a *balloon* payment — a one-time larger payment (if you're certain you'll be able to afford that payment).

Managing Debt
Debt
FOR
DUMMIES®

by John Ventura and Mary Reed

BICENTENNIAL

1807

WILEY

2007

BICENTENNIAL

Wiley Publishing, Inc.

Managing Debt For Dummies®

Published by
Wiley Publishing, Inc.
111 River St.
Hoboken, NJ 07030-5774
www.wiley.com

WILEY

About the Authors

John Ventura: John is a best-selling author and a nationally board-certified bankruptcy attorney. He is also an adjunct professor at the University of Houston Law School and the director of the Texas Consumer Complaint Center at the Law School.

As a young boy, John dreamed of becoming a Catholic priest so he could help everyday people, and he spent his high school years in a Catholic seminary. After graduating, however, John decided to achieve his dream by combining journalism with the law. Therefore, he earned an undergraduate degree in journalism and a law degree from the University of Houston Law School. Later, he and a partner established a law firm in Texas, building it into one of the most successful consumer bankruptcy firms in the state. He subsequently began a successful consumer law firm in South Texas.

Today, as Director of the Texas Consumer Complaint Center, he supervises law students as they help consumers with their legal problems. He is also a regular speaker at law conferences around the country and serves on the Bankruptcy Council for the Texas Bar Association.

John is the author of 13 books on consumer and small business legal matters, including *Law For Dummies,* 2nd edition; *The Everyday Law Kit For Dummies; Divorce For Dummies,* 2nd edition; and *Good Advice for a Bad Economy* (Berkeley Books). John has been interviewed about consumer money matters by numerous national media including CNN, NBC, NPR, Bloomberg Television & Radio, *The Wall Street Journal, USA Today, Newsweek, Kiplinger's Personal Finance, Money, Inc. Martha Stewart's Living, Bottomline, Entrepreneur,* Bankrate.com, CBSMarketWatch.com, and MSNMoney.com. In addition, his comments and advice have appeared in major newspapers around the country, and he has been a frequent guest on local radio programs.

Mary Reed: Mary Reed is a personal finance writer who has coauthored or ghostwritten numerous books on topics related to consumer money matters and legal rights. The books she has coauthored with John Ventura include *The Everyday Law Kit for Dummies, Divorce For Dummies,* and *Good Advice for a Bad Economy* (Berkeley Books). Mary has also written for the magazines *Good Housekeeping, Home Office Computing,* and *Small Business Computing,* and she has ghostwritten numerous articles that have appeared in national and local publications.

Mary is also the owner of Mary Reed Public Relations (MR•PR), an Austin, Texas-based firm that provides public relations services to a wide variety of clients, including authors, publishers, attorneys, financial planners, healthcare professionals, retailers, hotels, restaurants, and nonprofits.

Prior to starting her public relations business and writing career 20 years ago, she was vice president of marketing for a national market research firm, marketing director for a women's healthcare organization, and public relations manager for *Texas Monthly,* a national award-winning magazine. She received her MBA from Boston University and her BA from Trinity University in Washington, DC.

In her free time, Mary serves on the board of a community development corporation in her neighborhood. She also enjoys long morning bike rides, road trips with her husband, gardening, working her way through the stack of books by her bed, taking care of her six cats, and spending time with her family and many friends.

Dedication

From John: To Mary Reed, my writing partner and friend.

From Mary: To my friend Ellen, who is always there for me. Your love and affection mean more than words can say.

Authors' Acknowledgments

Thanks to Joan Friedman, the editor for this book. Despite relocating to Texas from Indiana with her family in the middle of this project and having to get her family settled before the start of school, Joan made the editing process a breeze and was a pleasure to work with. This book is a far better product because of her. A big thanks as well to Kathryn Perron, our technical reviewer, for her queries and comments.

Mary would also like to thank her husband, Rodney Root, for his constant support while she toiled away for endless hours this summer in front of her computer and for his willingness to do more than his share of the housework and errand-running so she could enjoy her down time.

Publisher's Acknowledgments

We're proud of this book; please send us your comments through our Dummies online registration form located at www.dummies.com/register/.

Some of the people who helped bring this book to market include the following:

Acquisitions, Editorial, and Media Development

Project Editor: Joan Friedman

Acquisitions Editor: Tracy Boggier

Technical Editor: Kathryn Perron, Momentive Consumer Credit Counseling Service, Inc.

Editorial Manager: Michelle Hacker

Editorial Supervisor: Carmen Krikorian

Editorial Assistant: Erin Calligan, Joe Niesen, Leeann Harney

Cartoons: Rich Tennant (www.the5thwave.com)

Composition Services

Project Coordinator: Adrienne Martinez

Layout and Graphics: Stephanie D. Jumper, Barry Offringa, Laura Pence, Alicia B. South

Anniversary Logo Design: Richard Pacifico

Proofreaders: Techbooks

Indexer: Techbooks

Publishing and Editorial for Consumer Dummies

    Diane Graves Steele, Vice President and Publisher, Consumer Dummies

    Joyce Pepple, Acquisitions Director, Consumer Dummies

    Kristin A. Cocks, Product Development Director, Consumer Dummies

    Michael Spring, Vice President and Publisher, Travel

    Kelly Regan, Editorial Director, Travel

Publishing for Technology Dummies

    Andy Cummings, Vice President and Publisher, Dummies Technology/General User

Composition Services

    Gerry Fahey, Vice President of Production Services

    Debbie Stailey, Director of Composition Services

Contents at a Glance

Table of Contents

Introduction

● ●

Call us clairvoyant: You're concerned about how much you owe to your creditors. Join the crowd! We won't even try to guess how many people are worried about their debts as we write these words. Suffice it to say the number is staggering, and it keeps on growing.

As we write, total consumer debt has skyrocketed to a whopping $2.2 trillion dollars. Data from the Federal Reserve Board shows that the annual rate of consumer debt has risen throughout this decade, driven primarily by revolving credit — mostly credit card debt. Statistics show that people in the United States now spend more than they take home; they make up the difference by drawing down their savings, using credit, or not paying all their financial obligations. These dismal facts are fueled by a variety of factors, including higher energy and healthcare costs; stagnant wages; easy access to credit; rising interest rates; inadequate savings; and poor understanding of basic money management.

Whether you picked up this book because you're drowning in debt and looking for a financial life raft or because you're just feeling uncomfortable about the amount you owe to your creditors, we're here to help. In this book, we show you how to assess the state of your finances; live on what you make; get your debts paid off as quickly as possible; and deal with high-risk debts like your mortgage, car loan, and federal taxes.

When your financial problems are behind you (which *will* happen if you put our advice into action), we prepare you for your financial future. We walk you through the credit rebuilding process and explain the basics about credit and debt and money management.

About This Book

You won't find any how-to-get-out-of-debt-overnight advice in *Managing Debt For Dummies.* We know that slow and steady wins the race. Getting out of debt takes time — months or even years, depending on how much you owe relative to your income. Despite what some ads claim, there are no shortcuts to debt reduction.

Getting out of debt may also require a lot of hard work and sacrifice. For example, for your family to meet its financial obligations without using credit, you may have to slash your spending to the bare bones and work at a second (or even a third) job.

But here's the great news: If you follow the advice in this book, your debt will diminish. Eventually, you'll have more disposable income, and you'll start to gain financial peace of mind. You'll even be able to put money away for your family's financial future and work toward such goals as buying your own home, taking a vacation, helping pay for your kids' college educations, and funding your retirement.

As you already know, getting into debt is easy. Getting out is not. In this book, we provide everything you need to meet that challenge.

Conventions Used in This Book

We've tried to make *Managing Debt For Dummies* as user friendly as possible. After all, you have enough stress in your life; you don't need a book that's tough to navigate! Here are some of the conventions we use throughout the book:

- ✔ When we introduce a new term, it appears in *italics*. We provide a definition or explanation nearby.

- ✔ We use *sidebars* (gray boxes with their own headings that are set apart from the rest of the text) to share information that isn't crucial but may be interesting to you.

- ✔ All Web addresses appear in monofont so they're easy to pick out if you need to go back and find them.

Keep in mind that when this book was printed, some Web addresses may have needed to break across two lines of text. If that happened, rest assured that we haven't put in any extra characters (such as hyphens) to indicate the break. When you use one of these Web addresses, type in exactly what you see in this book, pretending as though the line break doesn't exist.

What You're Not to Read

Of course, we think that every word in this book is essential reading. But we're not going to check up on you to make sure you're studying each chapter in depth!

You can certainly skip the sidebars if you're crunched for time, and we hope that some chapters in Part III of this book don't apply to you. (If every one of them does apply to you, you have our sympathy — your stress level must be extraordinary!)

Foolish Assumptions

We assume that because you're taking the time to read these words, you're serious about wanting to get out and stay out of debt, and you're willing to do whatever it takes to achieve that goal. That's great, because the road to financial health is not always smooth.

We also assume that you don't know very much about money management. Don't be embarrassed, and don't let that fact prevent you from taking action against your debt. Most U.S. consumers need help with basic money management and in this book, we offer exactly that.

How This Book Is Organized

We've packed this book full of information and advice to help you tackle your debts and move your finances onto sounder ground, and we've organized everything into five parts.

Part 1: Getting a Grip on Your Finances

We have three goals for this part of the book: give you an overview of what's involved in getting control of your finances and dealing with your debts; guide you through the preliminary steps in the debt management process; and help you get your game face on.

Maybe you have been determinedly uninformed about exactly how much you owe to your creditors and how that compares to your income. Maybe you haven't wanted to know how badly your debts have damaged your credit history. We help you face facts about the state of your finances.

We encourage you to take a hard look at your relationship with money and to determine whether that relationship has contributed to your debt problems. We also help you develop a can-do attitude about getting out of debt because your attitude can mean the difference between success and failure.

Part II: Going on a Debt Diet

In this part, you find the nuts and bolts of debt management. We walk you through the budget-building process and explain how to use your budget to manage your money. We suggest ways to spend less and make more, and we show you how to use a variety of debt management strategies that make it easier to keep up with your debt payments. We also show you how a credit counseling agency can help you (and how to find a good one), and we explain how to act when debt collectors come calling.

Part III: Tackling Your High-Stake Debts

In this part, we focus on specific kinds of debts, like mortgages, car loans, rent, court-ordered child support, federal taxes, and federal student loans. We tell you what's at stake when you fall behind on each type of debt, and we offer options for avoiding the negative consequences.

Part IV: Avoiding Debt Problems down the Road

Ah, here's where things get easier. In this part, we assume that most of your debt problems are in the past and, having followed the advice in this book, you're wiser about your money now. We show you how to rebuild your credit history, build your savings, set financial goals, and use credit as a tool for managing your money and building your wealth. Here's to a happier and financially healthier future!

Part V: The Part of Tens

What would a *For Dummies* book be without this part? Not a *For Dummies* book, we guess. First, we turn you on to an array of free and low-cost resources for finding out more about debt management and financial management in general. Then we help you avoid some of the more common mistakes consumers make when they owe too much money to their creditors.

Icons Used in the Book

Throughout this book, you find eye-catching icons that call your attention to especially important or helpful information. Here's what each icon indicates:

The Remember icon highlights information that's crucial. We suggest you make an effort to tuck it into your mental filing cabinet for future use.

The Tip icon alerts you to advice that can save you time, money, and legal hassles.

Make sure you read the text next to each Warning icon! If you don't, you could face some serious consequences.

Where to Go from Here

Your debt situation may be daunting, but don't be daunted by this book. What we explain here isn't tough to understand. It can be tough to implement, but that's why we help you gather your inner strength early on.

So plunge in. We suggest that you get your feet wet by starting at the very beginning of the book; in Chapter 1, we give you an overview of everything you'll find in *Managing Debt For Dummies*.

But if there's a particular type of debt keeping you awake at night, or if you're haunted by never-ending phone calls from debt collectors, jump right to the chapters that deal with those subjects. You can always back up and read earlier chapters that provide the basic tools for debt management.

Wherever you start reading, know this: If you follow the advice in our book and stay focused and disciplined, you *will* overcome your debts and emerge with a brighter financial future.

Part I

Getting a Grip on Your Finances

The 5th Wave   By Rich Tennant

"I bought a software program that should help us monitor and control our spending habits, and while I was there, I picked up a few new games, a couple of screen savers, 4 new mousepads, this nifty pullout keyboard cradle..."

In this part . . .

*O*ur goal in this book is to help you work your way out of debt, and we start that process by tackling some preliminaries. First, you need to get clear about the facts of your financial situation: Exactly how much are you spending each month relative to your household income? How much debt do you have? What do your credit report and credit score say about the state of your finances? And how do your finances stack up against the standard ratios that financial professionals use to evaluate someone's financial health?

Facing the truth about your finances is tough, and mustering the self-discipline to make necessary sacrifices is even tougher. But don't despair: In this part, we also give you lots of advice and encouragement to help you develop a get-out-of debt mindset.

Chapter 1

The Basics of Managing Too Much Debt

. . . .

In This Chapter

▶ Figuring out where you stand financially

▶ Knowing what to do when you owe too much

▶ Dealing with debt collectors

▶ Handling your most important debts

▶ Building your financial future

. . . .

Going into debt is as American as Mom's apple pie and fireworks on the Fourth of July. It's the American way! Unfortunately, if it's also *your* way, you may be so deep in debt that you live paycheck to paycheck, using credit cards and home equity loans to make ends meet and pay for unexpected expenses. Maybe you despair of ever being able to buy a home, have a comfortable retirement, or take a vacation with your kids. (Are we hitting a nerve?) You've probably just about given up on the American Dream.

Many creditors claim that consumers owe too much because they're irresponsible spenders, but recent studies tell a different story. For example, a 2006 study based on information from the Federal Reserve Board reveals that U.S. wages have been flat (after adjustments for inflation) since 2001, while the costs of such basics as housing, medical care, food, and other household essentials have increased. In other words, not all U.S. consumers are in debt because they're spendthrifts; instead, we've all taken a national pay cut.

Okay, so consumers at all income levels are being stretched to their limits — including you, which is undoubtedly why you picked up this book. But chances are that you haven't yet taken decisive action to improve your financial situation. Maybe you haven't even acknowledged the state of your finances, much less changed your lifestyle and become more careful about your spending. Even if you're well aware that you're in financial jeopardy, chances are you don't know what to do about your situation. You may be frozen by fear and confusion.

If you're trying to keep up with your financial obligations but you feel like poor Sisyphus, struggling to keep the boulder he's pushing uphill from rolling over him, you're in the right chapter. Starting here, we give you the information you need to take control of your finances and turn them around.

Taking Stock of Your Finances

You need a clear idea of the current state of your finances in order to figure out the best way to deal with your debts. Here's how you can begin to take stock of your finances (a topic we discuss in detail in Chapter 2):

- ✔ **Compare your monthly spending to your monthly income.** Prepare yourself for a shock. Most people underestimate the amount that they actually spend relative to what they earn. By doing this comparison, you may quickly realize that you're using credit to finance a lifestyle you can't afford, and you're spending your way to the poorhouse. If that's the case, you must reduce your spending to meet your financial obligations, and you may need to do a lot more than that depending on the seriousness of your financial situation.

- ✔ **Order copies of your credit histories from the three national credit-reporting agencies: Equifax, Experian, and TransUnion.** We provide the contact information in Chapter 2. Your credit history is a warts-and-all portrait of how you manage your money: to whom you owe money, how much you owe, whether you pay your debts on time, whether you are over your credit limits, and so on. Being charged higher interest rates on credit cards and loans is a direct consequence of having a lot of negative information in your credit history.

- ✔ **Find out your FICO score.** Your FICO score, which is derived from your credit history information, is another measure of your financial health. These days, many creditors make decisions about you based on this score rather than on the actual information in your credit history. See Chapter 2 for instructions on ordering this score.

We understand that things beyond your control — like bad luck and rising prices — may be partly to blame for your debt. We also know that chances are you're at least partly responsible as well. For example, you may

✔ Pay too little attention to your finances. You forget to pay your bills on time; you don't pay attention to the balance in your checking account so you bounce checks a lot; and/or you have a lot of credit accounts.

✔ Maintain high balances on your credit cards. As a consequence, you can afford to pay only the minimum due on the cards, you pay a lot in interest on your credit card debts, and all that debt has lowered your FICO score.

✔ Have little (or nothing) in savings so you have to use credit to pay for every unexpected expense.

✔ Mismanage your finances because you don't know how to manage them correctly.

The National Foundation for Credit Counseling surveyed its member credit counseling agencies in early 2006 to determine the key reasons consumers were filing for bankruptcy. The survey showed that 41 percent of consumers blamed their bankruptcy on poor money management skills; 34 percent attributed it to lost income; and 14 percent cited an increase in medical costs.

If compulsive spending is the cause of your financial problems, get help from an organization like Debtors Anonymous (www. debtorsanonymous.org) or from a mental health therapist. Compulsive spending is an addiction just like alcoholism, and you can't beat it on your own. You'll always have debt problems if you can't control your spending.

Using a Budget to Get Out of Debt

After you assess the seriousness of your financial situation, you need to prepare a plan for handling your debt, including keeping up with your creditor payments — or at least keeping up with payments to your most important creditors. One of the first things you should do is prepare a household budget (or *spending plan*, as some financial experts euphemistically call it). Whether your annual household income is $20,000 or $100,000, living on a budget is probably the single most important thing you can do to get out of debt and to avoid debt problems down the road.

A *budget* is nothing more than a written plan for how you intend to spend your money each month. It helps you

✔ Make sure that your limited dollars go toward paying your most important debts and expenses first.

✔ Avoid spending more than you make.

> ✔ Pay off your debts as quickly as you can.
>
> ✔ Build up your savings.
>
> ✔ Achieve your financial goals.

In Chapter 4, we walk you through the budget-building process from start to finish.

Reducing your spending and making more money often go hand in hand with creating a budget. We provide lots of practical suggestions for doing both in Chapter 5.

Getting out of debt usually requires that you change your spending habits. Because those changes may affect everyone in your family, if you have children (especially preteens or teens), you and your spouse or partner should invite them to help you create your household budget. They can suggest expenses to cut and things they can do to improve your family's financial situation. By involving them, your kids will be less apt to resent the effects of budget cuts on their lives. Also, you'll be giving your kids the education they need to become responsible money managers as adults.

Taking the Right Steps When You Have Too Much Debt

If you don't owe a ton of money to your creditors, living on a budget may be all that it takes for you to whittle down your debts and hold on to your assets. If you owe a lot, living on a budget is only the first step in the get-out-of-debt process. You may also need to do some or all of the following:

✔ **Cut deals with your creditors.** Ask your creditors to help you keep up with your debts by lowering your monthly payments on a temporary or permanent basis, reducing the interest rate on your debts, or letting you make interest-only payments for a limited period of time. Before you approach any of your creditors, you've got homework to do. For example, you need to

• Create a list of all your debts and the relevant information pertaining to each debt. In Chapter 6, we explain the specific information to include on your list.

• Review your budget to figure out how much you can afford to pay on your debts every month, starting with the ones that are the most important. Don't allow a creditor to pressure you into agreeing to pay more than you think you can afford.

Whenever you talk with a creditor, explain why you're calling and exactly what you're asking for. If the first person you speak with says *no* to your request, politely end the conversation and ask to speak with a manager or supervisor.

✔ **Borrow money to pay off debt.** When you get new debt in order to pay off existing debt, the process is called *consolidating debt*. We realize that going into debt to get out of debt may not sound sensible, but if it's done right, it can be a smart debt-management strategy. To do it right, however, all the following should apply when you consolidate:

- The interest rate on the new debt is lower than the rates on the debts you pay off.

- The monthly amount of the new debt is lower than the combined monthly total for all the debts you consolidate.

- The new debt has a fixed interest rate.

- You commit to not using credit again until you've paid off the new debt.

In Chapter 7, we explain the various ways to consolidate debt, including transferring credit card debt to a lower rate card and getting a bank loan. We also discuss debt consolidation offers that will do you more harm than good.

✔ **Get help from a credit counseling agency.** The advice and assistance of a credit counseling agency can be a godsend when you have a lot of debt and are struggling to take control of it. This kind of agency can especially help when you are confused about what to do or lack confidence about your ability to improve your finances on your own. As you find out in Chapter 8, a credit counseling agency can

- Help you set up a household budget.

- Evaluate a budget you have already created to suggest changes that will help you get out of debt faster, avoid the loss of assets, and so on.

- Negotiate lower payments with your creditors and put you into a debt management plan.

- Improve your money management skills.

Not all credit counseling agencies are on the up and up, so take time to choose one that is reputable. First and foremost, that means working with a nonprofit, tax-exempt agency that charges you little or nothing for its services. In Chapter 8, we offer a complete rundown of all the criteria to consider when you are choosing a credit counseling agency.

Also in Chapter 8, we warn you against mistaking a debt settlement firm for a credit counseling agency. If you're not careful, it can be an easy mistake to make because some debt settlement firms try to appear as though they are credit counseling agencies. However, there are big differences between the two. The goal of debt settlement firms is to profit off of financially stressed consumers — not help them improve their finances. They charge a lot for their services, and many of them don't deliver on their promises. Consumers who work with debt settlement firms often end up in worse financial shape than they were before.

✔ **File for bankruptcy.** When you owe too much relative to your income, your best option sometimes is to file for bankruptcy, especially if you're concerned that one of your creditors is about to take an asset that you own and don't want to lose. You can file a *Chapter 7 liquidation bankruptcy,* which wipes out most but not all of your debts, or a *Chapter 13 reorganization bankruptcy,* which gives you three to five years to pay what you owe and may also reduce the amounts of some of your debts. Throughout this book, we explain how bankruptcy can help you deal with various types of debts.

Handling Debt Collectors

Being contacted by debt collectors can be unnerving, especially if they try to pressure you into paying more than you think you can afford by calling you constantly, threatening you, and using other abusive tactics. Some debt collectors can be so difficult to deal with that you may promise them just about anything to make them leave you alone.

Realizing your rights

Debt collectors don't like taking *no* for an answer. Most of them are paid according to how much they collect, and they know from experience that pushiness pays off. They also know that most consumers are unaware of the federal Fair Debt Collection Practices Act (FDCPA), which gives them rights when debt collectors contact them and restricts what debt collectors can do to collect money. For example, the FDCPA says that you have the right to

✔ Ask a debt collector for written proof that you owe the debt he's trying to collect from you. The debt collector is obligated to comply with your request.

✔ Dispute a debt if you do not think that you owe it or if you disagree with the amount. You must put your dispute in writing and send it to the debt collector within 30 days of being contacted by the debt collector for the first time.

- ✔ Write a letter to a debt collector telling him not to contact you again about a particular debt. After the debt collector receives your letter, he cannot communicate with you again except to let you know that he'll comply with your request or to inform you of a specific action he's about to take in order to collect the money you owe.

The FDCPA also says that a debt collector cannot

- ✔ Call you before 8 a.m. or after 9 p.m. unless you indicate that it's okay.

- ✔ Contact you at work if you tell the collector that your employer doesn't want you to be called there.

- ✔ Call you constantly during a single day or call you day after day. That's harassment!

- ✔ Use profane or insulting language when talking to you.

- ✔ Threaten you with consequences that are not legal or that the debt collector has no intention of acting on.

Many states have their own debt collection laws. Sometimes those laws provide consumers with more protections from debt collectors than the federal law. Contact your state attorney general's office to find out if your state has such a law.

If a debt collector violates the law, get in contact with a consumer law attorney right away. The attorney will advise you of the actions you may want to take.

We're not suggesting that you should never deal with a debt collector. If you agree that you owe a debt, and if your finances allow, you may want to work out a plan with the debt collector for paying your debt over time, or the debt collector may agree to let you settle your debt for less than the full amount you owe.

Understanding why debt collectors behave like they do

The adage *know thy enemy* certainly applies to debt collectors. Understanding why debt collectors behave like they do helps take some of their power away and empowers you in return.

One of the main reasons debt collectors are so darn persistent (and can be quite aggressive at times) is money. Most of them are paid according to the amount of money they collect: The more they collect, the more they earn; if they collect nothing on your debt, they get nothing. Other debt collectors actually purchase your bad debt from the creditor you originally owed the money to. These collectors need to recoup the investment they've made by purchasing your past-due debt.

A second explanation for the behavior of debt collectors is one we address in the previous section: They know that most consumers don't have a clue about their legal rights related to debt collection. Debt collectors are more than willing to push the legal envelope because experience shows that a lot of consumers will pay at least a portion of what they owe if collectors harass them enough and scare them into submission.

There is a third reason for pushy collection practices as well: If the debt collector's phone calls and letters don't get you to pay your past-due debt, he has to invest additional time and money to take further action. This situation applies specifically to the collection of *unsecured* debts, like credit card debts or unpaid medical bills. When you acquire an unsecured debt, you don't have to give the creditor a *lien* on one of the assets you own (which would give the creditor an automatic right to take the asset if you didn't pay your debt). If you can't or don't pay a past-due unsecured debt, the debt collector has to sue you for the money, which costs him time and money. Then if the debt collector wins the lawsuit, he has to try to collect the money you owe by doing one of the following:

- ✔ Seizing one of your assets (assuming you have an asset that the debt collector can take)

- ✔ Having your wages garnished (if your state allows wage garnishment)

- ✔ Placing a lien on one of your assets so you can't sell it or borrow against it without paying the debt first

All three options cost the debt collector more time and money. If your debt is small, the debt collector may decide it's just not worth the effort to sue you; his time is better spent going after other consumers with debts that he thinks will be easier to collect. The same is true if you are *judgment proof,* meaning that you don't have any assets the debt collector can take or put a lien on, you are unemployed, or your state doesn't permit wage garnishment.

Paying Special Attention to High-Stake Debts

Some debts deserve special attention because the consequences of falling behind on them are especially serious. For example, depending on the type of debt, you may risk losing an important asset, being evicted, having your income tax refunds taken (or intercepted), and maybe even serving jail time. In later chapters, we give you detailed guidance regarding how to handle debts such as the following:

✔ A mortgage (see Chapter 10)

✔ A car loan (see Chapter 11)

✔ Rent or utility bills (see Chapter 12)

✔ Medical bills and court-ordered child support obligation (see Chapter 13)

✔ Federal income taxes (see Chapter 14)

✔ Federal student loans (see Chapter 15)

 Talk with a consumer law attorney as soon as you become concerned about your ability to keep up with payments on a high-stake debt. The attorney can help you figure out a way to avoid a default. If you're already in arrears and being threatened with a foreclosure, repossession, lawsuit, or some other serious legal action, run — don't walk — to the attorney's office.

Getting a Financial Education

What would you do if you had no debt? Would you buy a new house? Take a great vacation? Boost your retirement savings? We've got great news: If you follow the steps we outline in this book, you'll eventually have to answer that question for yourself because your debt will disappear and you'll have money to put toward your financial goals. Getting from here to there won't be easy, but you can do it. If you're having trouble getting yourself psyched up for the challenge, take a look at Chapter 3.

To make sure you succeed, we encourage you not only to deal with your debt head-on but also to become the smartest money manager you can be. After all, when you get to the other side of your debt problems, you never want to return.

In the sections that follow, we give your financial education a quick jump-start. To get more details, see Chapters 16 and 17.

Good debt, bad debt: What's the difference?

Considering that you have serious problems with debt, you may be surprised to hear this: We eventually want you to use credit cards and get loans again. Why on earth would we steer you back into debt when getting out of it is such hard work? Because owing money to creditors is not necessarily a bad thing.

Whether debt is good or bad depends on why you took on the debt in the first place and how you manage it — whether you make your payments on time, for example. It also depends on how much debt you have relative to your income because too much debt, even if you're able to keep up with your payments, harms your credit history and brings down your credit score (see Chapter 2).

Why debt can be a good thing

Going into debt can be a good thing in many circumstances. For example, you could go to your grave trying to save up enough money to purchase a home, so a mortgage is a wonderful thing — especially if the value of your home grows over time. Also, a home equity loan is a good financial tool when you use it to improve or maintain your home (again, with the goal of increasing its value).

A car loan is another example of good debt because most of us need a vehicle to get to and from work, and most of us can't afford to purchase a car for cash. Debt is also good when it helps you build your wealth; for example, you borrow money to purchase your home or rental property. Some debt helps you save money in the long run, like getting a loan to make your home more energy efficient so you can reduce your energy bills.

When debt isn't so good

Debt is detrimental to your finances when you run up your credit card balances in order to live beyond your means or to purchase goods and services that don't have any lasting value for you or your family. For example, restaurant meals, happy hour drinks, clothing, jewelry, and body care services don't have any lasting value, but they sure can run up your credit card balances.

Debt is also a negative thing when you have so much that you can't afford to repay it (especially when your home is at risk), when the amount you owe lowers your credit score, or when you borrow money from shady operators (like finance companies or payday loan companies) who charge high interest rates.

Distinguishing between types of credit

You may think that all credit is created equal. Lots of people think so, which is one of many reasons they run into debt problems. In this section, we brief you about various types of credit. They definitely aren't created equal, and you should get familiar with these terms so you can become a better credit consumer.

Here are the types of credit you should be familiar with:

✔ **Secured:** With this kind of credit, the creditor guarantees that it will be paid back by putting a *lien* on an asset you own. The lien entitles the creditor to take the asset if you don't live up to the terms of your credit agreement. Car loans, mortgages, and home equity loans are common types of secured credit.

✔ **Unsecured:** When your credit is unsecured, you simply give your word to the creditor that you will repay what you borrow. Credit card, medical, and utilities bills are all examples of unsecured credit.

✔ **Revolving:** If your credit is revolving, the creditor has approved you for a set amount — your *credit limit* — and you can access the credit whenever you want and as often as you want. In return, you must pay the creditor at least a minimum amount on your account's outstanding balance each month. Credit cards and home equity lines of credit are examples of revolving credit.

✔ **Installment:** With installment credit, you borrow a certain amount of money for a set period of time and you repay the money by making a series of fixed or installment payments. Examples of installment credit include mortgages, car loans, and student loans.

We give you the complete credit rundown (not runaround!) in Chapter 16.

Seeing yourself through a creditor's eyes

To be a savvy consumer, you also need to know the criteria that creditors use to evaluate you when you apply for new or additional credit. Although creditors may take other factors into account, following are the three biggies:

✔ **Your character:** Does your credit history show that you've got a history of repaying your debts?

✔ **Your financial capacity:** Can you afford to repay the money you want to borrow?

✔ **Your collateral:** If you have a poor credit history, or if you are asking to borrow a lot of money, creditors want to know whether you have assets that you can use to secure your debt or guarantee payment on it.

These criteria not only determine whether a creditor will approve or deny credit; they also impact how much credit you're given, what your interest rate is, and what other terms of credit apply. See Chapter 16 for details.

Building a better credit history

Right now, when you're smothered by debt, you may not be able to think about improving your credit history — you've got too many other immediate concerns. But tuck this topic into the back of your mind because when you've had money troubles, rebuilding your credit history should be one of your first goals. Having a positive credit history is essential to getting new credit with attractive terms. (And as we explain in the section "Good debt, bad debt: What's the difference?", you do want to have access to credit again down the road.)

The credit rebuilding process, which we walk you through in Chapter 16, is quite simple: You get small amounts of new credit and repay the debt on time. For example, you get a MasterCard or Visa card, use it to purchase some goods or services you need, and pay off your card balance according to your agreement with the card issuer. You should also borrow a small amount of money from a bank and pay off the loan according to the terms of your agreement with the lender.

As you do these things, you add new positive information to your credit history. Meanwhile, the negative information in your credit history gradually begins to disappear because, with a few exceptions, most damaging credit record information can be reported for only seven years and six months. As time passes, your credit history will gradually contain more positive than negative information, assuming that you manage your finances responsibly.

Why is rebuilding your credit history so crucial? First, if you have a negative credit report, you won't qualify for a credit card with a low interest rate, and you'll have trouble borrowing a significant amount of money from a bank. Here are some other potential consequences of a negative credit history:

✔ Potential employers who review your credit record as part of the job application process may not hire you. You could also be denied a promotion with your current employer if it checks your credit report as part of the process.

✔ Life insurance companies may penalize you by charging you a higher premium or not selling you as much insurance as you would like.

    ✔ Landlords may not want to rent to you.

    ✔ You may not be able to get a security clearance or certain types of professional licenses.

Avoid companies that promise to rebuild your credit or promise to *presto chango* make all the negatives in your credit history disappear. Not only are you wasting your money, but (depending on the tactics a credit repair firm uses) you also may violate federal law if you do what the firm tells you to do. See Chapter 16 for details.

Using other financial management basics

As you know all too well, life is full of twists and turns. You may initiate some of these changes, but others come at you with no warning. Either way, having a good handle on the basics of money management helps you keep your finances on track and cope with the inevitable bumps in the road.

Here are some of the financial basics you should have under your belt (see Chapter 16 for details):

    ✔ **Setting and achieving your financial goals.** The problem: There's a gap between what you'd like to achieve with your money and the actual money you've got available. The solution: Set (and work methodically toward) financial goals.

    Goal setting involves deciding what you want to do with your money, setting realistic time frames for achieving each goal, and deciding how you'll accomplish them. You may decide to work toward achieving several goals at the same time, or you may focus all your efforts on attaining one very important and relatively costly goal, like owning your own home.

    ✔ **Building a financial safety net.** As you start your financial recovery, one of your first goals should be growing the balance in your savings account. Having money in savings means that you can pay cash instead of going into debt for expenses such as car repairs and home maintenance. The money in your savings account can also help you weather a job loss. Financial experts advise that you stash away a minimum of 10 percent of your take-home pay every month.

    ✔ **Using a budget.** Even as your finances improve, don't throw away your budget! As we explain in Chapter 4, there is no better money management tool than a budget. Even if you're so successful at conquering your debt that you end up with lots of disposable income, we want you to continue to use a budget to plan your spending and monitor what you actually do with your money each month.

You're far more likely to achieve the financial goals you set for yourself if you build them into your budget than if you just wing it.

✔ **Being a responsible money manager.** As your finances improve, don't get sloppy about the way you manage your money. If you do, you could end up right back where you are today as you're reading these words. Avoid backsliding by setting financial goals, having enough money in savings, and living on a budget. Also, make these truisms part of your daily life:

- Whenever possible, pay with cash, not credit.

- Pay your bills on time.

- Don't run up your credit card balances.

- Don't treat your home equity like it's a piggy bank.

✔ **Becoming a lifelong money learner.** The financial management guidance we provide in this book is really only the tip of the iceberg. There is a lot more to uncover, and fortunately, you've got access to countless resources for additional education — books, magazines, newspapers, the Web, classes at your local college, and so on. For a sampling of the possibilities, see Chapter 18.

Being smart with your money requires a lifelong commitment because the laws that pertain to credit and debt change over time, as do laws that apply to other aspects of money management, such as taxes and investments. Also, as you age, you'll have different financial needs and a different relationship with your money. For example, even if you aren't thinking about retirement today, we promise you will someday!

✔ **Relying on professional advice and assistance.** No matter how much you learn about money management, you're never going to know as much as financial professionals like CPAs, financial planners, insurance agents and brokers, and estate-planning attorneys. At times, you're going to need the advice and assistance these pros can give. For example, they can help you avoid paying too much in taxes, get your retirement planning on track, save for your child's college education, purchase the appropriate types and amounts of insurance, avoid costly money mistakes, and tackle estate planning (Your *estate* is simply all the assets you own, regardless of their value.)

In Chapter 17, we explain how each type of financial pro can help you, and we highlight various resources you can use to identify the specific advisors you need on your financial team.

Chapter 2

Facing Financial Facts

. . . .

. . . .

*Y*ou've bought our book, so we assume that means you're at least a little worried, maybe *really* worried, about your debts, and you're not sure what to do about them. We seriously doubt that you're reading this book just for the fun of it!

Here's something else we assume: You probably don't have a good handle on the true state of your finances. After all, it's human nature to try to avoid bad news.

We understand. Facing financial facts can be unsettling and even scary. Also, when you know the state of your finances, you probably can't ignore the fact that improving your financial situation requires changing your lifestyle and making some big sacrifices.

But no matter how scary it is, confronting the reality of your financial situation is essential. You have to take that first step before you can create an effective plan of action for dealing with your debts. Unless you know where you are, it's hard to know where you need to go. And until you come face to face with the facts of your finances, you may find it impossible to develop the resolve and self-discipline you need to implement your plan of action.

In this chapter, we guide you through a series of financial fact-finding exercises. They include answering some questions about your money situation and how it's affecting your life, evaluating your relationship with money, checking out your credit history information, ordering your FICO credit score, and comparing your family's spending to your household income.

The more bad news you get as you complete these exercises, the more critical it is that you get serious about dealing with your debts. The sooner you do, the quicker and easier it will be to improve your finances and the less likely that your creditors will take some of your assets or that you'll have to file for bankruptcy. So let's get going!

Answering Some Questions

You'll get a general sense of the severity of your debt problem by honestly answering the following questions. The more often you answer 'yes," the more you have cause for concern.

- ✔ Are you clueless about how much money you owe to your creditors?

- ✔ Over time, is a growing percentage of your household income going toward paying your debts?

- ✔ Do you ever pay your bills late because you don't have enough money?

- ✔ Have you stopped paying some of your debts?

- ✔ Are you paying only the minimum due on some of your credit cards because you can't afford to pay more?

- ✔ Are you using credit and/or credit card cash advances to help pay debts and/or your basic living expenses, like groceries, rent, utilities, and so on?

- ✔ Have you maxed out any of your credit cards, or have any of your cards been cancelled for nonpayment?

- ✔ Do you have little or nothing in savings?

- ✔ Have you borrowed money from friends or relatives to pay your bills?

- ✔ Have debt collectors begun calling you, and/or are you receiving threatening notices from some of your creditors?

- ✔ Are you having a hard time concentrating at work because you are worried about money?

- ✔ Are you losing sleep because of your finances?

- ✔ Have you and your spouse or partner begun fighting about money?

✔ Are you drinking more or using illegal drugs in order to try to cope with your money worries?

✔ Are you an overspender? Answering the 15 questions at the Debtors Anonymous Web site can help you decide. According to the site, most compulsive spenders answer *yes* to at least 8 of the 15 questions. Go to www.debtorsanonymous.org and click on "Take a Debt Quiz."

Evaluating Your Relationship with Money

Some serious soul-searching is in order if you're worried about how much you owe to your creditors. If you are really honest with yourself, you may conclude that *you* are the reason you've got a debt problem. Here are two good books that can help you honestly evaluate your relationship with money and change the way you think about it:

✔ *Your Money or Your Life: Transforming Your Relationship with Money and Achieving Financial Independence* (Penguin) by Joe Dominguez and Vicki Robin. This personal finance classic helps you evaluate the role that money plays in your life, reorder your priorities, and live on what you make.

✔ *The Financial Wisdom of Ebenezer Scrooge: 5 Principles to Transform Your Relationship with Money* by Ted Klontz, Rick Kahler, and Brad Klontz (Hci Publishing). This book combines quotes from Charles Dickens's *A Christmas Carol,* real stories of people with money problems, and the authors' own advice to help you figure out how your attitudes about money affect your life and to help you change destructive patterns.

Equating stuff with success

You may have the misconception that you are what you buy, which means the more you spend, the more successful and important you are. It's easy to develop that mindset because we are bombarded with messages that equate money and stuff with success. How often do you see ads promoting frugality, saving, or self-denial?

If you're hanging with a fast set and struggling to keep up, it may be time to reevaluate your friendships. Trying to keep up with the Joneses may be driving you into the poor house.

Recognizing emotional spending

Maybe you spend money for emotional reasons. For example, think about what you do when you feel sad or disappointed, or when you want to celebrate a success. Do you head to the mall or click on your favorite retail Web site? Do you treat yourself to an expensive meal or enjoy a weekend getaway even though you really can't afford it?

If this describes your behavior, you need to get a handle on why you're overspending. Meet with a mental health professional; you may qualify for help from a low-cost/no-cost clinic in your area. Or get involved with Debtors Anonymous (DA). DA uses the time-tested methods of Alcoholics Anonymous to help people understand why they spend and to gain control over their spending. To find a DA chapter in your area, go to www.debtorsanonymous.org, or call 781-453-2743.

Living for the moment

Maybe your problem is that you live for today and don't think about tomorrow. In some ways, living in the moment is great, but not if you turn a blind eye toward your future. How do you know if you've got this attitude toward money? You probably

- ✔ Use credit too much.
- ✔ Don't try to pay off your credit balances as quickly as possible, using the rationale that there will be plenty of time to do that later.
- ✔ Save little, if anything.
- ✔ Rarely if ever take time to balance your checkbook and check out your credit reports and credit score, much less develop and use a household budget.

These money attitudes are self-destructive, and they do catch up with you eventually. Since you're reading this book, they probably already have.

Checking Out Your Credit Reports

There are three national credit reporting companies: Equifax, Experian, and TransUnion. Reviewing the information in your credit report from each is an excellent way to get a clear picture of how you fare financially.

Getting copies of your credit reports

For a comprehensive picture of your creditworthiness, order a copy of your credit report from each of the national credit reporting agencies, not just from one. Each report may contain slightly different information about you, in part because all creditors do not necessarily report all consumer account payment information to each of the three agencies.

You are entitled to one free copy of each of your credit reports every 12 months. To order your free reports, go to www.annual creditreport.com, or call 877-FACT-ACT.

If you've already obtained copies of your free credit reports during a particular 12-month period, you must pay a fee to order additional copies. In most states, the cost will be $10 per report. (Some states also charge a sales tax.) However, depending on your state, you may be entitled to pay less for additional copies of your credit reports. Call your state attorney general's office to find out.

Also, you are always entitled to a free credit report if

- ✔ You are unemployed and intend to apply for a job within the next 60 days.
- ✔ You are receiving public welfare assistance.
- ✔ You believe that you have been the victim of identity theft.
- ✔ You have been denied credit, employment, insurance, or a place to rent within the past 60 days because of information in your credit report.

To order additional copies of your credit reports after you've obtained your free annual credit reports, you must contact each of the three credit reporting agencies individually. You can order the copies via the mail, by phone, or online. Here's the ordering information you need:

- ✔ **Equifax:** www.equifax.com; 800-685-1111; Disclosure Department, P.O. Box 740241, Atlanta, GA 30374
- ✔ **Experian:** www.experian.com; 888-397-3742; P.O. Box 2104, Allen, Texas 75013
- ✔ **TransUnion:** www.transunion.com; 800-888-4213; P.O. Box 1000, Chester, PA 19022

If you order additional copies by mail, put your request in a letter that includes the following information, and be sure to sign your letter:

- ✔ Your full name (including Jr., Sr., III, and so on)
- ✔ Your Social Security number
- ✔ Your date of birth
- ✔ Your current address and previous addresses for the past five years
- ✔ Your phone number, including area code
- ✔ The name of your current employer

Knowing why your reports matter

The credit report you get contains the very same information that your current creditors and potential future creditors review to make decisions about you. The more negative information that is contained in your credit histories (such as past-due accounts, accounts in collection, accounts that your creditors have charged off as uncollectible, tax liens, and so on), the worse your finances are.

Your existing creditors may use the information to decide if they will raise the interest rates you are paying, lower your credit limits, or even cancel your credit. And whenever you apply for new credit, the creditors review your credit record information to decide whether to approve your application, how much credit to give to you, the interest rate you must pay, and so on.

Many insurance companies, landlords, and employers also review your credit record information to make decisions about you. If they find a lot of negative information, insurance companies may not agree to insure you or may charge you higher than normal premiums; landlords may refuse to rent to you; and employers may not want to hire you or to give you the promotion you applied for.

Most negative information remains in your credit reports for seven years and six months. A Chapter 7 liquidation bankruptcy and a Chapter 13 reorganization of debt will linger for ten years. A tax lien will stick around until you pay it.

For more detailed information about credit reporting, including advice on understanding your credit reports and correcting problems in them, pick up a copy of *Credit Repair Kit For Dummies* by Steve Bucci (Wiley).

Finding Out Your FICO score

A growing number of creditors, as well as insurance companies, employers, and landlords, use your credit score together with (or rather than) your credit history to make decisions about you. Your credit score is a numeric representation of your credit-worthiness, and the number is derived from your credit history information. Like your credit history, the score is a snapshot of how you've managed credit in the past, and it is generally considered to be an indicator of how well you are likely to manage credit in the future.

There are a variety of different credit scores. For example, Equifax, Experian, and TransUnion have each developed their own credit scores. (Each credit-reporting agency sells its credit score on its own Web site.) But the FICO score has become the industry standard. You can order your FICO score by going to www.myfico.com.

Your FICO score will range from 300 to 850. The higher your score, the better: A score of at least 720 is considered to be very good.

If your score is well below 720, you may still qualify for credit from some creditors, but you'll be charged a higher interest rate, and you may not qualify for as much credit as you would like. Likewise, insurance companies may be willing to sell you insurance, but you'll probably pay extra for the coverage, and you may not be able to purchase as much insurance as you would like. And when you have a low FICO score, some landlords will not rent to you, and you may not qualify for certain kinds of jobs, especially those that involve handling money.

You can raise your FICO score by improving the state of your finances. For example, your credit score will go up if you

✔ Pay down your account balances.

✔ Begin paying your debts on time.

✔ Build up your savings.

✔ Minimize the amount of credit you apply for.

✔ Correct problems in your credit histories.

Comparing Your Spending to Your Income

Now comes the *real* measure of the state of your finances: Figuring out how your total spending compares to your total household income. You may be in for a shock. Are you ready?

Gathering the necessary materials

To complete this exercise, you need a pad of paper, a pen or pencil, and a calculator. You also need the following financial information:

- ✔ Check registers
- ✔ Bank statements
- ✔ Receipts for major purchases not made with a credit card
- ✔ Credit card account statements
- ✔ Other expense records for the past 12 months

You also need records of your income for the past 12 months, such as pay stubs and deposit slips or direct deposit information. If you're self-employed, you need your business records.

Your spouse or partner should gather up the same information because the goal of this exercise is to give you as complete a picture as possible of how your *household* spending compares to your *household* income.

Categorizing your expenses

Create a worksheet modeled after the one at the end of this chapter. Doing so will help you organize your spending and income information and make sure that you don't overlook anything. (This worksheet will also come in handy if you read Chapter 4, where we help you build a budget.)

The worksheet divides your spending into three categories:

- ✔ **Fixed expenses:** These are expenses that stay the same from month to month. Examples include your rent or mortgage, car loan, home equity loan, and insurance.

✔ **Variable expenses:** These types of expenses tend to vary from month to month. Examples include groceries, gas, utilities, restaurant meals, movies, CDs, books, and so on.

✔ **Periodic expenses:** These kinds of expenses may be fixed or variable. The difference is that you pay them just once in a while, such as quarterly, every six months, or annually. Tuition, some insurance premiums, property taxes, and dues are common examples of periodic expenses.

Some of the expenses listed as *fixed* spending on the worksheet may actually be *periodic* expenses for you. For example, instead of paying your auto insurance every month, you may pay it every quarter.

After you've calculated total annual amounts for each of your debts and for all your living expenses, transfer those dollar amounts to the appropriate lines on your worksheet.

Figuring out the fritter factor

It's easy to fritter money away: a latte here, a happy hour drink or two there, lunch out with the girls, some new clothes. Before you know it, it's the end of the month and you don't have any money left in your checking account. Where did it all go? Most likely, you unconsciously frittered it away on unnecessary, miscellaneous items. Each purchase may not have cost much, but together over a month's time, they add up to a significant amount.

For example, let's assume that every workday you spend $3 on a latte. In a month, you spend $60, and in a year that tiny daily purchase adds up to $720! If you also spend $2.50 per day for a bagel or pastry to go with the latte, you're spending $110 each month and more than $1,300 per year!

To help you get a handle on how much you fritter away, for one month we want you to write down *everything* you purchase with cash, a debit card, or a credit card. Your spouse or partner should do the same. Carry a small notebook with you whenever you leave the house so you can record every expenditure right away instead of trying to remember it later.

After the month is up, add up everything you spent on nonessential items. We bet you'll be surprised to see how much it amounts to.

Multiply this number by 12, and put that number in your worksheet under "Other" in the "Variable Spending" section.

Totaling spending and earnings

Add up the numbers in each of the three spending categories to get a subtotal for each category. Then add up the subtotals. The final number represents the amount you are currently spending each year.

Next, add up all the income you received during the same 12-month period. Take into account not just your net household income (which is your *take-home pay:* your gross income minus all deductions), but also any other income you or your spouse or partner may receive: government benefits, investments, royalties, child support or spousal support, income from a family business, and so on. Record that total on your worksheet too.

If you are entitled to receive child support and/or spousal support but the payments rarely come, don't include those amounts when you calculate a total annual income number for your household. If it's unreliable income, you can't count on it to help cover your spending.

Calculating your financial bottom line

After you have a total annual income amount and a total annual spending amount, subtract your spending total from your income total.

If the final number you calculate is negative, that means the amount you are spending is more than your annual household income. You may be financing your lifestyle by using credit cards and cash advances, and/or you may be falling behind on some of your obligations. Furthermore, you may not be paying some of your bills at all, which means that if you add the amount of those bills into your calculations, you have an even bigger deficit.

If you ended up with a positive number, your finances may be in better shape than you think. Or not. If the number is small, you may be just barely staying ahead. And if your bottom line is positive only because you're paying just the minimum due on your credit cards each month or because you've stopped paying some of your debts, you have no cause for celebration. If this describes your situation, you are treading water at best, and a financial setback like a job loss or an expensive illness could be financially devastating.

Annual Income and Spending Worksheet

Annual Income

Your household take-home pay	$_____
Child support income	$_____
Alimony income	$_____
Other income (specify the source)	$_____
Other income (specify the source)	$_____
Other income (specify the source)	$_____
Total Annual Income	$_____

Annual Spending

Fixed Spending

Rent	$_____
Mortgage	$_____
Home equity loan	$_____
Condo or homeowners' association fee	$_____
Car payment	$_____
Other loans	$_____
Homeowner's insurance	$_____
Renter's insurance	$_____
Health insurance	$_____
Auto insurance	$_____
Life insurance	$_____
Other insurance	$_____
Childcare	$_____
Dues and fees	$_____
Cable/satellite service	$_____
Internet access	$_____
Child support obligation	$_____

Alimony obligation $_____

Other fixed expenses (specify type) $_____

Other fixed expenses (specify type) $_____

Other fixed expenses (specify type) $_____

Other fixed expenses (specify type) $_____

Total Annual Fixed Spending $_____

Variable Spending

Groceries $_____

Cigarettes $_____

Alcohol $_____

Utilities $_____

Cellphone $_____

Gas for car $_____

Public transportation $_____

Tolls and parking $_____

Newspapers, books, and magazines $_____

Allowances $_____

After-school activities for kids $_____

Babysitting $_____

Entertainment $_____

Restaurant meals $_____

Personal care products $_____

Clothing $_____

Body care (haircuts, manicures, massages) $_____

Laundry and dry cleaning $_____

Out-of-pocket medical expenses $_____

Lawn care $_____

Home repair and maintenance $_____

Other (specify type) $_____

Other (specify type) $_____

Other (specify type) $_____

Other (specify type) $_____

Total Annual Variable Spending $_____

Periodic Spending

Insurance $_____

Auto registration and inspection $_____

Subscriptions $_____

Charitable donations $_____

Tuition $_____

Dues and fees $_____

Income taxes $_____

Property taxes $_____

Other (specify type) $_____

Other (specify type) $_____

Other (specify type) $_____

Other (specify type) $_____

Total Annual Periodic Spending $_____

Total Annual Spending $_____

Total Annual Income $_____

minus -

Total Annual Spending $_____

equals =

Your Bottom Line $_____

Chapter 3

Adopting an Attitude for Success

In This Chapter

▶ Thinking positively

▶ Dealing with disappointments

▶ Making your family part of the solution

*G*etting out of debt can be no fun! We're the first to admit it because we've been there. Like countless other people, we've had our share of money troubles over the years, so we understand what a drag it is to pinch pennies, give up the things you enjoy, and work harder than ever. We've also counseled people whose finances were in such bad shape that getting out of debt meant having to take other steps like consolidating their debts, negotiating with their creditors, and even giving up some of their assets.

It can be daunting to owe a bundle to your creditors and to be faced with the change and sacrifices that are necessary to turn your finances around. Success may require every ounce of determination and self-discipline you can muster. It also requires that you be able to maintain a can-do attitude — a get-out-of-debt attitude — over a sustained period of time because your finances are probably going to improve gradually, not overnight.

In this chapter, we help you develop the right thinking for the challenges ahead. We tell you how to overcome self-doubt and set your mind to the job, and we provide advice and encouragement for staying the course despite any setbacks and disappointments you may encounter along the road to financial health. We also offer suggestions for alleviating the stress you may experience as a result of your get-out of-debt efforts. In addition, we explain the value of involving your family in those efforts. We provide specific advice for keeping the lines of communication open between you and your spouse or partner and for helping your kids cope.

Believing in Yourself

A positive, *I-can-get-out-of-debt* attitude is key to turning your finances around. You have to believe that you've got what it takes. Here are some proven strategies for helping you believe in yourself and set your resolve:

- ✔ **Draw strength from tough challenges you've faced in the past.** Maybe someone in your family had a serious illness, you went through a divorce, a close relative or friend died, or you experienced a major disappointment in your career. Think about what you did to get through those tough times. Use the memories to remind yourself of your strengths and abilities.

- ✔ **If you believe that you're largely responsible for your family's financial problems, don't beat yourself up about what you did or didn't do.** You can't change what happened, and letting feelings of self-recrimination and guilt bog you down makes it a lot harder to do what you need to do now. Benefit from your mistakes and move on. When negative thoughts come into your head, try to let them go.

A negative attitude can be contagious. If you act bummed out all the time about your family's financial situation, your bad attitude is likely to spread to everyone else in your household. Don't forget that your kids are observing how you behave in the face of adversity, so set a good example.

- ✔ **Remember that you're not the only person who has ever experienced financial problems.** Millions of people have been where you are and have had to do what you must now do to get out of debt. If they can do it, so can you!

- ✔ **Get inspired by reading a book or watching a TV documentary about someone who had to overcome something difficult.** These types of stories are plentiful, but if you need some suggestions, consider FDR, Nelson Mandela, Helen Keller, or Stephen Hawking.

- ✔ **Motivate yourself by visualizing your future.** Close your eyes and think about what life will be like when you don't have a lot of debt, you're not stressed out about money all the time, you've got a comfortable balance in your savings account, and you and your family can afford a few extras.

- ✔ **Don't stay silent about your money troubles.** You don't need to shout it from the rooftops, but let your close friends and family members know that you are going through some financially tough times, even if you have to swallow your pride and admit some mistakes. You may need their support and encouragement. If you've kept your financial problems a secret until now, telling people about them can take a huge load off your shoulders. And you just may discover that your friends or relatives have been in similar situations.

If some of your friends or family members are experiencing money problems, create your own support group. Get together regularly to share ideas about getting out of debt, to give one another encouragement, and to celebrate your successes.

✔ **Boost your self-confidence by getting smarter about money.** Enroll in a basic personal finance class; read a good book on the subject, like *Personal Finance For Dummies,* 4th Edition, by Eric Tyson, MBA (Wiley); or make regular visits to personal finance Web sites like www.bankrate.com for practical information about all aspects of everyday money management.

✔ **Be realistic about how long getting out of debt will take.** Don't expect to pay off your high-interest debts, build your savings account, and have extra money in your pocket by next week. Depending on the specifics of your finances, tackling your debt could take months or years. As long as you're serious about dealing with your debts, you'll see gradual improvement in your finances, but there's no quick fix for serious money problems.

✔ **Rethink your definition of success.** It's easy to get caught up in the idea that success means spending a lot of money. After all, the more stuff you have, the happier you'll be, right? That's certainly what credit card companies and advertisers want you to believe! But there are other ways to define success: being a good parent, spouse, and friend; helping the less fortunate; living an ethical life; making a difference in your community; and so on. Money can't buy any of these things, yet all of them can bring you profound and lasting happiness.

✔ **Stop making excuses.** Maybe you hear yourself saying, "Yes, but I don't have time to find cheaper insurance." "Yes, but living on a budget is too much work." Yes, but I can't earn more money right now." You *can* make the necessary changes in your life. You *can't* afford to make excuses.

Handling Setbacks

When you begin down the path toward financial health, you may get off course occasionally. If you do, don't beat yourself up. Instead, refocus, steel your resolve to do better from now on, and move forward.

Okay, that's great advice, but is it realistic? Negative thinking can creep up on any of us, making it seem impossible to move forward. Maybe you're tired of living on a budget, having to say no to your kids, and working all the time. Maybe you've been hit with a financial setback like a creditor who refuses to negotiate with you or the loss of an asset you wanted to hold on to. Of course you're going to feel blue once in a while. What can you do about it? Lots.

- ✔ **Celebrate each get-out-of-debt success.** At a minimum, take time to acknowledge what you've achieved. Maybe you got one of your creditors to agree to lower the interest you are paying, or you landed a part-time job that will allow you to pay off your debts faster. Celebrating your successes, no matter how small, can help motivate you to keep moving forward.

- ✔ **Stay active.** Exercise is a great way to get rid of stress, frustration, and negative thoughts. So when you're feeling down, don't plop yourself in front of the TV. Go for a run or walk, take a bike ride, swim, or play your favorite sport.

- ✔ **Find things to laugh about.** Rent a funny movie, spend time with a witty friend, watch your favorite sitcom, read the funny papers, or check out a jokes and humor Web site like the one at http://swcbc.org/humor. A good belly laugh is therapeutic.

- ✔ **Do something fun.** There are plenty of ways to have fun on the cheap. Read a good book, play board games, do puzzles with your kids, go for hikes, dig in the garden, invite friends over for a potluck meal, rent a movie, enjoy your local park, visit a museum, and so on.

- ✔ **Count your blessings.** Draw strength from the good things in your life. Volunteering (maybe at a food bank or homeless shelter) is an excellent way to get rid of a "poor me" attitude and to keep your situation in perspective.

- ✔ **Accept what you can't change.** If your financial problems are the result of things you had no control over (maybe you lost your job in a downsizing or had a bad accident that landed you in the hospital), railing against your fate is a waste of time. Accept what happened and move on. Say the Serenity Prayer used by Alcoholics Anonymous and other self-help organizations: "God grant me the serenity to accept the things I cannot change, the courage to change the things I can, and the wisdom to know the difference."

- ✔ **Find peace through prayer or meditation.** Whether it's a church or synagogue, your house, or the beach, find a quiet place where you can recharge your spirit regularly. Use prayer or meditation to detach yourself from the negatives going on in your life. Tell yourself, "All this will pass." And it will, eventually.

Signs of depression

Depression can be a debilitating disease, but in most cases it's also very treatable. If, after reading the following list of symptoms, you suspect that you may be depressed, schedule an appointment with a mental health therapist right away. Keep in mind that you don't have to have all these symptoms to be diagnosed as depressed.

The signs of depression include

✔ Feeling sad all the time.

✔ Feeling worthless, hopeless, and/or guilty for no rational reason.

✔ Constant anxiety and/or irritability.

✔ Lethargy.

✔ Loss of interest in the activities you used to enjoy.

✔ A change in your sleep patterns: You want to sleep all the time, you are having trouble falling asleep, or you're not getting a full night's sleep.

✔ Difficulty concentrating and making decisions.

✔ A lot of headaches or stomachaches.

✔ Loss of interest in eating or a need to overeat.

✔ Using alcohol and/or illegal drugs to avoid reality.

✔ Constantly thinking about death or even suicide. If you have these thoughts, get help immediately. The crisis hotline of the National Strategy for Suicide Prevention is a good resource: Call 800-273-8255. It will connect you immediately to someone with your local suicide crisis center who can help you deal with your feelings.

If you're experiencing more than the occasional blues — if you can't shake your negative feelings — you may be depressed. Depression will sap your energy and make it difficult, if not impossible, to move forward (see the "Signs of depression" sidebar). Get help by scheduling an appointment with a mental health professional. We can hear you saying, "But I can't afford that!" Your local chapter of the Mental Health Association is a good resource for finding the help you need at an affordable price. To locate the chapter nearest you, go to www.nmha.org/infoctr/FAQs/treatment.cfm. This site also provides contact information for other mental health resources you or someone in your family may need.

Asking for Help

You may find that you need more than pure willpower and resolve (coupled with the information in a good book like this) to help you handle your debt problems. If you are having trouble committing to a get-out-of-debt program and staying focused, or if you can't shake feelings of discouragement and hopelessness about your finances, take advantage of these resources:

- ✔ **Debtors Anonymous (DA):** Drawing on the time-tested principles and approach of Alcoholics Anonymous, DA chapters around the country help consumers with spending problems. DA meetings are free and open to anyone. Hearing other DA members talk about their own struggles and successes can be inspiring. And having a sponsor — someone to call when you feel discouraged or want to spend money that you shouldn't — can help you stay in control of your life and get out of debt. To find a DA chapter near you, use your local Yellow Pages, go to the organization's Web site (www.debtorsanonymous.org), or call the organization at 781-453-2743.

- ✔ **Mental health professionals:** Individual or group therapy can be invaluable when emotional problems are getting in the way of your get-out-of-debt efforts. If you have medical insurance but it doesn't cover mental health therapy, or if you don't have insurance, find out about low-cost/no-cost mental health resources in your area. A good place to start is the Web site of the National Mental Health Association, www.nmha.org/infoctr/FAQs/treatment.cfm.

- ✔ **Other books about money and your relationship with it:** Reading books like *Your Money or Your Life: Transforming Your Relationship with Money and Achieving Financial Independence* (Penguin Books) by Joe Dominguez and Vicki Robin and *Mary Hunt's Debt-Proof Living: The Complete Guide to Living Financially Free* (Broadman & Holman Publishers) by Mary Hunt, a recovering credit card addict, can help you rethink your attitude toward spending and debt. They can also help you live a life that is simpler, more personally rewarding, and less focused on spending money.

- ✔ **Your friends and family:** Don't let pride and embarrassment keep you from letting the people closest to you know that you're having financial trouble. You'll isolate yourself when you are most in need of their moral support and encouragement.

Making Your Family Members Your Financial Allies

If you're the primary money manager in your family, you will probably shoulder most of the responsibility for turning your family's finances around. However, that does not mean you shouldn't involve the rest of your family in the effort. The cooperation of your spouse or partner is essential. Although you may pay the bills each month, you and your spouse or partner both spend your family's money, so he or she has a very direct effect on the success or failure of your get-out-of-debt program.

You should also be honest about your family's finances with your children. They don't need to know all the details, but if your children are old enough to sense money-related tension and anxiety in your household, you need to tell them what is going on and what you are doing to improve things.

Pulling together with your spouse or partner

The support and cooperation of your spouse or partner is essential to getting your family's finances back on track. One of you can't be pinching pennies while the other is spending like there is no tomorrow. Both of you should be totally committed to getting out of debt and not using credit.

If you and your spouse or partner have trouble talking calmly about your family's financial problems and what to do about them, avoid letting your conversations degenerate into arguments. You may find that talking about money is easier in a public place, such as a coffee shop or a park. If a change of venue doesn't improve your communication, consider scheduling an appointment with a marriage counselor or religious advisor so you can get at the root problems.

When you talk with your spouse or partner about your debts, try to stay focused on solutions to your financial problems instead of letting the conversation turn into a blame game. Both of you are probably responsible for your debts to some degree, and finger-pointing won't pay the bills.

But keep in mind that no matter how hard you try to cooperate with one another, money problems create a lot of stress in a relationship. We can't offer easy solutions for getting through the tough times ahead. We can only encourage you to work hard at keeping your relationship amicable.

If your spouse or partner is unwilling to work with you to help your family get out of debt, and if you are concerned that his or her spending will condemn you to a life of financial troubles, you may want to reevaluate your relationship. Although ending your relationship at the same time you are trying to resolve your family's financial problems won't be easy, you may conclude that it's best. If you are thinking about divorce, our book *Divorce For Dummies* (Wiley) explains how to prepare emotionally and financially for that process.

Talking money with your children

If you're like a lot of parents, your initial instinct may be to protect your children from your family's financial problems. Usually, that's not a good thing. Even very young children are amazingly perceptive about negative changes in their environment. They may not know exactly how things have changed or why, but they can sense the change and may develop problems as a result unless you help your kids understand and deal with what is going on.

Help your children maintain a sense of security by explaining your family's financial situation and what they can expect in the months ahead. Take their ages and maturity levels into consideration when you decide what to say and how to say it. Tell them as much as you think they need to know and can process intellectually, and be careful not to scare them.

You probably need to go into greater detail with a preteen or teenage child than you do with a younger child. Teen and preteen kids generally have more financial needs and wants than young children and are more subject to peer pressure, so they need a clear sense of how they may be affected by your efforts to get out of debt. For example, they may have to start bringing their lunches to school, or you may need them to get part-time jobs to help pay for their gas, auto insurance, or nonessentials.

Compared to your younger kids, your preteens and teenagers are most apt to have difficulty accepting the fact that they can't do and have all the things they have become used to. Peer pressure can be a powerful thing!

Regardless of the age of your children, reassure them that things may be different for a while, but you love them and everything will be okay. Help them feel safe by letting them know that you and your spouse or partner are putting a financial turnaround plan together, by keeping their day-to-day routines as unchanged as possible, and by doing fun things together.

 Be alert to signs that your family's financial problems are creating a lot of stress in your children's lives or that they are becoming depressed. Signs of trouble include crying, angry outbursts, withdrawal, behavior problems at school, headaches, stomachaches, not wanting to go to school . . . just about anything out of the ordinary. Try to get your kids to talk about what is bothering them. If they won't, or if their symptoms get worse, they probably need to meet with a mental health professional. Contact the psychologist at their school, and consider letting their teachers know what is going on so they can look for signs of trouble as well.

As you help your children cope with your family's financial circumstances, bear in mind that your money troubles offer you an opportunity to teach them important lessons about managing money and the dangers of too much debt. When they become adults, they may be able to use those lessons to avoid financial trouble. One good way to help them master these lessons is to involve them in creating a monthly household budget. We talk about budgeting and the role your children can play in that process in Chapter 4.

Part II
Going on a Debt Diet

In this part . . .

*I*t's time for action! In this part, we give you the fundamentals you need to take control of your debts. We cover preparing a household budget, reducing your spending, making more money, negotiating more affordable debt payment plans with your creditors, consolidating your debts, and more. We discuss when and how a credit counseling agency can be of help (and how to find a good one), and we tell you everything you need to know about those dreaded debt collectors.

Chapter 4

Building a Budget

*W*e know. You *hate* the idea of a household budget. However, it's a basic money management tool for getting out and staying out of debt. So if you're serious about improving the state of your finances and avoiding future problems, you need to lose your anti-budget bias.

A budget is nothing more than a written plan for how you intend to spend your money each month, how much you'll contribute to savings and retirement, and so on. A budget helps you live within your means. When you're drowning in debt, it's your financial life raft.

In this chapter, we show you how to create a monthly household budget and how to monitor your compliance with it from month to month. If you can't afford to pay all your obligations in a certain month, we tell you which debts to pay and which to put off. We also warn you against using certain types of loans to generate extra cash.

Over time, if you stick to your budget and follow the rest of the advice in this book, your financial situation will improve. But even after your financial outlook is rosier, you should continue to manage your money by using a budget. Otherwise, you may get careless about your spending or begin using credit too much, and the amount of your debt may begin creeping up to dangerous levels again.

Living on a budget will also make it easier for you to

✔ Build up your savings so you have money to fall back on if you are hit with a big unexpected expense, lose your job, or have to take a pay cut.

✔ Purchase big-ticket items with minimal use of credit.

✔ Help make your family's financial dreams come true — a new home, a great vacation, college educations for your kids, a comfortable retirement.

The benefits of living on a budget are huge, so let's get started creating one for your household.

Comparing Your Monthly Spending and Income

Creating a monthly budget for your household is not a complicated process, but it can be time consuming. Simply stated, here's what you need to do:

✔ Compare your current total monthly spending to your current total monthly income.

✔ Reduce your spending as necessary so it's less than your income.

✔ Allocate your dollars appropriately so you are able to pay all your living expenses and debts.

In Chapter 2, we ask you to compare your annual spending to your annual income in order to get a fix on the state of your finances. If you have not already completed that exercise, now's the time to do it; that information will be essential to the budgeting process in this chapter. Don't worry, we'll wait for you!

After you've completed that exercise, take these steps:

1. **Divide each of the annual dollar amounts on the Chapter 2 worksheet by 12 in order to come up with monthly amounts.**

2. **Make copies of the spending and income worksheet at the end of this chapter (so you can use the worksheet multiple times).**

3. **Record each monthly amount in the appropriate place on the worksheet.**

Making budgeting a family affair

As we discuss in Chapter 3, developing a budget and making it work is something that you and your spouse or partner should do together. After all, you're both spending your family's money. It's a good idea to involve your kids in the process too.

Sit down as a family and talk about why your family needs to live on a budget and what budgeting involves. Show your kids the income and expense worksheets you fill out as you work your way through the budgeting process. Share your current income and spending figures with them, let them know how much less your family needs to spend each month, and ask your kids for budget-cutting ideas, including things they are willing to give up. Also, discuss any budget cuts you plan to make that will directly affect them.

At the end of each month, sit down as a family and compare your budgeted spending to your actual spending. Celebrate if your family's spending is in line with its budget by doing something inexpensive together — maybe ice-cream cones for all or a picnic in the park. When your comparison shows that your family spent more than was budgeted, talk about why you went over budget and what all of you can do to ensure that it doesn't happen again.

When your children feel like an important part of your family's financial team and understand that you value their input, they will be more apt to pull with you, not against you. Also, they'll be less apt to resent changes that may affect them.

4. **Review the dollar amounts and adjust them up or down as necessary so they are as accurate as possible.** For example, the cost of your auto insurance may be about to increase, your child's tuition is going to go up next month, or your income is going to go down.

If your annual totals don't include living expenses and debts that you should be paying but aren't because you don't have enough money, be sure to add them to your annual totals before you divide by 12. For budget-building purposes, you must have an accurate picture of *all* your living expenses and debts.

5. **Subtract your total monthly spending from your total monthly income.** Record that amount on the worksheet. It will be either a positive or a negative number.

Tackling a Budget Deficit

If the bottom-line number on your worksheet is negative, you've got a budget deficit. You may be making up the difference between your total monthly income and your total monthly spending by using credit cards, getting credit card advances, borrowing money, writing hot checks, paying bills late, or not paying them at all. Stop doing those things! They're driving you deeper and deeper into debt.

Cutting expenses

Deal with your budget shortfall instead by reducing your spending. Review your budget, looking for expenses you can cut back or eliminate. Focus first on your discretionary spending because those are nonessential items. You'll find most of your discretionary spending items in the "Variable Spending" category on your worksheet; however, some of your fixed and periodic spending items may also be discretionary. For example, cable is not an essential expense, you may be able to find a less expensive Internet provider than the one you now use (or go to the library when you need to get onto the Internet), and maybe you can cancel some of your memberships.

If your deficit is small and most of it is due to waste and fluff, you may be able to move your budget into the black just by eliminating nonessentials. But you may not be that lucky. Instead, you may have to go through several rounds of budget cutting and do some serious belt-tightening before your household's total monthly spending is less than its total monthly income. Use your worksheet to calculate the impact of each round of cuts on your budget's bottom line.

If you need spending reduction suggestions, check out our ideas in Chapter 5.

Focusing on reducing debt rather than saving

If you are still contributing to savings and/or a retirement plan, stop doing that for now. Use that money to cover your living expenses and pay down your high interest debts. Why? The money in your savings and retirement accounts earns only a few percentage points of interest each month — most likely far less than the interest rates on your debts. Therefore, when you have debt, every month you pay more in interest than you can earn in interest on your savings.

When your financial situation improves, you can start contributing to savings and retirement again. For now, you must put every penny you have toward your essential living expenses and toward paying down your high interest debts.

Using other strategies

Moving your budget from red to black may require more than budget cutting alone. The same is true if you can afford to pay only the minimum due on your high interest debts. When you pay just the minimum each month, it takes months if not years to pay off those debts, and you pay hundreds of dollars in interest — dollars that you could put to better use.

Other get-out-of-debt strategies you may need to consider include

- ✔ **Increasing your household income:** Get a second job, turn your hobby into a part-time business, or let your boss know that you would like to work more hours. If your spouse or partner is not working outside the home, discuss whether a paying job makes sense — at least until your finances improve. In Chapter 5, we review your moneymaking options.

- ✔ **Negotiating with your creditors:** Some of them may be willing to lower your monthly payments or make other changes to help you afford to continue paying on your debts. In Chapter 6, we explain how to negotiate with your creditors.

- ✔ **Consolidating your debts:** Debt consolidation involves borrowing money to pay off high interest debt and to lower the total amount you pay on your debts each month. We explain how debt consolidation works and your consolidation options in Chapter 7.

- ✔ **Getting help from a reputable nonprofit credit counseling agency:** The agency can help you develop your budget and may also suggest setting up a debt management plan. In Chapter 8, we explain how credit counseling works and how to find a good credit counseling agency.

- ✔ **Filing for bankruptcy:** Bankruptcy should always be your option of last resort. When may it become your best option?

  - • If you're about to lose an important asset

  - • If your monthly expenses are so much higher than your income that it will take years of sacrifice and barebones budgeting before your debts are manageable and you have a little extra money left over each month

  After reviewing your financial information, a bankruptcy attorney can tell you whether you should file for bankruptcy and which type of bankruptcy to file: a Chapter 13 reorganization, which gives you three to five years to pay your debts; or a Chapter 7 liquidation, which wipes out most of your debts. For detailed explanations of your bankruptcy options and the bankruptcy process, read *Personal Bankruptcy Laws For Dummies* by James P. Caher and John M. Caher (Wiley).

Gauging your finances by using standard percentages

Financial experts agree that in general each of your basic living expenses, as well as the total amount of debt you owe (secured and unsecured), should equal no more than a certain percentage of your net household income. (*Net household income* is your income after deductions for taxes and other expenses; it's your take-home pay.) When you're developing your budget, one way to pinpoint expenses that need reducing is to compare your numbers to the standard percentages below. After you have a budget, you can also use the standard percentages to monitor the state of your finances over time.

If your percentages are a little higher than the ones on the following list, you don't necessarily have cause for concern because certain expenses may be higher in your part of the country. Housing, for example, varies greatly from place to place. Also, some financial books and Web sites may use slightly different percentages than the ones below. There is no one correct set of figures. These are just approximate amounts for you to use as spending guidelines:

- ✔ **Your monthly housing expense:** 25 percent of your net household income (35 percent if you take into account homeowner's insurance, property taxes, home maintenance, and repairs)

- ✔ **Consumer debt (credit cards, student loans, medical debts, and so on):** 10 percent of your net household income

- ✔ **Utilities:** 15 percent of your net household income

- ✔ **Transportation:** 15 percent of your net household income

- ✔ **Savings:** At least 10 percent of your net household income

- ✔ **Everything else (food, clothing, medical insurance, prescriptions, entertainment, and so on):** 25 percent of your net household income

Paying the Important Stuff If You Can't Pay Everything

If you've cut your budget to the bare bones and you still can't afford to pay all your debts and cover all your living expenses, you have to decide what you will and won't pay. Here's how to prioritize:

✔ **Essential living expenses:** Your essential living expenses belong at the top of your "Bills to Pay" list, including putting bread on your table, keeping a roof over your head, keeping your utilities on, and gassing up your car if you need it to earn a living. However, make sure that you have reduced those expenses as much as you possibly can.

✔ **Secured debts:** Your secured debts also belong at the top of the list of things to pay. Keep reading if you aren't sure what a secured debt is.

✔ **Certain unsecured debts:** Some of your unsecured debts should take priority over others. We go into detail in the upcoming section "Knowing when to prioritize an unsecured debt."

Distinguishing between secured and unsecured debt

A *secured* debt is a debt that you collateralized with an asset that you own. (The asset is often referred to as your *collateral.*) When you collateralize a debt, the lender puts a lien on that asset, which gives the lender the legal right to take the asset if you fall behind on your payments. For example, if you have a mortgage loan, your lender has a lien on your home. If you have a car loan, the lender has a lien on your vehicle.

A lot of your debt, like credit card debt, is probably *unsecured,* which means that the creditors do not have liens on any of your assets. If you don't pay an unsecured debt, the creditor will try to get you to pay up. If you don't, the creditor may bring a debt collector on board to try to get your money. If you still don't pay, the creditor must sue you to get the court's permission to try to collect what you owe. The creditor can ask the court for permission to

✔ Seize one of your assets

✔ Put a lien on an asset so you can't borrow against it or sell it without paying your debt

✔ *Garnish* your wages (taking a portion of them each pay period), assuming wage garnishment is legal in your state

Knowing when to prioritize an unsecured debt

Depending on your circumstances, certain unsecured debts should be treated as top priorities given the potential consequences of not paying them. Unsecured debts that deserve priority treatment include

- ✔ **Child support, especially if it's court ordered.** In Chapter 13, we provide advice for what to do if you've fallen behind on your payments, and we warn you about the potential consequences of not making them.

- ✔ **Federal income taxes.** Uncle Sam has almost unlimited powers to collect past-due tax debts. In Chapter 14, we review those powers and explain what to do if you fall behind on your taxes.

- ✔ **State income taxes.** If you don't pay these taxes, your state can sue you, garnish your wages, or seize your property.

- ✔ **Property taxes and homeowner's insurance, if these expenses aren't included in your mortgage payments.** When you don't pay your property taxes, the taxing authority will eventually take your home. If your homeowner's insurance gets cancelled for nonpayment, your lender will buy insurance for you, but the insurance will be very expensive, so the total amount of your monthly mortgage payments will increase.

- ✔ **Federal student loans.** The IRS can collect what you owe when you fall behind on your federally guaranteed student loans. In Chapter 15, we offer advice about how to avoid defaulting on your student loans.

- ✔ **Your health insurance, if you're responsible for the payments.** Keeping up with your health insurance is especially important if you or a family member has an ongoing health problem. Without insurance, an expensive illness or accident could push you into bankruptcy.

- ✔ **Medical bills.** A growing number of healthcare providers, including hospitals, are getting very aggressive about collecting on their patients' past-due accounts, even suing patients in some instances. If you owe money to a healthcare provider, contact the provider to try to work out a plan for paying what you owe.

If one of your unsecured creditors turns your debt over to a debt collector, no matter how much the debt collector may hound and threaten you, do not give in to the collector's demands if paying the unsecured debt means you can't pay your priority debts or living expenses. In Chapter 9, we tell you how to deal with debt collectors.

Examining a Budget Surplus

If your monthly spending and income comparison shows that you have money left over each month, you still may not have cause for celebration. For example, you may have a surplus because you're not paying some of your bills or you're meeting some of your obligations by using credit cards. If this is the case, you must still reduce your spending so your income covers all your bills and living expenses each month.

A key aspect of getting out of debt is not using your credit cards. We certainly understand that sometimes you may have to use a credit card to pay for a financial emergency if you have no extra money in your budget and nothing in savings. But you should resolve to pay off the amount you charge as quickly as possible: the next month, if possible. And you should try not to charge anything more until you've wiped out the new credit card debt.

You may also have a surplus because you're paying only the minimum due on your outstanding credit cards balances each month. You'll never get out of debt that way! If you have any surplus in your budget, use it to accelerate the rate at which you pay off the balances, starting with the highest rate card.

Even if you can cover your monthly obligations without using credit cards and while paying more than the minimum due on your card balances, don't assume that you shouldn't reduce your spending. You must be concerned about how much you owe to your creditors, or you probably wouldn't be reading this book. Cut back where you can, and use that additional money to pay off your debts as fast as you can, starting with the debt that has the highest interest rate. After you've paid off that one, focus on paying off the debt with the next highest rate of interest, and so on. When you've paid down your high interest debts, start building up your savings.

Finalizing and Sticking to Your Budget

After you've reduced your spending as much as you can and decided what you will and won't pay if you can't afford to pay everything, it's time to finalize your household budget. Make a fresh copy of the worksheet at the end of this chapter. Label the new worksheet "Monthly Household Budget," and record your revised monthly spending amounts, as well as your monthly income amounts. Now you have a written plan for what you're going to do with your money each month.

Review the budget with your family members, and post it in a visible location so everyone can see it — maybe on a bulletin board in your kitchen or family room or on the front of your refrigerator.

Steeling your resolve

Now comes the hard part: living according to your budget. There is no sense in having a budget if you and your family are not going to stick to it. Sticking to your budget won't be easy, but keep your eye on the prize: less financial stress, fewer debts, less damage to your credit history, and (eventually) more money to spend the way you want.

Leave these loans alone

If you don't have enough money to pay all your living expenses and debts, do *not* raise the money you need by getting one of the following types of loans. Although they may give you some temporary financial relief, in the end they'll make things worse — maybe a lot worse. When it comes to improving your finances, there are no easy answers or shortcuts. You've just got to bear down and do it.

✔ **Advance fee loan:** Just as its name implies, to get this kind of loan you must pay money upfront to the lender — sometimes as much as several hundred dollars. Some advance fee lenders will take your money and run, but others will give you a very high interest loan. Traditional lenders do not make advance fee loans.

✔ **Finance company loan:** Finance companies make relatively small, high interest loans. Some finance company loans are downright dangerous: The lender may be less than honest about all the fees associated with its loan; or it may mislead you into thinking that you're getting an unsecured loan when in fact the loan is secured by one or more of your household goods, such as your furniture, entertainment center, and so on. (This detail is usually buried in the fine print of the loan agreement.) If you default on the loan, you risk losing the asset(s). Some finance companies encourage consumers to get a bigger loan than the consumers can afford so they'll end up in default.

✔ **Payday loan:** This is a very short-term, high interest loan made by check cashing companies, some finance companies, and businesses that do nothing but make payday loans. To get this loan, you write a personal check to the lender for the amount of money you want to borrow plus the amount of the lender's fee — usually a percentage of the loan amount or a set amount for every $50 or $100 you borrow — and you agree to repay the loan on your next payday. The lender pays you the amount of the check less its fee but does not cash your check.

On your next payday when you repay the loan, you get the check back. If you can't repay the loan on the next payday, the lender rolls over the loan until the following payday in exchange for you paying the lender another fee, which will probably be higher than the first fee. Over time, if you keep rolling over the loan and paying higher and higher fees, the cost of the loan skyrockets, and you have a harder and harder time paying it off.

Some states have payday loan laws. Contact a consumer law attorney or your state attorney general's office to find out if your state has such a law and what your rights are.

✓ **Pawnshop loan:** This is a short-term loan (no more than three months in most states) with a very high interest rate. Here's how this kind of loan works: You give the pawnshop an item that you own, like a TV, DVD player, piece of jewelry, or computer. The pawnshop lends you a percentage of the item's value. At the end of the loan period, if you cannot afford to pay the loan plus interest, the pawnshop keeps your item and sells it.

✓ **Tax refund loan:** Also known as a *tax anticipation loan* or an *instant refund loan,* this kind of loan involves borrowing against your future IRS tax refund. Some tax preparers, as well as finance companies, car lenders, retailers, and check cashing companies, make this kind of loan. Usually the loan will be for no more than $5,000, and it will last for no more than ten days. In addition to having to pay a very high rate of interest on the loan, you must also pay the lender an upfront fee, and you must file your tax return electronically to the tune of about $40. So when you consider the loan's interest rate plus the fees involved, the effective rate of interest you pay to borrow against your own money may be in the triple digits. When the IRS issues your tax refund, it deposits the money directly into an account set up by the lender, who takes its money and gives you the rest.

✓ **Car title loan:** If you own your car free and clear, some lenders will make you a loan for a small fraction of what your car is worth. Usually the loan will be for no more than 30 days and will have a very high rate of interest. To get the loan, you must give the lender the title to your vehicle and a set of car keys. The major danger with this kind of loan is that if you miss a loan payment, you risk the loss of your car. Depending on the loan agreement, all it may take is one missed payment.

As you go through each month, be mindful of every dollar you spend, every check you write, and every time you use your debit card or go to an ATM machine. Refer to your budget regularly to make sure you are staying on track. If you find that you have over-spent in one area, try to compensate by reducing your spending in another area.

If your kids ask for things that you've not budgeted for, remind them why your family is trying to spend less. If they are older, maybe they can earn the money they need for what they want.

As we suggest in Chapter 2, carry a small notebook or some other small record-keeping device with you for writing down everything you purchase with cash, debit card, or credit card each day. Keep all your receipts as well. You need this information at the end of each month when it's time to evaluate how well you are doing.

Checking your progress each month

To live on a budget, each month you must compare your actual monthly spending to what you budgeted. Here's how:

1. **On your monthly budget, add a column to the right of each dollar amount that's labeled "Actual."**

2. **Compile all your spending records for the month (check registers, bank statements, receipts, the information in your spending notebook) and all your income records to figure out your actual expense and income numbers.**

3. **Record these amounts in the appropriate places in the "Actual" column of your budget for the month.**

4. **Calculate subtotals and grand totals for the month.**

If you spent more than you budgeted on something, or if your total spending exceeded what you budgeted, try to figure out why you spent more. Here are some possible explanations:

- ✔ **You overlooked a living expense or debt when you devel-oped your budget.**

- ✔ **Your budget isn't realistic.** It's too bare bones, so it's impossi-ble for you and your family to live on it.

- ✔ **Your family did not try hard enough to live according to your budget.** Making a budget work takes a 100 percent commitment from everyone in your household.

- ✔ **You were hit with an unexpected expense that month.** For example, you were working late at the office, so your childcare expenses increased, or your car broke down and you had to spend money getting it fixed.

- ✔ **Some of your expenses increased for reasons beyond your control.** The cost of gas went up or your insurance premium increased, for example.

- ✔ **Your income dropped.** Maybe you had to take a cut in pay, your sales commissions were lower than usual, or a client did not pay you that month.

Depending on your conclusions, you may need to revise some of the numbers in your household budget. If you have to increase the amount of an expense, try to decrease another expense by the same amount. If you have to revise your budget to reflect a decrease in your household's monthly income, try to offset the decrease with budget cuts as well.

If your monthly comparison shows that some of your expenses were lower than what you budgeted, don't revise your budget right away. Wait a month or two to see if the changes are permanent. If they are, put the extra money toward your high interest debts, focusing first on paying off the debt with the highest rate of interest. Do the same if your income increases permanently.

Your budget is a dynamic document that should change as your finances change, hopefully for the better. Gradually, if you stick to your budget, you'll start paying off your debts faster. Eventually, you'll also be able to add some extras to your budget (maybe some of the things you've had to give up for now) and start contributing to savings so you'll have a financial safety net. If you continue to be careful about your spending and to minimize your use of credit, before you know it, you family will be in a position to make its financial dreams come true.

Monthly Spending and Income Worksheet

Monthly Income

Your household take-home pay	$_____
Child support income	$_____
Alimony income	$_____
Other income (specify the source)	$_____
Other income (specify the source)	$_____
Other income (specify the source)	$_____
Total Monthly Income	$_____

Monthly Spending

Fixed Spending

Rent	$_____
Mortgage	$_____
Home equity loan	$_____
Condo or homeowners' association fee	$_____
Car payment	$_____
Other loans	$_____
Homeowner's insurance	$_____
Renter's insurance	$_____
Health insurance	$_____
Auto insurance	$_____
Life insurance	$_____
Other insurance	$_____
Childcare	$_____
Dues and fees	$_____
Cable/satellite service	$_____
Internet access	$_____
Child support obligation	$_____
Alimony obligation	$_____
Other fixed expenses (specify type)	$_____

Other fixed expenses (specify type)	$_____
Other fixed expenses (specify type)	$_____
Other fixed expenses (specify type)	$_____
Total Monthly Fixed Spending	$_____

Variable Spending

Groceries	$_____
Cigarettes	$_____
Alcohol	$_____
Utilities	$_____
Cellphone	$_____
Gas for car	$_____
Public transportation	$_____
Tolls and parking	$_____
Newspapers, books, and magazines	$_____
Allowances	$_____
After-school activities for kids	$_____
Babysitting	$_____
Entertainment	$_____
Restaurant meals	$_____
Personal care products	$_____
Clothing	$_____
Body care (haircuts, manicures, massages)	$_____
Laundry and dry cleaning	$_____
Out-of-pocket medical expenses	$_____
Lawn care	$_____
Home repair and maintenance	$_____
Other (specify type)	$_____
Other (specify type)	$_____
Other (specify type)	$_____
Other (specify type)	$_____
Total Monthly Variable Spending	$_____

Periodic Spending

Insurance	$_____
Auto registration and inspection	$_____
Subscriptions	$_____
Charitable donations	$_____
Tuition	$_____
Dues and fees	$_____
Income taxes	$_____
Property taxes	$_____
Other (specify type)	$_____
Other (specify type)	$_____
Other (specify type)	$_____
Other (specify type)	$_____
Total Monthly Periodic Spending	$_____

Monthly Contributions

Savings	$_____
Retirement	$_____
Other (specify type)	$_____
Other (specify type)	$_____
Other (specify type)	$_____
Other (specify type)	$_____
Total Contributions	$_____

Total Monthly Spending and Contributions	$_____
Total Monthly Income	$_____
minus	-
Total Monthly Spending and Contributions	$_____
equals	=
Your Bottom Line	$_____

Chapter 5

Slashing Your Spending and Making More Money

In This Chapter

▶ Cutting back on housing costs, utilities, food, and more

▶ Boosting your household income

*W*hen your monthly expenses are greater than your income, you must rein in your spending and stop using your credit cards. The same is true if you're just barely getting by each month, if you're paying only the minimum due on your credit cards, or if you have little or nothing in savings.

Finding ways to increase your family's income may also be essential, especially if you've cut your budget to the bare bones and you're still sliding backwards, just treading water, or paying for every unexpected expense with a credit card. Working at another job or working more hours at your current job are two options you may want to consider.

This chapter provides you with practical suggestions for reducing your spending *and* boosting your income. Although every idea in this chapter won't apply to you, the advice we offer here may help trigger other ideas that make sense for your particular situation.

Finding Ways to Spend Less

In this section, we offer a treasure trove of ideas for spending less, organized by category of everyday expense: housing, utilities, food, transportation, healthcare, and so on. Some of the ideas are small and simple but yield big benefits over time, especially when done in combination with other money-saving suggestions.

Don't reject any cost-cutting ideas right off the bat, even if implementing them means major changes in your lifestyle and a lot of sacrifice. Be open to anything and everything, and try to focus less on what you're giving up and more on where spending less will help get you in the end.

After you give up a few "essentials," you may discover that you don't even miss them. You may find that not having them actually improves your quality of life. For example, using public transportation to get to and from work gives you time to read, think, and maybe even relax. And cutting out some activities that have filled your kids' after-school hours and weekends may open up new opportunities for and your kids to interact.

Looking for good deals

Before we tackle specific areas of your household budget, we have a couple tips for getting the most out of your money no matter what you're buying.

First is a Web site that should be on your list of favorites: www. yokel.com. Whether you're in the market for a prom dress, a car, a DVD player, or a new refrigerator, you can locate the best deals in your area by going to this site.

Next is a piece of advice about advertising: Although you should always try to buy things when they're on sale, you shouldn't buy an item just because it's discounted. Instead, make purchases based on whether you truly need an item. If you scour the Sunday ad flyers in your newspaper looking for good deals, you're bound to be tempted to buy things you don't really need. Keep this in mind: That item that looks like such a good deal today may get marked down even more in a week or two.

If you can't resist a sale, you may have a spending problem. People with spending problems tend to buy for the sake of buying, even when they know they shouldn't. Spending makes them feel good at the time but lousy later. Even so, they spend again. If you think you may have a spending problem, don't be embarrassed. Get help from other overspenders by going to a Debtors Anonymous (DA) meeting in your area. To find a DA chapter in your area, go to www.debtorsanonymous.org or call 781-453-2743.

Spending less on your housing

Housing is probably the single biggest item in your budget, especially if you are a homeowner and you take into account the cost of maintenance, repairs, insurance, and taxes. You can rein in your housing costs in many ways.

✔ **Renters:** Following are some options to consider if you're renting:

- If you're close to the end of your lease, find a cheaper place to live. If you've got time left on your lease, read your lease agreement to find out how much it costs to break it so you can move out early.

- Move in with your parents or other relatives while you work on improving your finances.

- Stay where you are but get a roommate if your lease allows.

Read Chapter 12 for more information about breaking your lease or adding a roommate.

✔ **Homeowners:** If you own your home, consider the following possibilities:

- Look into mortgage refinancing to lower your monthly payments. Be careful, however, about refinancing with a mortgage that may create problems for you down the road, like an interest-only mortgage or one with a big balloon payment at the end. If you are confused about whether a particular mortgage is good or bad for your finances, talk to a financial advisor, a nonprofit credit counseling agency, or a real estate attorney.

- Rent out an extra room in your home.

- Lease your home to someone else and move into cheaper digs. Make sure the rent you charge covers your mortgage payments plus the cost of your home-owner's insurance, property taxes, and routine mainte-nance and repairs.

- Sell your home. We know this may be a lot to ask, but if you're paying for more house than you can truly afford, getting out from under the debt is a good thing.

Lowering your utility bills

The cost of heating and cooling a home always seems to go up, up, up. Add in the cost of water, wastewater, and lights, and you may find yourself gasping when you open your utility bills each month. Here are some suggestions for bringing down these costs:

✔ Use your heat and air conditioning less by keeping your home cooler in the winter and warmer in the summer. Keep your thermostat set at 68 degrees in the winter and at no less than 78 degrees in the summer.

✔ Lower the temperature on your water heater, but not to less than 120 degrees.

✔ Ask if your local utility company offers free energy audits. You'll find out where your house is losing energy and what you can do to make your home more energy efficient. The utility may also offer rebate programs that can lower the cost of your energy improvements, or you may qualify for a low-interest/no-interest home energy loan to finance expensive improvements like installing a more energy-efficient heating and cooling system.

✔ Find out if your utility offers an energy saving program. For example, some power companies automatically shut off your household appliances during peak use hours each day.

✔ Replace your commode with one that uses less water. Also, replace old showerheads with new, low-flow heads.

✔ Make your home more energy efficient by caulking, using weather stripping, and adding insulation, all of which are relatively easy do-it-yourself projects.

✔ Use fans, not AC, to cool your home.

✔ Hang up your clothes to dry. Not only is using a dryer expensive, but all that hot air makes your clothes wear out faster.

✔ If you have to replace your washing machine, get one that loads from the front rather than the top. You'll reduce your energy use by as much as 50 percent and save on water too.

✔ Take showers, not baths, and limit the length of your showers.

✔ Replace old-fashioned light bulbs with the new ultra-efficient fluorescent bulbs.

✔ Never run a dishwasher that is only half-full of dishes.

✔ Fix leaky faucets.

Eating for less

One of the easiest expenses to reduce is the amount you spend on food. Reducing your grocery bill may mean eating more homemade foods and less prepackaged items, which has some added bonuses: You'll be eating healthier, and you'll probably shed a pound or two!

✔ Plan out your meals for the coming week based on your budget, and go to the grocery store with a list of the items you need. Buy them and nothing more.

✔ Minimize your trips to the grocery store. The more trips you make, the more you are apt to spend. Also, never shop when you are hungry. You're more apt to load your cart up with items you really don't need.

✔ When you make a meal, double the recipe and store the extra half in your freezer. When you have to work late one night or are feeling frazzled after a difficult day at the office, you'll be less tempted to purchase prepared food or carryout on your way home because you have a meal waiting that you can just pop into the microwave.

✔ Clip coupons and read the grocery store inserts in your local newspaper for good deals on items you plan on buying.

Coupon Web sites like www.couponcabin.com, www.coupon-craze.com, and www.coolcoupons.com offer savings at specific stores and on popular national brands. Some offer free product samples too.

✔ Shop at several different grocery stores. Some may offer better deals on certain items that you use.

✔ Purchase house brands.

✔ Minimize your use of prepared foods and convenience items. You pay a premium for them.

✔ If you drink regularly, drink less and buy less expensive wine, beer, or hard liquor.

✔ Purchase groceries at warehouse stores, discount houses, and buying clubs. When practical, buy in bulk.

Don't buy perishable items in large quantities unless you are sure you will use them up before they spoil. Also, don't buy items in bulk or on sale that you're not sure your family will use; they're only good deals if you actually use them!

✔ Pack lunches for yourself and your family.

✔ Make your own morning coffee instead of buying it on your way to work.

✔ Eliminate sodas and junk food from your diet.

✔ Reserve dining out for special occasions only.

✔ Celebrate a special occasion with a picnic rather than with a restaurant meal.

✔ Pop your own popcorn for the movies. Old-fashioned home-made popcorn tastes a whole lot better than the prepopped stuff available at most movie theaters, and it's a lot cheaper too.

✔ When your family goes on a day trip, pack your meal instead of eating at a restaurant.

✔ Grow your own vegetables and herbs. If you don't have a green thumb or if you lack the space for a garden, buy your fruits and veggies at your local farmers' market.

Paying less for transportation

After the cost of housing, the cost of getting from here to there may be your second biggest monthly expense. You may already have found ways to trim your transportation budget since the cost of a tank of gas has been rising, but you may find some new ideas here.

✔ Use public transportation, ride your bike, walk, or carpool to work if possible. If you use public transportation or carpool, you may be able to read and enjoy the passing scenery. If you ride your bike or walk, you may even lose a few pounds.

✔ Shop around for the best deal on gas. Driving a little farther to fill up your tank for less may be worth the extra miles and time.

✔ If your vehicle is a gas guzzler or expensive to maintain, consider selling it and purchasing a reliable, less expensive used vehicle.

✔ Change your own oil, and do your own simple car repairs. Your local community college or an adult education program in your area may offer a class in basic car maintenance, or maybe a neighbor or friend can show you the basics. Also, the "Car Talk" guys on National Public Radio feature a humorous but down-to-earth do-it-yourself guide to car repair and maintenance at their show's Web site, www.cartalk.com/content/diy.

✔ Pump your own gas, and wash your own car. Also, don't buy a higher grade gas than your car really needs.

✔ Find a reliable mechanic who won't charge you an arm and a leg every time you bring your vehicle to the repair shop. Ask people you know, especially people who drive cars similar to yours, for the names of good mechanics. A *shade tree* mechanic — someone who maintains and repairs cars in his backyard — may provide affordable, high quality service. Avoid having your car repaired by a dealer or at a chain car repair shop.

 The experts on the "Car Talk" radio show maintain a "humongous database of over 16,000 great mechanics, recommended by — and for — the *Car Talk* community." Access their Mechanics File by going to www.cartalk.com/content/mechx.

✔ Ask your teenagers to pay for their own gasoline and auto insurance or to help contribute to the cost.

Just how much do your vices cost?

There may be a silver lining in your cash crunch if you are a regular smoker or drinker. Not having the money you need to pay your creditors and cover your basic living expenses may convince you that it's time to become a nonsmoker or to give up that glass or two (or three) of wine you sip at the end of each day, or that six pack of beer you throw back each evening.

Let's assume, for example, that you and your spouse or partner enjoy a $15 bottle of wine with dinner each night. In a week's time, your nightly bottle of wine costs you $105. That's $402 a month and nearly $5,000 a year! Now that's a lot of money to spend on the fruit of the vine!! Just think what you could do with that money instead.

Now, let's look at how much you're spending to smoke. Let's assume that you smoke half a pack of cigarettes every day, and you pay $5 for each pack. More than $900 of your money is going up in smoke each year, which doesn't even take into account how much extra you're paying for life insurance because of your unhealthy habit. If you give the habit up, you can reduce the cost of your premium by as much as 30 percent. You'll probably pay less for health insurance as well.

Having fun for less

Reducing your budget does not mean that you and your family have to eliminate fun from your lives. It means cutting out the frills and taking time to find affordable ways to have a good time. Think back to when you were just married and money was tight or to when you were a kid. What did you do for fun then? Do any of these cheap fun suggestions sound familiar?

- Use your public library instead of buying books and DVDs, or swap these items with your friends.

- Go to www.zunafish.com and exchange your used books, CDs, DVDs, and video games with others online for a buck a trade. As the Web site says, "Trade the stuff you're done with for the stuff you want!"

- Commune with nature. Go for a hike, ride your bike, have a picnic in the park, go fishing, enjoy the babble of a swift running creek, and take time to enjoy the sunset.

- Have fun the old-fashioned way: Put jigsaw puzzles together, play card and board games, do crossword puzzles, play charades, create a scrapbook, or put all your photos in an album.

- Use your community pool.

- Take advantage of free events in your community.

✔ Entertain with potluck meals.

✔ Invite your friends over for a backyard barbeque with a twist: Everyone brings something to throw on the grill.

✔ Curl up with a good book.

✔ Use two-for-one-coupons or share an entrée with your dinner companion when you want to dine out.

✔ Trade babysitting services with friends or relatives who also have young children so going out occasionally is more affordable.

Looking good for less

When you are rolling in dough, you can afford to spend a bundle on salons, spas, personal trainers, and so on. But those are all luxuries you can't afford right now. They gotta go! Here are suggestions for keeping yourself and your family looking good for less:

✔ Do your own manicures and pedicures, or get together with a girlfriend and do them for each other.

✔ Cut and color your own hair, get it cut and colored less frequently, or look in your Yellow Pages or on the Web for a beauty school in your area. Most beauty schools offer free or low-cost cuts and coloring so students can hone their skills while being supervised by experienced professionals.

✔ Cut your family members' hair.

✔ Get a massage at a massage school in your area. Find one in your local Yellow Pages, or go to www.naturalhealers.com.

✔ Eliminate expensive cosmetics, creams, and lotions. Although the packaging may not be as attractive as the high priced stuff, drug store cosmetics, creams, and lotions usually do the job.

✔ Minimize your use of dry cleaning, and wash and iron your own shirts, blouses, and pants. If you hate ironing, watch TV or listen to music while you work out those wrinkles.

✔ If you belong to a health club and your membership is about to expire, find a less expensive alternative or — if you rarely go to the club — cancel your membership. Your local YMCA or community center may be more affordable options.

✔ Speaking of health, give up those glasses of wine or bottles of beer you drink every night. Not only do they cost you money (see the sidebar "Just how much do your vices cost?"), but they also increase the number of calories you consume each day and jeopardize your health if you're a problem drinker.

Dressing for less

With a little planning and ingenuity, you and the rest of your family members can look like fashion plates without paying top dollar. The key is to plan ahead, eliminate impulse buying, and maybe rethink where you shop. Here are some suggestions for how to look like a million dollars on the cheap:

- Shop for clothes only when you truly need them, not for fun or out of boredom.

- At the end of each season, take an inventory of the clothing items you need to replace because they are worn out or because your kids have outgrown them. Then take advantage of end-of-season sales.

- Check out thrift shops, nearly new stores, and yard sales. You're likely to find some great deals.

- Buy on sale whenever possible, and shop at discount stores like T.J. Maxx, Target, Marshalls, and Kohl's.

- If you have young children, make their clothes last longer by buying them a little big. Then roll up the sleeves and pants bottoms, and shorten the hems on skirts and dresses.

- Swap clothes with friends or family members.

- If you've got the time and the skills, make some of your own clothes.

Reducing your phone costs

Over the past decade or so, the amount of money you spend to stay in touch has probably increased. Cellphones are ubiquitous, and phone companies offer a plethora of extras that are nice but unnecessary. Therefore, reducing the amount that you spend on your phone service each month may not be much of a challenge, and those reductions should have little or no real impact on your lifestyle. Here are some suggestions for staying in touch for less:

- Shop around for the best deal on phone service. If you're in the market for a cell phone and service plan, Web sites like www.letstalk.com and www.myrateplan.com can help you home in on your best options.

- Cancel your landline and go with Internet-based phone service through your cable company or a company like Vonage, SunRocket, or Skype. Typically, you pay a flat fee of about $25 for unlimited domestic calls. However, most of these companies require that you have high-speed Internet access, and you may need to purchase a headset, so before you ditch your landline put pencil to paper to be sure you'll save money.

✔ Make sure that your calling plan matches the way you use your phone. For example, if you make a lot of in-state calls, your calling plan should have a low intrastate rate, and if you frequently call out of state, be sure your plan offers low interstate rates. Some plans allow unlimited long distance calling on weekends, in the evenings, or 24/7. Call your service provider to make sure that your plan fits your needs.

✔ Consider a family plan for your cell phone service if multiple people in your household have wireless phones. Also, ask your teens to pay for the cost of having a cell phone.

✔ Get rid of your landline, if you have a cell phone with an unlimited calling plan.

✔ Review the extras you're paying for like voice mail, call waiting, caller ID, call forwarding, and so on. Do you *really* need them?

✔ Minimize your use of directory assistance.

Saving on prescription drugs

If the cost of prescription drugs is taking a big bite out of your budget, don't do without the drugs you need. Follow some of this advice for reducing what you pay for your pills:

✔ Ask your doctor for free samples whenever he prescribes a prescription drug for you or someone in your family.

✔ Ask your doctor if there is a generic alternative to the drug he prescribes, or whether he can prescribe a less expensive alternative. Many newer drugs are more expensive than their older equivalents, but they are not necessarily better.

✔ Buy 90-day supplies of the drugs you take regularly in order to save on the dispensing fee that many pharmacies charge each time they fill a prescription.

✔ Talk with your doctor about prescribing a higher dose of the pill you normally take, and use a pill splitter to split it in half. You pay for fewer refills this way. However, your doctor should have the final say on whether this is a good option for your particular medication.

✔ Shop around before you get a prescription filled. You may be surprised at the range in prices from drugstore to drugstore.

✔ Purchase your prescription drugs from an online pharmacy — one licensed by the National Association of Boards of Pharmacy through its VIPPS program. (The VIPPS seal of approval will be prominently displayed on the site.) Go to the association's Web site at www.nabp.net for a list of the online pharmacies it has licensed. Reputable online pharmacies include www.costco.com, www.drugstore.com, and www.familymeds.com.

✔ Buy in bulk, from a mail-order pharmacy, medications that you take regularly.

✔ Find out if you qualify for a drug assistance program. Some programs are income based, but others, like Merck's, offer prescription drug discounts to consumers who are uninsured regardless of their incomes. Partnership for Prescription Assistance at www.pparx.org offers an online databank of drug assistance programs.

Drug discount cards tend to be bad deals, in part because they have so many restrictions. For example, you may not be able to use your card to buy generic drugs or drugs online, or you may be able to use it only at certain pharmacies.

Inching down your insurance costs

Maintaining your insurance coverage is essential even when you need to cut back. Without it, a serious illness, a car accident, or flood or wind damage to your home could be financially devastating and push you into bankruptcy.

Shop around for the best deal on your insurance. An insurance broker can help you, or you can explore your options by using a Web site like www.insure.com. For example, you may be able to get less expensive coverage by switching to another provider, by raising your *deductibles* (the amount of money you have to pay out of pocket before your insurance company starts to pay) on your current policies, or by getting rid of any insurance bells and whistles you really don't need.

Also, make sure that you are getting all the insurance discounts you're entitled to. For example, you may be entitled to a discount if you don't commute to work in your car, if you take a class to refresh your driving skills and knowledge, if you purchase your home and auto insurance from the same company, if you're over 65, if you install certain safety features in your home, and so on.

Homeowners insurance
Following are specific tips for reducing your home insurance costs:

✔ When you insure your home, don't count the value of the land your home sits on. Insure the structure only.

✔ Find out if you'll save money by installing deadbolt locks and smoke detectors. If your home already has a security system, make sure it's reflected in your policy.

✔ If someone in your family was a smoker but has kicked the habit, find out if your insurance company will lower your premium costs. Households with smokers often pay a premium for insurance because burning cigarettes are a leading cause of house fires.

Auto insurance

Consider the following ways you may trim your auto insurance bill:

✔ If your vehicle is old and not worth very much, drop your collision coverage, especially if you're spending more on the coverage than your car is worth. Another option is to increase the deductible amounts for your collision and comprehensive coverage.

Blogs that can help you make every penny count

Blogs can be a great way to find out what other people in your same financial straits are doing to cut back and live on a budget. They can also provide you with moral support and encouragement. Here are a few of the blogs we think are worth a visit:

✔ *The Budgeting Babe* (www.budgetingbabe.blogspot.com). This blog claims that it's dedicated to "all of the young working women who want to spend like Carrie in a Jimmy Choo store, but have a budget close to Roseanne . . ."

✔ *Everybody Loves Your Money*, (www.everybodylovesyourmoney.com). The author of this blog grew up in a family where money was tight.

✔ *The Frugal Duchess* (www.sharonhr.blogspot.com). A *Miami Herald* personal finance columnist who claims that she has "fine tastes and a small budget" writes this blog.

✔ *Frugal for Life* (www.frugalforlife.blogspot.com). This blog is all about living a simple, frugal life.

✔ *Savvy Saver* (www.savvysaver.blogspot.com). This blog is dedicated to "making smart money decisions, living below your means, and increasing personal wealth."

✔ *Spending Wisely* (www.spendingwisely.com). For thoughts and musings on spending, saving, and simple living, check out this blog.

✔ *Stop Buying Crap* (www.stopbuyingcrap.com). The goal of this blog is to help people stop wasting money.

✔ Be sure that you are getting all the discounts you may be entitled to, such as discounts for

- Driving a car with antilock brakes, automatic seat belts, and airbags.

- Being in a particular profession. Statistics show that people in certain types of professions — engineers and teachers, for example — tend to have fewer accidents.

- Your military service. Some insurance companies give you a break on the cost of your insurance if you are currently in the military or if you used to be.

✔ If you have to purchase a new car, buy one like your granny might drive. High profile/high performance cars cost more to insure.

✔ Find out if your association membership entitles you to a discount on your auto insurance.

Health insurance

Health insurance costs continue to skyrocket, and finding ways to reduce them can seriously help your household budget. Here are some suggestions:

✔ Talk with your employer's health plan administrator, or with your insurance broker or agent if you are not part of a group plan, about what you can do to lower your monthly health insurance costs. Possibilities may include increasing your annual deductible, switching insurance companies, or changing plans. Keep the following in mind:

- If you're willing to sacrifice the freedom to go to whatever doctor, pharmacy, or hospital you want, you can save money. Sign up with a plan that limits your choices; the more flexibility, the more costly the plan.

- If someone in your family has a preexisting medical condition, don't change plans or insurers before you are clear about how coverage for that condition may be affected. Some plans or providers may refuse to cover the condition at all or may not cover it for a period of time — six months to a year, for example.

- Be aware that the insurance plan with the lowest premium cost is not a good deal if it doesn't offer the coverage and benefits you need. In the long run, paying a little extra to have the appropriate coverage may mean lower out-of-pocket expenses for doctors, hospitals, and prescription drugs.

✔ If your income is low and you have few if any assets of value, find out if you qualify for *Medicaid,* a federal/state health

> insurance program that is state administered. To check on your eligibility, go to www.familiesusa.org, click on "Consumer Assistance Program Locator," and choose your state. You'll get a direct link to your state's Medicaid office.

> ✔ If you don't qualify for Medicaid, you may be able to get health coverage for your children through the federal State Children's Health Insurance Program (SCHIP). Go to www.insurekidsnow.gov for information about the program in your state.

Bringing in More Bucks

If slashing your spending doesn't free up all the money you need to meet your financial obligations *and* accelerate the rate at which you pay off your debts, look for ways to increase your household's monthly income. Maybe what it will take to improve your financial outlook is working extra hours at your current job (if you're paid by the hour), taking a second job, or working for yourself as a freelancer. This section discusses the in and outs of each of these income boosters.

If your spouse or partner is a stay-at-home parent and he or she is considering getting a paying job, take into account the costs of working outside the home, such as childcare and transportation, so you can be sure that the change makes financial sense. The online calculator at www.fincalc.com/bud_06.asp?id=6 makes that analysis easy.

If making more money will be an uphill battle because demand for your skills is declining or because the industry you work in is depressed, consider getting trained for a new career by attending your local community college or a reputable trade school. Before you leap into anything, however, find out where the experts expect future job opportunities to be. Start your research by looking through the *Occupational Outlook Handbook* and the *Career Guide to Industries,* two publications available at the Web site of the U.S. Department of Labor's Bureau of Labor Statistics, www.bls.gov.

Earning more at your current job

Your current employer may be an immediate source of additional income. If you are paid by the hour, let your boss know that you want to work additional hours. If demand for your employer's product or service is growing or if your employer is opening a new office or store, you may be able to add another shift to your schedule, work longer each day, or work on weekends, especially if you have a good reputation as an employee.

Asking for a raise is another option, assuming you can justify your request. For example, a raise may be in order if you have not received one in a long time, if you have assumed new responsibilities without additional compensation, or if you recently completed an important project. Other possible reasons to ask for a raise include a stellar performance review and the fact that co-workers in your same position may be paid more than you.

Another way to earn more money at your current place of employment is to apply for a promotion. Let your boss know that you want to be considered for a higher paying job in your same department. If you're qualified to work in other departments, schedule a time to meet with the managers of those departments to let them know that you are interested in working for them.

Looking for a new job

Getting a better paying job with a new employer is another obvious way to boost your income. In this section, we share tips for starting a job search.

Doing your homework

Prepare for your job hunt by whipping your résumé into shape, writing a short but snappy cover letter, and honing your interview skills. If you need help doing any of these things, you'll find a wealth of free information on the Web. Here are a few sites to check out:

- ✔ **The Writing Center at Rensselaer Polytechnic Institute:** This site (www.wecc.rpi.edu) offers a clear, step-by-step process for creating a winning résumé. Click on "E-handouts," and look for "Resumes."

- ✔ **The Career Advice section of Monster.com:** At www.monster.com, you can find résumé assistance, help figuring out how much salary to ask for, and a self-assessment center for evaluating your skills and abilities. You also get career-specific advice based on whether you want to change careers, are looking for a job, or are 50 years old or over. You can even go through a virtual interview to help prepare for the kinds of questions you're likely to be asked in a job interview.

- ✔ **Career Builder:** This Web site helps you build an online résumé from scratch or improve the one you already have. Then you can post it at the site so employers who are looking for someone like you can see it. To access the site's résumé building help, go to www.careerbuilder.com and click on "Post Resumes" at the top of the home page. Then click on "Build Your Resume."

- ✔ **The *Wall Street Journal's* Career Journal:** The site www.careerjournal.com/jobhunting features a "Job-Hunting

Advice" section that is full of useful articles and tips on using the Internet to find a job, creating effective résumés and cover letters, job search strategies, interviewing tips, strategies for negotiating your salary, and more.

Finding out about new job opportunities

So when your résumé and cover letter are up-to-date, and you're ready to turn a practice interview into a real one, how do you find potential employers? Here are some ideas:

✔ **Let your friends know that you're in the market for a better paying job.** They can keep their eyes and ears open for opportunities at their workplaces.

✔ **Visit job search Web sites.** Scope out a variety of job sites to figure out which ones best meet your needs and are easiest to use. Here are some possibilities:

- National online job Web sites like CareerBuilder (www. careerbuilder.com), Job-Hunt.org (www.job-hunt. org), Monster.com (www.monster.com), and America's Job Bank (www.ajb.dni.us). Some of these sites will send you e-mail alerts to let you know about new job listings that match your job search criteria.

- Niche online job sites that focus on a narrowly defined type of job or on jobs within a specific industry. For example, www.dice.com focuses on high tech jobs; www. bankingboard.com zeroes in on jobs in the mortgage banking, title, escrow, and real estate fields; and www. allretailjobs.com focuses on — you guessed it — all types of positions in the retail world.

- Your state's employment office. Most of these sites include a job bank of openings with local and national private sector employers, nonprofits, state government, and sometimes local governments.

- The Web sites of your local and county government. These sites may feature job banks with a focus on government job openings in your specific locale.

- The Web sites of any professional or trade organizations you belong to. Many of these organizations list job openings of specific interest to their members.

- www.craigslist.com. Craigslist features traditional and offbeat job listings for many larger cities.

Visit the QuintCareers Web site (www.quintcareers.com/ top_50_sites.html) for descriptions and links to 50 great job sites. Also, search for jobs by industry type — from jobs in the airline industry and law enforcement to jobs in academia, fashion, retail, finance, and advertising — at www. quintcareers.com/indres.html.

✔ **Read the employment listings in your local newspaper or in newspapers in nearby areas.**

✔ **Attend job fairs.** Job fairs are a great way to meet employers in your area who are hiring. You may even have the opportunity to do some initial interviews at the job fairs or to set up interviews for a later date. You can find out about job fairs through your local media; by visiting www.careerfairs.com, www.careerbuilder.com, or other Web sites dedicated to job fairs; and by searching the Internet.

✔ **Network.** Many great jobs are never advertised online or in newspapers. Instead, they are filled via word of mouth, through networking. Networking involves letting anyone and everyone know that you are looking for a job, including your former bosses, professional associates, friends, relatives, neighbors, elected officials you may know, and even people you just happen to meet. Any of these individuals may know about a job opening that would be perfect for you.

You can also network by attending networking events. For example, your local Chamber of Commerce may sponsor breakfasts, luncheons, or happy hours that are organized to help professionals network. Other good networking opportunities include meetings of your alumni association, meetings of clubs and associations you may belong to, community events, cocktail parties and dinner parties, and conferences — just about anywhere that you are going to be with other people.

When you are networking, be prepared to explain in concise terms exactly what type of job you are looking for and to describe your skills and experience. You may have only a few minutes to make a good first impression.

Carry business cards with you at all times in order to take full advantage of every networking opportunity that comes your way, and whenever you meet people who could be helpful in your job search, get their business cards so you can follow up. You may even want to carry copies of your résumé with you whenever you leave your home so you can pass them out when appropriate. For more information about all aspects of networking, go to www.careerjournal.com/jobhunting/networking.

✔ **Schedule an appointment with an employment agency in your area or with an executive recruitment firm (also known as a *headhunter*) if you are looking for a mid- to upper-level management position.**

Employment agencies and executive recruitment firms are paid a fee for linking up employers and employees. Typically, employers pay the fees of executive search firms, but you may have to pay the fee if an employment agency finds you a job. Be clear about who will pay before you sign an agreement with a business that says it will try to help you find employment. If you'll be responsible for the fee, make certain you understand the amount and the conditions of the fee you'll owe.

Getting (and surviving) a second job

Thinking about making more money by working at another job, known as *moonlighting*? Join the crowd. According to the U.S. Department of Labor, about 7.2 million Americans hold down more than one job. You can find a second job by using the same job-hunting resources we suggest in the previous section.

Moonlighting can be a great way to make some extra bucks, as long as your second job doesn't interfere with your ability to be effective at your primary job. You also need to make sure that you'll come out ahead financially after taking into account any additional expenses you may incur by working two jobs: transportation, childcare, food costs, and so on.

If you signed a contract with your current employer, read it before you take a second job. The contract may prohibit you from working for specific types of employers or from moonlighting at all.

If you feel like your life is already a juggling act, a second job is going to make keeping all your balls in the air even more of a challenge. However, you can take steps to alleviate some of the stress that working multiple jobs may create. For example,

- ✔ Ask your spouse or partner and your older children to assume more of the day-to-day household chores if you are the one who is responsible for most of them.

- ✔ Create a schedule of when things need to be done, and post it on your family's bulletin board or refrigerator.

- ✔ Accept the fact that for now, some things at home will fall through the cracks, and everything may not get done according to your standards.

- ✔ Make casseroles, soups, and other nutritious one-pot meals that you can freeze and that will feed your family for several days.

- ✔ Try to find a second job you enjoy doing — maybe a job that relates to a hobby or special interest of yours. You won't be as likely to resent the extra work if what you are doing is fun.

- ✔ Avoid taking a second job that involves a lot of pressure and stress, especially if you're already under a lot of pressure and stress at your main job. You'll quickly burn yourself out, and you may begin having health problems.

> ✔ Look for a second job that is relatively close to either your home or your main job so you are not spending a lot of time commuting.

> ✔ Grab naps when you can!

Considering freelancing

Depending on what type of skills you have, you may be able to boost your income by doing part-time freelance work. When you are a freelancer, you are self-employed and offer your services to other businesses. For example, you may be a freelance copywriter, graphic designer, software designer, CPA, and so on.

Working for yourself may sound appealing and can be quite profitable, but if you need an immediate infusion of cash, it's probably not your best bet. Usually, before you can expect to see any money from freelancing, you have to

> ✔ Prepare information explaining your services.

> ✔ Decide how you will charge for your services (by the hour, by the project, or on a monthly retainer basis, for example) and how much you will charge.

> ✔ Let potential clients know about your services and then hope that some of them will contract with you.

> ✔ After you are hired, invoice your clients and cross your fingers that they'll pay you quickly.

Obviously, being a successful freelancer, especially when you're holding down a regular job, takes organization, self-discipline, the ability to manage numerous tasks simultaneously, and a little bit of luck. However, if freelancing appeals to you, here are some ways to find out more about the process and about potential freelancing opportunities:

> ✔ Talk to people you know who are already freelancing.

> ✔ Let your former employers know you would like some freelance work.

> ✔ Visit www.quintcareers.com/freelancing_career.html.

> ✔ Read *Freelancing For Dummies* by Susan M. Drake (Wiley). There is a *For Dummies* book for everything, isn't there?

> ✔ Register at www.guru.com so that businesses looking for someone who offers your type of service know how to find you.

When you freelance, your clients won't deduct taxes from the money they pay you. Therefore, you owe those taxes to Uncle Sam on April 15. If you are making a considerable amount from freelancing, it's a good idea to pay your taxes quarterly. Otherwise, you may end up in hot water with the IRS if your tax return shows that you owe more taxes than you can afford to pay when April 15 comes around. Meet with your CPA to figure out the best way to handle your taxes as a freelancer.

The skinny on business scams

Beware of business "opportunity" scams that you may find out about on the Internet, in your local newspaper, through the mail, and so on. Typically, the promoters of these scams promise that you'll earn big bucks after you pay them for equipment, software, supplies, training materials, and/or business leads. Typically, the value of what they sell you is negligible and far less than the fee you pay to the business promoters. Two of the most common work-at-home scams are envelope stuffing and medical billing.

If a business opportunity sounds interesting, ask the promoter to send you printed information about its offer. Among other things, the information should

- Indicate the promoter's name, address, and phone number.

- Explain the business opportunity in detail — what you will get for your money and what assistance the promoter will give you.

- State the opportunity's total cost, as well as how and how often you'll be paid, who will pay you, and all terms and conditions for getting paid.

Ask for the names and phone numbers of people who have pursued the business opportunity, and contact them to find out if it lived up to their expectations. If the business promoter offers instead to provide you with a list of testimonials from happy business owners, don't accept it. The testimonials may be made up. Don't work with a business opportunity promoter who has no information to send you or no references you can contact.

Also, ask to see a copy of the contract you will have to sign if you agree to work with the promoter. The contact information should match the company's printed information and whatever you may have been told via an e-mail or over the phone.

Federal law requires promoters who charge more than $500 for a business opportunity to also tell you how much you can earn from the opportunity and the number and the percentage of individuals who have earned at least that much recently.

Never pay any money to one of these companies without checking first with your local Better Business Bureau and with the Better Business Bureau where the company is located, as well as with your state attorney general's office and with the Federal Trade Commission. They can tell you if they've received complaints from consumers who feel that a business opportunity promoter ripped them off. Contact these same organizations if you get ripped off by a business opportunity scam, and talk to a consumer law attorney if you lost a substantial amount of money as a result.

Chapter 6

Negotiating with Your Creditors

*I*f slashing your spending, making more money, and living on a strict budget are not enough to resolve your financial problems, it's time to bite the bullet and contact your creditors. You want to find out if they will negotiate new, more affordable debt payment plans so you can get caught up with whatever is past due and continue paying on your debts. You may resist the idea of negotiating, but getting some relief from your debts can mean no more futile struggles to keep up with what you owe, an end to threatening letters and calls from annoying debt collectors, and less damage to your credit history.

We can't guarantee that 100 percent of your creditors will agree to sit down at the bargaining table with you. But if you contact them soon enough — as soon as you realize it's going to be a struggle to keep up with your debts, or as soon as you begin to fall behind on your payments — we bet that most creditors agree to work with you. They may not give you everything you ask for, but just a few concessions from your creditors can make a big difference to the state of your finances and, ultimately, can help keep you out of bankruptcy court.

In this chapter, we tell you about the preparation you should do before you contact any of your creditors, and we fill you in on how to contact them and who to speak with. We also explain what you should and should not say during your negotiations and highlight the importance of putting in writing the details of any agreement you may reach with a creditor.

Getting Ready to Negotiate

Upfront planning and organizing is essential to the success of any negotiation, whether you're trying to negotiate world peace or convince one of your creditors to let you pay less each month or have a lower interest rate.

Your upfront planning and organizing should include

- ✔ Creating a detailed list of your debts.

- ✔ Deciding which debts to negotiate first and what you want to ask from each of your creditors.

- ✔ Reviewing your budget (or creating one if you don't have one yet — see Chapter 4).

- ✔ Pulling together your financial information.

In this section, we walk you through each of these steps. If you don't do the necessary planning and organizing, you won't have any idea what you really need from each creditor and what you can offer in return. You'll be shooting in the dark, and the results could be disastrous for your finances.

If you don't feel comfortable about doing your own negotiating, you may want to ask your attorney or CPA to handle it for you if you have a long-established relationship with that person. Assuming you have that kind of relationship, the CPA or attorney may agree to help you out for very little money. Another option is to get negotiating help from a nonprofit credit counseling agency in your area. (In Chapter 8, we explain how to choose a credit counseling agency and review the various ways that it can help you with your debts.) You can also ask a friend or relative for help, especially if you know someone who is good at making deals.

Listing all your debts

Create a list of all your debts, separating the ones that are high priority from the ones that are low priority. (In Chapter 4, we distinguish between these two types of debt.) For each debt on your list, record the following information:

- ✔ The name of the creditor

- ✔ The amount you are supposed to pay every month

- ✔ The interest rate on the debt

- ✔ The debt's outstanding balance

Also, note whether you are current or behind on your payments. If you are behind, record the number of months you are in arrears and the total amount that is past due.

You should also note whether a debt is secured or unsecured. For each secured debt, write down the asset that secures it. For example, your car secures your auto loan, and your house secures your mortgage and any home equity loans you may have. (In Chapter 4, we explain the differences between secured and unsecured debts.)

When you list your unsecured debts, like your credit card debts and past-due medical bills, list them according to their interest rates. Put the debt with the highest rate at the very top of the list, followed by the one with the next highest rate, and so on.

Leave space next to each debt on your list for recording the new payment amount you would like each creditor to agree to, or for recording any other changes you want from a creditor, such as a lower interest rate or the ability to make interest-only payments for a period of time. You will record this information after you have reviewed your budget.

Zeroing in on certain debts first

As we explain in Chapter 4, all debts are not created equal. Some debts are more important than others because the consequences of falling behind on those obligations are a lot more severe. For example, if you don't keep up with your secured debts, the creditors may take back their *collateral:* the assets you used to guarantee payment. You could also lose assets if you don't pay the taxes you owe to the IRS. (Part III of this book offers specific information about negotiating various types of high priority debts.) Therefore, when you are preparing to negotiate with your creditors, negotiate these debts first:

- ✔ Your mortgage
- ✔ Your past-due rent
- ✔ Your car loan
- ✔ Your utility bills
- ✔ Your court-ordered child support obligation
- ✔ Your past-due federal taxes
- ✔ Your federal student loans

During your negotiations, don't be so eager to reach an agreement with one of your creditors that you offer to pay more than you really can afford. Also, don't agree to a temporary change in how you pay a debt if you really need the change to be permanent. If you can't live up to the agreement as a result, most creditors probably won't negotiate with you again.

When you negotiate your lower priority debts, which will probably all be unsecured debts (such as credit card debt and medical bills), start by negotiating the one with the highest rate of interest. That's because the debt is costing you the most each month.

Reviewing your budget

After you create your list of debts, it's time to review your household budget. You need to figure out exactly what you need from each creditor in order to be able to pay off any past-due amounts and keep up with future payments. For example, you may want a creditor to agree to

✓ Lower the amount of your monthly payments on a permanent or temporary basis.

✓ Lower your interest rates.

✓ Let you make interest-only payments for a while.

✓ Waive or lower certain fees.

✓ Let you pay the amount that is past due by adding that total to the end of your loan rather than paying a portion of the past-due amount each month.

If you are at least 120 days past due on a debt, you may want to ask the creditor to let you settle the debt for less than the full amount you owe on it. The creditor may be willing to do that if it's convinced that settling is its best shot at getting at least some of what you owe. For example, the creditor may know that suing you for the full amount of your debt would be a waste of time because you are *judgment proof:* You have no assets that the creditor can take, and your state prohibits wage garnishment.

There can be federal tax ramifications to settling a debt for less. The amount the creditor writes off is treated as income to you and may increase the amount you owe to the IRS when your taxes are due. For example, if you owe $10,000 to a creditor and the creditor agrees to let you settle the debt for $6,000, it sends the IRS a 1099 form reporting the $4,000 difference as your income. However, you may not be affected if you are insolvent by IRS 1099 standards. A CPA can tell you if the IRS considers you to be insolvent.

When one of your creditors agrees to let you settle a debt for less, ask the creditor to report the debt as current and to remove all negative information related to the debt from your credit report. The creditor may or may not comply with your requests, but you won't know unless you ask.

Negotiating basics

When they sit down at the bargaining table, savvy negotiators employ some basic rules to increase their chances of leaving with a deal that makes them happy. So take a cue from them by keeping the following in mind when you negotiate with your creditors:

✔ **Never put all your cards on the table.** When you tell a creditor how much you can afford to pay on a debt each month, the number of months that you want to make interest-only payments, and so on, always hold a little back. By not letting the creditor know right away what your bottom-line offer is, you give yourself some room to negotiate. If you are lucky, the creditor will accept your initial offer. But if the creditor responds with a counteroffer — maybe he wants you to pay a little more each month than you've suggested, or he offers to lower your interest rate two percentage points when you had asked for a four-point reduction — you can either respond with another offer or accept the creditor's offer and still be better off financially than you are now.

✔ **Know your bottom line.** Know the minimum that you need to get out of your negotiations and the most that you can afford to give to a creditor. Never agree to more than that.

✔ **Understand that you have to give a little to get a little.** A negotiation is successful when both parties leave the bargaining table with something. For example, in exchange for a creditor agreeing to lower your monthly payments, you may have to give the creditor a lien on another one of your assets. However, your goal is to give as little as possible in exchange for getting as much as possible.

✔ **Recognize who has the edge in your negotiations.** Whoever has the edge will have a stronger bargaining position, and the other person will have to give a little extra in order to have any chance of leaving the bargaining table with something. Your creditors will almost always be in a stronger position than you. That's certainly true for your secured creditors because if you can't strike a deal with them, they know they can always take your collateral back.

✔ **Never be demanding, and never get angry or confrontational.** If you do, the creditor may simply cut off the negotiations. When you feel like you are about to lose your cool, end the conversation and resume it after you've had an opportunity to clear your head and calm down.

Pulling together your financial information

Some creditors may want to review your financial information before they agree to negotiate with you or agree to the changes you request. Prepare for that possibility by gathering together the following information and putting everything in one place for easy access:

- Your household budget
- The list of all your debts
- A list of your assets and their approximate values

Sharing information about your assets with your creditors can be dangerous. If one of them decides to sue you to collect on your debt, you've made it easy for that creditor to figure out which asset(s) to go after. However, if you are anxious to strike deals with your creditors so you can continue paying off your debts, you are between a rock and a hard place; you may have no option but to share the information with them. Another risk you take by sharing information about your assets is that a creditor may demand that you sell one of your assets and give it the sale proceeds. However, you don't have to take that step unless you want to and unless doing so is in your best financial interest.

- Copies of your loan agreements

After you have pulled together your financial information, review your list of assets to determine if you can use any of them as collateral. (Ordinarily, you must own the assets free and clear in order to use them as collateral.) Perhaps you own a boat, motorcycle, or RV, for example. As a condition of agreeing to lower your monthly payments or to let you make interest-only payments for a couple months, one of your secured creditors may require that you increase your collateral. If you do not have any assets that you can use as collateral, the creditors may decide it is too risky to work with you, and they may decide to take back the collateral you've already used to secure your debts with them.

A creditor may make having a cosigner a condition of any new agreement. We suggest that you determine ahead of time if a friend or relative would be willing to cosign for you. As a cosigner, your friend or relative will be as responsible for living up to the agreement as you are, which means that if you default on the agreement, the creditor can look to your cosigner for payment. To be fair, before you ask someone to cosign for you, be sure that you can live up to the terms of the agreement. Also, make your friend or relative aware of the risks of cosigning before she signs any paperwork related to the agreement.

Getting Down to Business: Contacting Creditors

After you've completed all your upfront planning and organizing, you're ready to begin contacting your creditors. How you contact them — in person or by phone — and who you talk to will depend on the type of creditor. For example, if the creditor is local (and not part of a national chain), an in-person meeting is appropriate, and you probably want to meet with the owner, credit manager, or office manager. However, if you want to negotiate your MasterCard or Visa bill, your mortgage, or the debt you owe to a national retail chain, for example, you start negotiating by calling the company's customer service number.

If a creditor asks you to put your negotiating request in writing, send the details of your request via certified mail and request a return receipt. That way, you have confirmation that your letter was received, and you will know when to follow up.

 Whenever you speak with someone, maintain a record of who you spoke to (name and title), the date of your conversation, what you asked for, how the creditor responded, and the specifics of any agreement you reached. You should also file away all correspondence related to your negotiations that you send or receive.

When you contact a creditor for the first time, explain that you are having financial problems and provide a general explanation of why the problems have occurred. For example,

✔ You lost your job.

✔ Your child is ill, and you have been saddled with a lot of unreimbursed medical expenses.

✔ Your former spouse is not paying you the child support you're entitled to.

✔ You took on too much credit card debt.

Give the creditor confidence that you'll be able to live up to any agreement you may reach with one another by explaining what you are doing (or have already done) to improve your financial situation and to minimize the likelihood that you'll develop money problems in the future. For example,

- ✔ You are living on a strict budget.
- ✔ You have enrolled in a money management class.
- ✔ You are working at a second job.
- ✔ Your spouse has taken a job outside the home.

Tell the creditor that you want to continue paying on your debt, but in order to do so you need the creditor to agree to some changes. Be specific about exactly what you want the creditor to agree to. For example, you would like to pay $100 less each month on your debt or to make interest-only payments for three months.

If you get nowhere with the first person you speak with, end your conversation and try negotiating with someone higher up, like a supervisor or a manager. That person is likely to have more decision-making authority and to be in a position to agree to your request. In fact, when you call a creditor for the first time, you may want to ask the person you speak with if he has the authority to negotiate with you. If that person does not, ask who does.

Some of your creditors may refuse to negotiate directly with you and may indicate that you should contact a credit counseling agency and let it do the negotiating for you. In Chapter 8, we tell you how credit counseling agencies work.

If the person you are negotiating with tries to pressure you into paying more than you can afford, stick to your guns.

Making the Agreement Official: Putting It in Writing

Whenever you and a creditor reach an agreement, ask for the agreement to be put in writing. If the creditor refuses, prepare the agreement yourself, date and sign it, and then send a copy to the creditor. The agreement should include

- ✔ Its duration.
- ✔ All deadlines.
- ✔ All payment amounts.

✔ Applicable interest rates.

✔ The amount of any fees you have agreed to and under what circumstance you must pay each fee.

✔ Everything the creditor has agreed to do or not do. For example, the creditor may agree to waive certain fees, forgive a past-due amount, or not report to the credit bureaus that your account is delinquent.

✔ When you and the creditor will be considered in default of the agreement and the consequences of the default

If a problem develops with your agreement after it is official — if your creditor violates some aspect of the agreement or accuses you of doing the same thing — and you do not have the terms of the agreement in writing, resolving your differences may be difficult. Each of you is apt to have different memories of the agreement details. As a result, you may both have to hire attorneys to help you work out your disagreement, and you may end up in court where a judge will decide what to do.

Before you sign any agreement that you may reach with a creditor, especially if it involves a lot of money or an asset that you do not want to lose, ask a consumer law attorney to review the agreement. You want to be sure that you are adequately protected and that the agreement does not have the potential to create future problems for you.

Don't hire an attorney until you have found out how much he will charge to do the review, which should not take more than one hour of his time. Most attorneys charge between $100 and $500 per hour for their services, depending on where they practice law and the size of the law firms they work for: Attorneys in metropolitan areas on the East and West coasts tend to charge more than attorneys in rural areas or in the Midwest. Attorneys who work for large firms tend to charge more per hour than attorneys with smaller firms.

If you cannot afford to hire an attorney, you may be able to get help from the Legal Aid Society in your area, which is essentially a law firm for poor people. Also, if there is a law school in your area, it may run a legal clinic, and an attorney or law school student with the clinic can review your agreement for free. Another option is to contact your local or state bar association to find out if it can refer you to a consumer law attorney who does a lot of pro bono work for financially strapped consumers.

After you have a final agreement with a creditor, revise your budget accordingly. When you are ready to contact another creditor, be sure that you prepare for your negotiations by working with the revised budget, not with your old one.

Chapter 7

Consolidating Your Debts

· ·

In This Chapter

▶ Understanding when debt consolidation makes sense

▶ Getting a rundown on your consolidation options

▶ Steering clear of options that can make your finances worse

· ·

Debt consolidation is another option for managing your debts when you owe too much to your creditors. It involves using new debt to pay off existing debt. When done right, it can help you get out of debt faster and pay less in interest on your debts. Although debt consolidation is not *the answer* to your money problems, in many situations it can help when you use it together with other debt management strategies in this book. However, if your finances are in really bad shape, consolidating your debts probably won't help much, if at all.

In this chapter, we explain when debt consolidation is and isn't a good debt management strategy. We also review the various ways you can consolidate your debts, explain how each option works, and review its advantages and disadvantages. We then warn you against dangerous debt consolidation offers that harm, not help, your finances.

Knowing When Debt Consolidation Makes Sense

When you consolidate debt, you use credit to pay off multiple debts, exchanging multiple monthly payments to creditors for a single payment. When done right, debt consolidation can help you accelerate the rate at which you get out of debt, lower the amount of interest you have to pay to your creditors, and improve your credit rating. However, to achieve these potential debt consolidation benefits, the following criteria need to apply:

✔ **The interest rate on the new debt is lower than the rates on the debts you consolidate.** For example, say you have debt on credit cards with interest rates of 22 percent, 20 percent, and 18 percent. If you transfer the debt to a credit card with a rate of 15 percent, or you get a bank loan at a rate of 10 percent and use it to pay off the credit card debt, you improve your situation.

✔ **You lower the total amount of money you have to pay on your debts each month.**

✔ **You don't trade fixed-rate debt for variable-rate debt.** The risk you take with a variable rate is that although the rate may start out low, it could move up. Worst-case scenario: The rate could increase so much that you end up paying more each month on your debt.

✔ **You pay off the new debt as quickly as you can.** Ideally, you apply all the money you save by consolidating (and more, if possible) to paying off the new debt.

✔ **You commit to not taking on any additional debt until you pay off the debt you consolidated.**

Paying less on your debts isn't the only benefit of debt consolidation. Another advantage is that by juggling fewer payment due dates, you should be able to pay your bills on time more easily. On-time payments translate into fewer late fees and less damage to your credit history.

However, too many consumers consolidate their debts and then get deep in debt all over again because they are not good money managers, because they have spending problems, or because they feel under less pressure after they've consolidated, so they get careless about their finances. For these consumers, debt consolidation becomes a dangerous, no-win habit.

Considering Your Options

You can consolidate your debts in several ways. Your options include

✔ Transferring high interest credit card debt to a credit card with a lower interest rate.

✔ Getting a bank loan.

✔ Borrowing against your whole life insurance policy.

✔ Borrowing from your retirement account.

Deciding if debt consolidation is right for you and which option is best can be confusing. If you need help figuring out what to do, talk to your CPA or financial advisor, or get affordable advice from a reputable nonprofit credit counseling organization (see Chapter 8). The more debt you are thinking about consolidating, the more important it is to seek objective advice from a qualified financial professional. Otherwise, you may make an expensive mistake.

Transferring balances

Transferring high interest credit card debt to a lower interest credit card — the lower, the better — is an easy way to consolidate debt. You can make the transfer by using a lower rate card that you already have, or you can use the Web to shop for a new card with a more attractive balance transfer option. Sites to shop at include www. cardtrak.com, www.cardweb.com, and www.cardratings.com.

Before you transfer balances, read all the information provided by the card issuer that explains the terms and conditions of the transfer — the stuff in tiny print. After you review it, you may conclude that the offer isn't as good as it appeared at first glance. For example, you may find that the transfer offer comes with a lot of expensive fees and penalties and that the interest rate on the transferred debt can skyrocket if you are just one date late with a payment.

Also, higher interest rates (not the balance transfer interest rate) will apply to any new purchases you make with the card, as well as to any cash advances you get from it. If the credit card offer does not spell out what the higher rates are, contact the card issuer to find out.

When a credit card company mails you a preapproved balance transfer offer, the interest rate on the offer may not apply to you. That's because most offers entitle the credit card company to increase the interest rate after reviewing your credit history.

To be sure that a balance transfer offer will really save you money, ask the following questions:

 ✔ **What's the interest rate on the offer, and how long will the rate last?** Many credit card companies try to entice you with a low rate balance transfer offer, but the offer interest rate may expire after a couple months, and then it may increase considerably. In fact, you could find yourself paying a higher rate of interest on the transferred debt than you were paying before. If you can't afford to pay off the new debt while the low rate offer is in effect, don't make the transfer unless the higher rate will still be lower than the rates you are currently paying.

Some people try to avoid higher rates on transferred credit card debt by regularly moving the debt from one card to another. Doing so damages your credit history and hurts your credit scores.

✔ **What must I do to keep the interest rate low?** Know the rules! Usually, a low rate will escalate if you don't make your card payments on time. However, if the card you use to consolidate debt includes a *universal default clause,* the credit card company can raise your interest rate at any time if it reviews your credit history and notices that you were late with a payment to another creditor, took on a lot of new debt, bounced a check, and so on.

The method you use to transfer credit card debt — going to the bank to get a cash advance through your credit card, writing a convenience check, or handling the transfer by phone or at the Web site of the credit card company — can affect the interest rate you end up paying on the new debt, as well as the fees you're charged as a result of the transfer. Typically, getting a cash advance at your bank is the most costly option. Before you transfer credit card debt, get clear about the interest rate and fees associated with each transfer option, and choose the one that costs the least.

If you decide to use one of the convenience checks you receive from a credit card company, be aware that some of those checks may have lower interest rates than others, and the interest rates associated with some of the checks may last longer than others. The terms associated with each check should be spelled out in the information the credit card company mailed with the checks. If you are confused, call the credit card company.

✔ **When will interest begin to accrue on the debt I transfer?** Usually, the answer is "right away."

✔ **How much is the balance transfer fee?** Fees vary, but typically they are a percentage of the amount you transfer, usually with a max of $50 to $75. Some credit card companies charge a flat balance transfer fee.

✔ **What method will the credit card company use to compute my monthly payments?** Credit card companies use one of several types of balance computation methods to determine the amount you must pay each month, and some methods cost you more than others.

Look for a card that uses the *adjusted balance* or the *average daily balance (excluding new purchases)* method to figure out your minimum monthly payments. Avoid credit cards that use the *two-cycle average daily balance* method if you can.

Also note whether the card has a 20- or a 30-day *billing cycle* — the number of days between statements. You pay more to use a card with a 20-day cycle.

If you plan to make purchases with the credit card after you've paid off the transferred card balances, also pay attention to the interest rate that applies to new purchases.

Getting a bank loan

Borrowing money from a bank (or a savings and loan or credit union) is another way to consolidate debt. However, if your finances are not in great shape, you may have a hard time qualifying for a loan with an attractive interest rate.

You can use different types of loans to consolidate debt: debt consolidation loans, loans against the equity in your home, and loans to refinance your mortgage.

When you're in the market for any type of loan, it pays to shop around. Some lenders offer better terms on their loans, and some loan officers may be more willing than others to work with you. However, if you have a good long-standing relationship with a bank, contact it first.

Taking out a debt consolidation loan

As the name implies, a debt consolidation loan has the specific purpose of helping you pay off debt. Depending on the state of your finances and how much money you want to borrow, you may qualify for an *unsecured* debt consolidation loan — one that doesn't require a lien on your assets. But under the best of circumstances, most banks won't lend you more than $5,000 unsecured.

If you qualify only for a *secured* debt consolidation loan, you have to let the bank put a lien on one of your assets. That means if you can't keep up with your loan payments, you risk losing the asset. It also means that if you have no assets to put up as collateral, getting a debt consolidation loan is out of the question.

If a lender tells you that the only way you can qualify for a debt consolidation loan is to have a friend or family member cosign the note, think twice before you do that. As cosigner, your friend or family member will be as obligated as you are to repay the debt. If you can't keep up with your payments, the lender will expect your cosigner to finish paying off the note, and your relationship with the cosigner may be ruined as a result. Plus, making the payments could be a real financial hardship for your cosigner, and if she falls behind on them, her credit history could be damaged.

Borrowing against your home equity

If you're a homeowner and you are current on your mortgage payments, some lenders may suggest that you consolidate your debts by borrowing against your home's equity. *Equity* is the difference between your home's current value and the amount of money you still owe on it. Most lenders will loan you up to 80 percent of the equity in your home.

Some lenders let you borrow more than the value of your equity in some cases. Never do that! If you borrow more than the value of your equity and then you need or want to move, you won't be able to sell your home because you owe more on it than it is worth.

Pros and cons

Consolidating debt by using a home equity loan can be attractive for a couple reasons:

- ✔ It's a relatively easy way to pay off debt, and the loan's interest rate will be lower than some other debt consolidation options.

- ✔ Assuming you're not borrowing more than $100,000, the interest you pay on the loan is tax deductible.

However, and this is a really big *however,* your home secures the loan, which means that if you can't make the loan payments, you can lose your home. If your finances are already going down the tubes, borrowing against the equity in your home is risky business and just doesn't make sense. And even if you're able to meet your financial obligations right now, if you owe a lot to your creditors and you have little or nothing in savings, a job loss, an expensive illness, or some other financial setback could make you fall behind on your home equity loan.

Also, be aware that if you sell your home and you still owe money on your mortgage and on your home equity loan, you have to pay back both loans for the sale to be complete. In other words, if your home doesn't sell for enough to pay off everything you owe on your home, you have to come up with enough money to pay the difference. If the housing market in your area is cooling off, and especially if you paid top dollar for your home, consolidating debt by tapping your home's equity is probably not a good move.

If you do decide that a home equity loan makes sense for you, keep the following in mind:

✔ Borrow as little as possible, not necessarily the total amount that the lender says you can borrow.

✔ Pay off the debt as quickly as you can. Lenders typically offer very relaxed home equity loan repayment terms, and why not? The longer it takes you to repay your home equity debt, the more money the lender earns in interest.

✔ Know your rights. When you borrow against your home, the Federal Truth in Lending Act requires lenders to give you a three-day cooling off period after you sign the loan paperwork. During this time, you can cancel the loan in writing. If you do, the lender must cancel its lien on your home and refund all the fees you've paid.

✔ Beware of predatory home equity lenders who encourage you to lie on your loan application so you can borrow more money than you actually qualify for. These lenders gamble that you'll default on the loan and they'll end up with your home. The same is true of unscrupulous home equity lenders who *over-appraise* your home (give it a greater value than it's really worth) in order to lend you more money than you can afford to repay.

Also, steer clear of lenders who want you to sign loan agreements before all the terms of the loan are spelled out in black and white, and avoid loans with prepayment penalties.

Two ways to borrow against your home equity

You can tap the equity in your home in one of two ways: by getting a home equity loan or by using a home equity line of credit. Here's a quick overview of how each option works:

✔ **Home equity loan:** The loan has a fixed or variable interest rate, and you repay it by making regular monthly payments for a set amount of money over a specific period of time. If you apply for a variable rate loan, be sure you understand what will trigger rate increases and the likely amount of each increase. If you're not careful, the initial rate can increase so much that you may begin having problems making your loan payments.

✔ **Home equity line of credit (HELOC):** A HELOC functions a lot like a variable rate credit card. You're approved to borrow up to a certain amount of money — your credit limit — and you can tap the credit whenever you want, usually by writing a check. Typically, a lender calculates the total amount of your credit line by taking a percentage (usually between 75 and 80 percent) of your home's appraised value and then subtracting from it the outstanding balance on your mortgage. The lender also reviews your credit history and/or credit score and takes a look at your overall financial condition.

While you have to repay a home equity loan by making fixed monthly payments that include both interest and principal, with a HELOC you usually have the option of making interest-only payments each month or paying interest and principal on the debt. If you opt to make interest-only payments, the amount of the payments depends on the applicable interest rate and on how much of your total credit limit you are using. For example, if you have a $10,000 HELOC but you've borrowed only $5,000 of that money, the amount of interest is calculated on the $5,000.

The problem with making interest-only payments is that the longer the principal is unpaid, the more your HELOC costs you, especially if the interest rate starts to rise. Also, if your HELOC expires after a certain number of years and there is no provision for renewing it, the lender will probably want you to pay the total amount you still owe in a lump sum, also known as a *balloon payment*. If you can't afford to pay it, you may lose your home.

Federal law requires lenders to cap the interest rate they charge on a HELOC. Before you sign any HELOC-related paperwork, get clear on the cap that applies. Also, find out if you can convert the HELOC to a fixed interest rate and the terms and conditions that apply if you do.

Refinancing your mortgage and getting cash out

If you are still paying on your mortgage, refinancing the loan at a lower rate and borrowing extra money to pay off other debts may be another debt consolidation option to consider. (The new mortgage pays off your existing mortgage.) However, refinancing is a bad idea if

✔ You've been paying on the mortgage for more than 10 years, assuming it's a 30-year note. During the first 10 years of a loan, you mostly pay interest on the loan, but after 10 years, you begin paying on the loan's principal. This means that you are closer to having your mortgage paid off and to owning your home outright. If you refinance, you start all over again with a brand-new mortgage.

✔ You can't afford the payments on the new loan. If you fall behind, eventually your mortgage lender will initiate a foreclosure.

Shopping for a home equity loan or line of credit

When you're in the market for a home equity loan or a home equity line of credit, you're not obligated to apply only to the lender who holds your home mortgage. You can apply to any lender who does home equity lending. So shop around for the best deal by using the following terms of credit to compare your options:

✔ **Annual percentage rate (APR):** This is the cost of your borrowing expressed as a yearly rate. It includes all fees and other costs that you must pay to obtain the credit.

✔ **Monthly periodic rate:** Also referred to as a *finance charge,* this is the rate of interest you'll be charged each month on your outstanding debt. The higher the rate, the more the debt will cost you.

✔ **Fees:** The more fees and the higher the fees you have to pay, the more it will cost you to borrow against your home equity. Fees are usually negotiable, but if you're not in a strong financial position, you won't have much bargaining power. Many home equity loans come with the fees built in. This means that you end up borrowing more money but getting less cash and paying more in interest.

✔ **The amount of your monthly payments:** If you start to fall behind on your payments because they are more than you can afford, your interest rate may increase. If you fall too far behind, you may lose your home.

✔ **How long you have to repay the borrowed money:** The longer you take to repay it, the more interest you pay and the greater your risk that something will happen in your life that will make it impossible for you to repay your debt.

✔ **Whether you have to make a balloon payment:** A *balloon payment* is a lump sum payment that you may owe at the end of a loan or when a home equity line of credit expires. If you can't afford to make the payment, you risk foreclosure, even if you've made all your monthly payments on time.

It may make sense to consolidate debt by going from a 30-year note to a 15-year note, assuming you can afford the higher monthly payments. (You pay less interest on a 15-year mortgage, so going from a 30-year to a 15-year loan won't mean doubling your monthly payments.) Run the numbers with your loan officer.

You're playing with fire if you use a mortgage refinance to consolidate debt by trading a traditional mortgage for an interest-only mortgage! Sure, your monthly payments may be lower initially, but after five years (or whenever the interest-only period ends), they will increase substantially, maybe far beyond what you can afford.

Borrowing against your life insurance policy

If you have a whole life insurance policy, you can consolidate your debts by borrowing against the policy's cash value. If you have this kind of policy, you pay a set amount of money each month or year, and you earn interest on the policy's cash value.

Here are two advantages of this option:

- ✔ There is no application to complete and no credit check.
- ✔ After you borrow the money, you won't have to repay it according to a set schedule. In fact, you won't have to repay it at all.

But there's a catch, of course. After you die, the insurance company will deduct the loan's outstanding balance from the policy proceeds. As a result, your beneficiary may end up with less than he or she was expecting, which can create a financial hardship for that person. For example, your surviving spouse or partner may need the money to help pay bills after your death, or your child may need the policy money to attend college.

Before you borrow against your life insurance, read your policy so you understand all the loan terms and conditions. Also, be clear about any fees you may have to pay because they will affect the loan's total cost. If you are unsure about anything, talk with your insurance agent or broker.

Borrowing from your 401 (k) retirement plan

If you're employed, you may be enrolled in a 401(k) retirement plan sponsored by your employer. If your employer is a nonprofit, you may have a 403(b) retirement plan, which works like a 401(k). The money you deposit in your retirement plan is *tax-deferred* income. In other words, whatever you deposit in the account each year won't be recognized as income until you begin withdrawing it during your retirement years. Your employer may match a certain percentage of your deposits.

Most employers that offer 401(k) plans allow their employees to borrow the funds that are in their retirement accounts, up to $50,000 or 50 percent of the value of the account, whichever is less. If the value is less than $20,000, your plan may allow you to borrow as much as $10,000 even if that represents your plan's total value.

No matter how much you borrow, you have five years to repay the money, and you're charged interest on the unpaid balance.

Borrowing against your 401(k) plan may seem like an attractive way to consolidate debt — after all, you're just borrowing your own money! There's no loan application to complete and no credit check. However, unless you are absolutely sure that you can and will repay the loan within the required amount of time, taking money out of your retirement account to pay off debt is a *really* bad idea. Here's why:

✔ If you don't repay every penny within five years, and assuming you are younger than 59½ when you borrow the money, you have to pay a 10 percent penalty on the unpaid balance. On top of that, the IRS treats whatever money you don't repay as an early withdrawal from your retirement account, which means that you're taxed on it as though it's earned income. As a result, on April 15 you can end up owing Uncle Sam a whole lot more in taxes than you anticipated, and you may not have enough money to pay them. (In Chapter 14, we explain your options for paying your taxes and tell you what the IRS may do to collect any taxes you don't pay.)

You may promise yourself that you'll repay your retirement account loan, but with no lender (or debt collector) pressuring you into paying what you owe, are you disciplined enough to do that? If you're like a lot of consumers, you'll keep promising yourself that you'll pay back the loan, but you'll never get around to it. Or if you begin having trouble paying for essentials, those expenses will take priority, and you may have no money left to put toward repaying your retirement account loan.

✔ Every dollar you borrow represents one less dollar you'll have for your retirement if you don't repay the loan. Using your retirement account like a piggy bank could make your so-called *golden years* not so golden.

✔ While the loan is unpaid, your retirement account earns less tax-deferred interest. Therefore, there is less money in the account when you retire.

✔ If your employer matches the contributions you make to your retirement plan, those contributions may end while you're repaying the loan. This also means less money for your retirement.

✔ Your employer may charge you a steep loan application fee — a couple hundred dollars or more. The fee increases the total cost of the loan.

✔ If you leave your job before you've paid off the loan — regardless of whether you leave because you found a better job, you were fired or laid off, or your employer went belly up — your employer will probably require that you repay the full amount of your outstanding loan balance within a very short period of time, somewhere between 30 and 90 days. If you can't come up with the bucks, the IRS will treat the unpaid money as an early withdrawal for tax purposes, and you'll also have to pay the 10 percent early withdrawal penalty.

Use the online calculator at `www.bankrate.com/brm/calc/401kl.asp` to figure out whether borrowing from your 401(k) is a good idea.

If you are younger than 59½, you may qualify for an early hardship withdrawal from your 401(k), even if your plan does not permit you to borrow from it. A withdrawal differs from a loan because you take the money out of your account without the option of repaying it. Therefore, you are permanently reducing the amount of money you'll have for your retirement. To be eligible for a hardship withdrawal, you must prove to your employer that you have "an immediate and heavy financial need" and that you've exhausted all other financial avenues for handling the need. Although your employer determines what constitutes "an immediate and heavy financial need," avoiding an eviction or foreclosure or paying steep medical bills almost certainly qualifies. You have to pay federal taxes on the money you take out for the year in which you get the money, and you also have to pay a 10 percent early withdrawal penalty. There's no free lunch in life, is there!

Avoiding Dangerous Debt Consolidation Possibilities

When your debts are creating a lot of stress, your judgment may get clouded. You may start grasping at straws and do something really stupid that you would never do if you were thinking clearly — like fall for one of the many debt consolidation offers out there that are outrageously expensive and maybe even scams. Here are some of the worst offenders to avoid:

✔ **Debt counseling firms that promise to lend you money to help pay off your debts.** If you get a loan from one of these outfits, it will not only have a high interest rate, but you may have to secure the loan with your home. Watch out! In Chapter 8, we tell you how to find a reputable nonprofit counseling agency that can help you deal with your debts. That chapter also explains how to avoid agencies that pretend to be nonprofits.

✔ **Finance company loans:** These companies often use advertising to make their debt consolidation loans sound like the answer to your prayers. They are not. Finance company loans typically have high rates of interest and exorbitant fees. As if that's not bad enough, working with a finance company will further damage your credit history.

✔ **Lenders who promise you a substantial loan (probably more than you can afford to repay), no questions asked, in exchange for your paying them a substantial upfront fee:** No reputable lender will make such a promise. Not only will these disreputable lenders charge you a high percentage rate on the borrowed money; they will also put a lien on your home or on another asset you don't want to lose.

✔ **Companies that promise to negotiate a debt consolidation loan for you and to use the proceeds to pay off your creditors:** In turn, they tell you to begin sending them money each month to repay the loan. The problem with many of these companies is that they never get you a loan or pay off your creditors. You send the company money every month while your credit history is being damaged even more, and you're being charged interest and late fees on your unpaid debts.

Chapter 8

Using Credit Counseling to Get a Grip on Your Finances

In This Chapter

▶ Getting help from a credible credit counseling agency

▶ Paying off your debts with a debt management plan

▶ Recognizing the dangers of debt settlement firms

▶ Knowing what to do if you get ripped off

*F*eeling overwhelmed by your debts and unsure how to take control of your finances despite the advice you've read in this book so far? Have you tried without success to pursue the self-help options we discuss in other chapters? Take heart; there is a calm port in the storm called a *credit counseling agency.* Among other services, the agency can help you develop a budget and figure out a way to deal with your debts.

The benefits of credit counseling presume that you work with a reputable, nonprofit credit counseling agency that employs trained and certified credit counselors and that charges fairly for its services. Many credit counseling agencies talk a good game and have impressive Web sites, but they charge an arm and a leg for their services and deliver little in return. If you work with one of them, your finances could end up worse, not better. Yikes!

If you're in the market for credit counseling, this chapter is for you. We give you the information you need to locate a reputable organization. We explain how good credit counseling agencies operate, and we provide you with a set of questions to ask before you agree to work with an agency. We also give you the lowdown on debt management plans in case a credit counseling agency suggests that it set one up for you, and we tell you how to get the most benefit from such a plan.

We also illuminate the dangers of working with a *debt settlement firm*: a firm that agrees to settle your debts for less than what you owe on them. Some consumers confuse debt settlement for credit counseling; we explain how they differ. Finally, we tell you what to do if you are ripped off by a credit counseling agency or a debt settlement firm.

Finding a Reputable Credit Counseling Agency

A reputable credit counseling agency evaluates your finances and comes up with a plan for helping you get out of debt and avoid financial problems in the future. Among other things, the agency

- **Reviews your budget to make sure it is realistic and suggests improvements and/or additional cuts.** If you do not already have a budget, the agency helps you develop one.

- **Assesses the state of your finances.** After reviewing your financial information, the agency gives you a realistic picture of where you are right now financially: no better or worse off than a lot of consumers, on the brink of bankruptcy, or somewhere in between.

- **Figures out how you can keep up with your debts.** The agency may revise your budget in order to generate more *cash flow* (the amount of money you have to spend) each month so you can pay your debts off faster. Or it may recommend that you participate in a debt management plan in order to lower your monthly debt payments to amounts you can afford. If your finances are in really bad shape, the agency may suggest that you meet with a consumer bankruptcy attorney.

  If the credit counseling agency advises you to pay off your debts through a debt management plan, the agency will explain how the plan works and review its pluses and minuses. Also, the agency should give you a general idea of how much you'll have to pay on your debts each month if it sets up a debt management plan for you.

When a credit counseling agency sets up a debt management plan for you, the plan will address your *unsecured* debts, like credit card debts, unpaid medical bills, and student loans. Most credit counseling agencies will not help you with your *secured* debts, such as your mortgage, home equity loan, and car loan. In Chapters 10 and 11, we help you figure out what to do about your mortgage and your car loans when you can't keep up with them.

> ✔ **Helps you set financial goals and provides you with financial education.** The financial education may include workshops and seminars on various aspects of money management, as well as brochures and workbooks.

Telling the good from the bad

Most credit counseling agencies are truly interested in helping consumers get a handle on their debts and develop a solid foundation for a financially sound future. However, some agencies are mostly out to make a buck (or lots of bucks) off consumers who are desperate for help and unaware of the differences between reputable and disreputable credit counseling agencies.

Sadly, consumers who work with a bad apple agency are apt to pay it a lot of money — money they could have used to pay their debts or their living expenses — and get little or nothing in return. In fact, many of these consumers end up worse off financially than they were before. For example, bad apple credit counseling agencies may charge excessive fees, push consumers into debt management plans when they don't need them (so the agencies can charge plan administration fees each month), and offer no financial education or goal-setting assistance.

That's the bad news. The good news is that it's relatively easy to find a good credit counseling agency, assuming that you know the questions to ask and the telltale signs that an agency may not be on the up and up.

If an agency's promises about what it can do for you sound too good to be true, watch out! No matter how much you may want to believe what it says, look for another credit counseling agency to work with.

Avoid credit counseling agencies that solicit your business by phone or e-mail. Also, don't be impressed by agencies that spend money on glossy print ads and regular ads on TV or radio. Reputable organizations do not spend a lot of money on advertising and rely mostly on referrals and word of mouth.

Locating agencies in your area

When you look for a credit counseling agency to work with, check out a couple so you can feel confident that you are going to get good help. Ask friends or relatives who have had a good past experience with credit counseling for a referral. Don't know anyone who's worked with this kind of agency? Here are two other excellent resources for finding a good one:

✔ **The National Foundation for Credit Counseling:** www.nfcc.org or 800-388-2227

✔ **The Association of Independent Consumer Credit Counseling Agencies:** www.aiccca.org or 800-450-1794

The counselors who work for credit counseling agencies that are affiliated with these two organizations are trained and certified.

Another excellent source of reputable credit counseling agencies is the Web site of the United States Trustee. These days, people who want to file for bankruptcy have to obtain a *certificate to file* from a credit counseling agency. Only credit counseling agencies that have been certified by the federal Trustee's office can issue this type of certificate. We think it's safe to assume that the certified agencies are reputable. To find a certified credit counseling agency in your state, go to www.usdoj.gov/ust and click on "Credit Counseling and Debtor Education."

If you don't find credit counseling agencies in your area, or if you will have a difficult time going to a credit counseling agency's office during business hours, many good agencies offer online counseling that can be just as effective as meeting face to face with a credit counselor. However you choose to get the counseling, your method of selecting a credit counselor and your expectations should be the same.

Knowing what to ask and the answers to expect

After you have the names of some agencies, ask each the following set of questions by meeting with a representative from each agency, e-mailing them from their Web sites, or talking with them on the phone. Do not pay a credit counseling agency any money or sign any paperwork until you have received satisfactory answers to each of these questions:

✔ **Are you a federally approved, nonprofit, tax-exempt credit counseling agency?** Nonprofit agencies will charge you the least for their services and provide you with the most in return. Some credit counseling organizations are for-profit businesses even though their names make them sound like they are nonprofits.

Get proof that a credit counseling agency is truly a nonprofit by asking for a copy of its IRS *approval of nonprofit status* letter. The letter is a one-page document. Don't work with an agency that refuses to let you look at this letter or never provides it.

✔ **Do you have a license to offer credit counseling services in my state?** Although some states do not license credit counseling organizations, many do. You can find out if your state requires licensing by contacting your state attorney general's office. If your state does issue licenses, ask for the name of the licensing agency and then get in touch with it to confirm that the credit counseling agency has a valid license.

✔ **What services do you offer?** The upcoming section "Working with a Credit Counselor" describes the services the agency should offer.

✔ **How do you charge for your services?** Reputable credit counseling agencies charge little or nothing for most of their services. However, if you participate in a debt management plan, you will be charged a small monthly administrative fee — probably $40 per month tops. Less reputable agencies charge substantial upfront fees — as much as several hundred dollars — as well as steep monthly fees if they put you in a debt management plan.

Some credit counseling agencies that are not on the up and up don't charge large fees but charge a lot of small fees instead. Over time, all those small fees really add up. Ask the credit counseling agency for a comprehensive list of fees. If it refuses to provide a list or tells you it does not have one, steer clear!

Some states regulate the amount of money a credit counseling agency can charge to set up a debt management plan and to administer it. Contact your state attorney general's office to find out if it regulates these fees.

Watch out for credit counseling agencies that encourage you to give them voluntary contributions. The *contributions* are nothing more than fees to make the agencies more money at your expense.

✔ **Will I be assigned a specific credit counselor to work with?** You should expect to work with one credit counselor.

✔ **How do you pay your credit counselors?** Reputable agencies pay their counselors a salary or pay them by the hour. Avoid agencies where the credit counselors make money by selling services to consumers. The counselors are nothing more than commissioned sales people who have a financial incentive to get you to buy as many services as possible whether you need them or not.

✔ **Can I see a copy of the contract I must sign if I work with you?** Don't work with an agency that does not use a contract or that won't share a copy with you. The contract should clearly state exactly what services the agency will be providing to you, a timeline for those services, and any fees or expenses you must pay. It should also provide information about any guarantees the credit counseling agency is making to you, as well as the name of the credit counselor you'll be working with and the counselor's contact information.

✓ **How will you keep my personal and financial information private and secure?** With identity theft on the rise, you must feel confident that the agency has a strong policy in place to protect your information from strangers.

After you find an agency you'd like to work with, check it out with your local Better Business Bureau and with your state attorney general's office. If either organization indicates that numerous consumers have filed complaints against the agency, reconsider your decision.

You should also check with the Federal Trade Commission (FTC) at www.ftc.gov or by calling 877-382-4857. The FTC is aggressively cracking down on businesses that pretend to be nonprofit credit counseling agencies.

Working with a Credit Counselor

After you have chosen a credit counseling agency, your assigned credit counselor will spend time becoming familiar with you and your finances. If you meet face to face with the counselor, you should expect your initial meeting to last about an hour, and you should expect to have a couple follow-up meetings. If you get your counseling online, you will exchange information and get your questions answered via e-mail.

Sharing your financial situation

At your first meeting (or soon after), be prepared to provide your counselor with such information as

✓ Your household budget, if you have one

✓ A list of your debts, including whether they are secured or unsecured (see Chapter 4)

✓ The amount of money due on each debt every month

✓ The interest rate for each debt

✓ Which debts you are behind on

> ✔ The assets you own and their approximate *market values* (meaning how much you could sell them for)
>
> ✔ Copies of your most recent tax returns or pay stubs reflecting your monthly take-home pay

The counselor uses all this information to prepare a get-out-of-debt plan that is customized just for you. Not only will the plan provide you with a road map for getting out of debt; it should also help you work toward your financial goals like buying a home, saving for your retirement, helping your children pay for their college educations, and so on.

As part of your plan, the credit counselor may suggest that you enroll in one or more of the agency's money management seminars and workshops so you can gain the information and tools you need to avoid debt problems in the future and achieve your financial goals. The seminars and workshops may focus on topics like smart budgeting, managing debt, financial goal setting, and so on. Also, the counselor may give you free money management materials to read.

Whittling down your debt with a debt management plan

If your counselor is unable to figure out a way for you to pay off your debts by reducing your expenses and maybe making more money, the counselor may recommend that you participate in a debt management plan. When you participate in such a plan, the counselor tries to negotiate smaller monthly payments with your creditors.

Getting creditors to buy in

The counselor determines exactly how much you can afford to pay to your unsecured creditors each month in order to eliminate each debt over a three- to five-year period. Then the counselor contacts the creditors to find out if they will agree to let you pay the amounts you can afford. In some instances, the counselor may also ask the creditors for other concessions, such as lowering your interest rates and reducing or waiving any fees you may owe to them.

If your unsecured creditors believe that giving you what you need is their best shot at getting the money you owe, and if they believe you are likely to file for bankruptcy otherwise (which means they may not get a penny from you), they will probably agree to the

plan the credit counselor has proposed. However, most large creditors will have a minimum amount that they expect you to pay on
your debts each month; unless you commit to paying it, they won't
agree to participate in your plan. If some of your creditors refuse
to work with you, you have to continue paying them according to
the original agreements with them.

Many creditors are willing to offer special concessions to consumers who pay off their debts through a debt management plan.
In return, they expect that consumers will not incur additional
debt while they are in their plans.

Working the plan

After the credit counselor has prepared your final debt management plan, ask for a copy. Do not sign it until you have read it carefully, understand everything in it, and are sure that you can live up
to it. Note any restrictions in the plan. For example, it may prohibit
you from taking on additional credit with your current creditors or
applying for new credit while it is in effect. If you violate any aspect
of your plan, you risk having it cancelled.

When your plan is official, you pay your credit counselor every
month the amount of money you have agreed to pay on your
debts, as well as the required monthly fee. In turn, the counselor
pays your creditors.

Make sure your debt management plan says that your credit counselor will send you regular monthly updates on the status of your
debt management plan, including confirmation that each of your
creditors was paid according to the terms of the plan.

Beware of credit counseling agencies that spend little or no time
evaluating your finances before advising you to enroll in a debt
management plan or that ask you to begin paying on a debt management plan before your creditors have agreed to work with you.

Also, be aware that some creditors who agree to be part of your
plan may report you as slow paying or as paying through a debt
management plan, which will damage your credit history a little.
However, statistics show that successfully completing a debt management plan actually increases your *FICO score*: the numeric representation of your creditworthiness that is derived from the
information in your credit history. (For more information about
FICO scores, see Chapter 2.)

Actively managing your plan

Even when you are careful about choosing a credit counseling agency to work with, if you participate in a debt management plan, problems can develop that may undermine the plan benefits. Follow these tips to minimize the potential for problems:

✔ After your counselor tells you which of your unsecured creditors have agreed to participate in your debt management plan, contact them to confirm their participation before you send the counselor any money.

However, taking this step before paying any money may not always be possible. Due to cost constraints, a nonprofit credit counseling agency may not contact your creditors to find out if they will participate in your debt management plan until you have given the agency an initial month's payment on the plan. The agency wants to be sure that you are serious about paying your debts before it spends time negotiating the plan details with your creditors.

✔ If your counselor tells you that one of your creditors won't agree to participate in your plan until you send the counselor an upfront payment, contact the creditor to confirm that what the counselor says is true.

✔ Make sure that the schedule your counselor sets up for paying your debts provides enough time for your creditors to receive what they are owed each month before the payment due dates. Otherwise, you risk racking up late fees and penalties.

✔ Every month, just after the date that your counselor is due to make a payment, confirm with the counselor that the payment was made on time.

✔ Whenever you receive a monthly statement of your account from one of the creditors participating in your debt management plan, review it carefully to make sure your account was credited appropriately. Also, make sure that each creditor made whatever concessions it agreed to make, such as lowering your interest rate, waiving certain fees, or allowing you to make reduced payments or interest-only payments for a while.

Avoiding Debt Settlement Firms

Some people confuse debt settlement firms, also known as *debt negotiation firms,* with credit counseling agencies. Don't make this mistake. Although a debt settlement firm may try to confuse you by choosing a name that sounds like a nonprofit credit counseling agency, debt settlement companies are in business to make money.

The services they offer are very different from those of a legitimate credit counseling agency. Also, if you work with a debt settlement firm, you risk harming your finances and damaging your credit history and your FICO score.

Being wary of false promises

Debt settlement firms claim that they can settle your unsecured debts for less than the full amount you owe on them. In other words, after you pay the settlement amounts, your creditors will consider the debts to be paid in full. For example, if you owe $10,000 in credit card debt, a debt settlement firm may tell you that it can get the creditor to agree to let you pay the debt off for $6,000.

You can try to settle your own debts, for free. You don't need a debt settlement firm to do it for you. In Chapter 6, we tell you how to negotiate with your creditors.

(But keep in mind that if a creditor agrees to forgive part of your debt, the IRS will probably treat that forgiven amount as income to you, and you will be taxed on it. If you receive an IRS 1099 form related to a debt that you settled, talk to a CPA. If the CPA can prove that you were insolvent at the time that the amount of the debt was forgiven, you won't be taxed on that amount. You're *insolvent* if you don't have enough money to pay your debts and living expenses and you don't have any assets you can sell to pay off the debts.)

Some debt settlement firms also promise that after they settle your debts, they can get all the negative information related to those debts removed from your credit history. Not true! Only the creditors that reported the negative information can remove it.

If you agree to work with a debt settlement firm, you may be told to stop paying your unsecured creditors and to begin sending that money to the firm itself. The problem is that a debt settlement firm may be all talk and no action. It may not be able to settle your debts for less. In fact, it may not even try. Furthermore, if it does intend to try to settle your debts, it may take months for the firm to accumulate enough money from the payments you are sending to be able to propose settlements to your creditors. Meanwhile, your debts are going unpaid, your credit history is being damaged further, and the total amount you owe to your creditors is increasing because late fees and interest are accumulating.

If you question a debt settlement firm about the consequences of not paying your debts, you may hear that your unsecured creditors won't sue you for their money. That is flat-out wrong.

Preventing worse financial problems

Debt settlement firms charge much more money than legitimate credit counseling agencies. If you work with a debt settlement firm, you may have to pay one or more substantial upfront fees, as well as additional fees that may be based on the number of unsecured credit accounts you have, the amount of debt you owe, or the amount of debt that the firm gets your creditors to forgive. In the end, the cost of working with a debt management firm may be more than the amount of money you save from settling your debts.

Be careful if a debt settlement firm offers to loan you money, maybe more than you can really afford to pay. Not only is the loan likely to have a very high interest rate and other unattractive terms of credit, but if you are not careful, you may sign paperwork giving the firm the right to put a lien on an asset you own. The firm is hoping that you'll fall behind on your loan payments so it can take the asset from you.

Getting Relief If You Get Ripped Off

If you get taken by a disreputable credit counseling organization or by a debt settlement firm, contact a consumer law attorney right away. The attorney will advise you of your rights. He may recommend sending a letter on his law firm stationery to the credit counseling organization or debt settlement firm threatening legal action unless the firm makes amends to you (such as by giving you your money back). The credit counseling organization or debt settlement firm may agree to the attorney's demands in order to avoid a lawsuit. If it does not respond or refuses to do what the letter asks, you can decide if you want to go forward with a lawsuit.

Assuming that you have a strong case, the attorney will probably represent you on a *contingent fee* basis. This means that you won't have to pay the attorney any money to represent you. Instead, the attorney gambles that you will win your lawsuit, and the attorney will take his fee from the money that the court awards you as a result. If you lose your lawsuit, you do not have to pay the attorney a fee. However, depending on your agreement with one another, win or lose, you may have to pay the attorney's court costs and any other fees and expenses related to your case.

Regardless of whether you sue the credit counseling organization or debt settlement firm, you should file a complaint against it with your state attorney general's office, your local Better Business Bureau, and the Federal Trade Commission (FTC). Although none of these organizations can help you get your money back or undo any damage done to your credit history and your FICO score, other consumers who may be thinking about working with the same credit counseling agency or debt settlement firm may think twice after reading your complaint. Also, if your state attorney general's office or the FTC receives a lot of complaints about the credit counseling agency or debt settlement firm, it may take legal action against it. For example, it may file a class action lawsuit on behalf of everyone who was ripped off.

Chapter 9

Dealing with Debt Collectors

. . . .

. . . .

*D*ebt collector. If you've ever been contacted by one (or heard horror stories from people who have), just reading those two words may give you a queasy feeling in the pit of your stomach. Even dealing with relatively friendly and polite debt collectors can be downright intimidating. And if you've ever had the misfortune to be contacted by aggressive, high-pressure debt collectors, you know all too well that they are willing to harass and threaten you with all sorts of dire consequences, like jail time, in an effort to get you to pay up.

This chapter arms you with the information and the tools you need to take control when debt collectors come calling. The goal is to ensure that they don't make your life totally miserable or pressure you into paying debts you really can't afford to pay. We explain how debt collectors operate so you understand why they act the way they do, what the law says debt collectors can and can't do in order to collect money from you, and some disturbing new trends in debt collection that it pays to know about.

The chapter also spells out your debt collection rights and your options for responding to a debt collector's demands, including meeting with a consumer law attorney — something that we frequently advise you do. Many debt collectors have become so aggressive and brazen that even when you let them know they have violated your rights, they keep on violating them. Therefore, we believe that you must arm yourself with the information in this chapter *and* consult with a consumer law attorney. Otherwise, aggressive, arrogant debt collectors are going to victimize you.

You probably won't have to pay a consumer law attorney any money to represent you if you've got a strong case against a debt collector because the attorney will charge on a *contingent fee* basis. In other words, the attorney takes his fee out of whatever money the court awards you if you win your lawsuit and gets no fee at all if you lose. Even better, the Fair Debt Collection Practices Act, the federal law that regulates the activities of debt collectors, says that if you win the lawsuit, the debt collector must pay your attorney's fees.

Understanding How Debt Collectors Operate

When you fall behind on the payments you are obligated to make to a creditor, you receive an increasingly serious-sounding series of notices demanding payment. If you don't pay, the creditor is likely to turn your debt over to an outside debt collection agency. When this happens, it won't be long before a debt collector who works for the agency contacts you.

First impressions

Some debt collectors are difficult and demanding right from the start. Others may start out acting relatively friendly on the phone, but if you do not agree to pay what you owe right away, they ratchet up the pressure the next time they get in touch.

Some debt collectors have a deliberate strategy of starting out being really friendly in order to encourage you to let your guard down and say something that could help them collect from you. Other debt collectors have the opposite strategy; they are aggressive and insulting from the get-go. They want to make you cry or feel so guilty about owing money that you will agree to pay your debt regardless of whether doing so is a wise financial move.

Why are debt collectors generally so unpleasant and pushy? Most are paid according to how much they collect, usually on a percentage basis. In other words, the more money they collect, the more money they make. Other debt collectors are paid according to the number of collection calls they place or the number of demand letters they send out, another method that provides them a financial incentive to be persistent, pushy, or even worse. Still others don't work for creditors at all; they buy creditors' old debts, often at a discount. Then the debt collectors try to make a profit by collecting as much as possible as quickly as possible.

Debt collectors also know that statistically, the longer a debt goes unpaid, the less likely it is that they will ever collect it. This knowledge motivates them to start out strong and also encourages them to create a false sense of urgency when they talk to you. For example, they may pressure you to commit to paying your debt by a specific deadline or according to a very short timetable. If you don't agree to their demands, they may try to scare you into capitulating by threatening you with a lawsuit, the loss of your personal property, the garnishment or seizing of all your income, even jail time — regardless of whether these consequences are likely to happen or are even legal. In the upcoming section "What debt collectors can do," we review exactly what actions debt collectors can take if you don't pay a debt and under what circumstances.

What debt collectors can't do

Knowledge is power, and that truth certainly applies to dealing with debt collectors. Knowing how they operate and what they can and can't do to collect a debt from you should make it easier to deal with them and help protect you from their bluster, bullying, and threats.

The Fair Debt Collection Practices Act (FDCPA) is the federal law that applies to debt collection. It clearly states what debt collectors *cannot* do in order to collect money from consumers. The law applies to the collection of personal, household, and family debts like your mortgage and car loan, other personal loans, your credit card debts, past-due utility bills, past-due student loans, medical and insurance debts, condo fees, unpaid legal judgments against you, and bounced checks.

The FDCPA applies to outside debt collectors but not to a creditor's own in-house debt collectors (meaning debt collectors who are employees of a creditor). However, if your state has its own debt collection law, it may cover in-house as well as outside debt collectors. The FDCPA also governs the debt collection activities of attorneys who collect debts for their clients, but it does not apply to employees of federal and state agencies who collect debts for those agencies.

If your state has its own law that applies to debt collectors, it may be tougher and more comprehensive than the federal law. Contact your state attorney general's office to find out if your state has a law and about the protections it provides you.

Debt collectors who are covered by the FDCPA cannot do any of the following to collect a debt from you:

✔ Call you before 8 a.m. or after 9 p.m. unless you tell them it is okay to do so. Also, they cannot contact you at any time that you indicate is inconvenient. For example, if you work the night shift and normally sleep from 8 a.m. to 4 p.m., you can tell debt collectors not to call you during those hours. If they do, they are breaking the law.

In fact, you don't have to talk to debt collectors any time of the day or night if you don't want to. To put an end to their calls, the FDCPA entitles you to tell debt collectors not to call you again. If you say "Stop," they must stop.

✔ Call you on a Sunday.

✔ Contact you at work if the debt collector knows that your employer does not want you to be contacted there during working hours.

✔ Get in touch with your employer about a debt you owe, unless the debt is past-due child support.

✔ Contact your relatives, friends, or neighbors about the money you owe in order to embarrass you into paying your debts. Debt collectors *can* contact these people to obtain information about how to contact you, such as your address or phone number, but they are not permitted to say why they want that information.

✔ Communicate with you about your debt by using a postcard or an envelope that clearly indicates that a debt collector sent it.

✔ Use a letter or envelope to communicate with you that appears to have come from a government agency or a court.

✔ Call you over and over again during a relatively short period of time. For example, they cannot call you repeatedly during a single morning or afternoon or call you day after day. Such behavior is harassment, and the FDCPA makes harassment illegal.

✔ Swear or insult you when you are having a conversation, or threaten you with the loss of your reputation or with jail time. However, debt collectors can threaten you with specific consequences if you don't pay what you owe, assuming that the consequences are legal and that they intend to make good on their threats. For example, they can threaten to garnish your wages unless your state prohibits it, or to take an asset that you own if they are legally entitled to take it. Again, it pays to know your state laws; your state may have a law that protects you from the loss of your home unless you have failed to keep up with your mortgage.

✔ Order you to accept collect calls from them.

✔ Deposit a post-dated check you have given them before the date on the check.

✔ Collect more than you owe on a debt, unless the contract you have with the creditor that turned your debt over to collections allows the debt collector to do that.

As soon as a debt collector does anything that violates the FDCPA and/or your state debt collection law, begin keeping a detailed record of exactly what the debt collector did, including the date and time of each illegal action. Also, save all correspondence you receive from a debt collector, including envelopes. This information can be invaluable if you meet with a consumer law attorney and the attorney advises that you sue the debt collector.

Some debt collectors are so aggressive that when you tell them they have broken the law or threaten to sue you, they adopt a "So what?" attitude and just continue the same behavior. The only effective way to deal with them is to get in touch with a consumer law attorney.

What debt collectors can do

Some debt collectors harass and threaten people with dire consequences to get them to pay their debts. But in reality, if a debt collector is trying to collect an *unsecured* debt (one not collateralized with an asset), such as a credit card debt, medical bill, or small personal loan, he is quite limited in terms of the legal actions he can take to collect from you. This is important information to have when you are deciding how best to respond to a debt collector's demands. In the next section, we review various ways you can respond to a debt collector when he tries to get you to pay a past-due unsecured debt.

If the debt is secured, the story is quite different. A *secured* debt is one collateralized with an asset that you own, like your mortgage and your car loan; you could lose that asset if you do not take care of the debt. Part III of this book zeros in on the collection of secured debts like your home mortgage and car loan, as well as other high-stake debts. The rest of this chapter focuses on the collection of unsecured debts.

If the amount of your debt is relatively small, the debt collector is likely to give up trying to collect it if you don't agree to pay what you owe right away. Most debt collectors are paid based on the amount of money they collect. When it becomes apparent that collecting from you is going to take time and effort, they are likely to move on to greener pastures. However, you don't get off scot-free:

The fact that the debt was sent to collections and remains unpaid will further damage your credit history and your credit score.

Debt collectors will go to considerable lengths to collect large debts. In fact, they may sue you in order to try to collect the money you owe. If a debt collector sues you, you will be notified of the lawsuit via a *summons,* which tells you why you are being sued and for how much, who sued you, and on what date you must appear in court.

 Get in touch with a consumer law attorney as soon as you receive a summons. The attorney may be able to negotiate a settlement with the debt collector, which would bring an end to the lawsuit and mean that you avoid the costs of a trial. If the negotiations are unsuccessful, the attorney can represent you in court. Trying to defend yourself is foolhardy.

Should the debt collector win the lawsuit, the judge awards him a certain amount of money. However, the debt collector cannot collect the money from you right away. Instead, he must get the court's permission to take specific actions in order to try to collect from you. For example, the debt collector may ask the court for permission to

- ✔ **Garnish your wages if wage garnishment is legal in your state.** (It is not legal in Pennsylvania, South Carolina, or Texas.) If the court gives the debt collector permission to garnish your wages, it will issue an order requiring your employer to withhold a certain amount of money from each of your paychecks for a set period of time. That money goes toward paying down your debt.

  If the debt collector is trying to collect unpaid child support that a court ordered you to pay, a past-due federal student loan, or unpaid taxes that you owe to the IRS, the debt collector may get permission to garnish a portion of a pension you may be receiving and even some of your monthly Social Security income. Under certain circumstances, a portion of your Social Security income can also be garnished to pay past-due spousal support.

- ✔ **Take one or more of your assets.** If a debt collector gets permission to take an asset that you own, such as a boat or motorcycle or real estate other than your home, the asset is sold in a public auction and the proceeds are applied to your debt. If the proceeds are not enough to pay off the debt in full, the debt collector is entitled to try to collect the deficiency amount from you.

> ✔ **Put a judgment lien on one of your assets.** When a lien is
> placed on one of your assets, you cannot sell it or borrow
> against it without paying the debt collector the money you
> owe so the lien can be removed.

If you have no assets, and if your state does not permit wage garnishment, you are *judgment proof.* In other words, a debt collector
can do nothing to collect the money you owe.

Depending on the amount of the debt you are being sued for, your
case may be heard in small claims court. The maximum amount
you can be sued for in a small claims court ranges widely from
state to state, from $1,500 to $15,000. When your case is heard in
small claims court, you may have to represent yourself because
many states do not allow attorneys in that kind of court. In that situation, we encourage you to consult with an attorney about how to
defend yourself.

Knowing Your Options When a Debt Collector Calls

The FDCPA gives you a number of different ways to respond to a
debt collector. In other words, you don't have to pay a debt just
because a debt collector demands that you do.

The best option for you depends on a number of factors, including
the kind of debt the debt collector is trying to collect, your financial situation, and whether you agree that you owe the debt. If you
are not sure about how to respond to a debt collector, talk to a
consumer law attorney.

Never voluntarily offer information to a debt collector, and do not
allow yourself to be drawn into a conversation with one. The
FDCPA does not require that you provide any information to a debt
collector or answer any questions a debt collector may ask you. By
talking to a debt collector, you may unwittingly provide information that she can use against you later. As they say, loose lips sink
ships! For example, never give a debt collector your bank account
numbers or any information about your assets.

When a debt collector calls you, ask him for his name and phone
number and tell him that you'll call him right back. By doing so,
you gain time to collect your thoughts and decide how best to
respond to the debt collector. Plus, simply by placing the call,
you're likely to feel more in control of the conversation.

Asking for proof

When a debt collector contacts you about a debt for the first time, that person is legally obligated to send you a written statement within five days indicating how much money you owe and to whom you owe it. The notice must also inform you of your right to request written verification of the debt and your right to dispute the debt.

It's a good idea to request verification of a debt, whether you are sure that you owe it or not. If you know that you owe the money, requesting verification buys you some time to figure out how to deal with the debt. If you are not sure that the debt is yours or you think that you owe less money than the debt collector wants you to pay, you *must* ask that the debt be verified. Always put your verification request in writing, and ask the debt collector to respond to you in writing. Ask the collector to verify not only the original amount of the debt that is still owed, but also any interest, late fees, and collection fees; ask him to itemize each amount instead of presenting the debt as a lump sum.

According to the Federal Trade Commission, which enforces the FDCPA, the number-one complaint it receives about debt collectors is that they try to collect more money than the consumers really owe.

Make a copy of the letter for your files, and send the request via certified mail with a return receipt requested. That way, you know when the letter was received. If the debt collector never responds with the verification, you have proof that the debt collector violated the FDCPA.

Some states limit the kinds of debt-related expenses a debt collector can charge consumers. Find out if your state has such limits by getting in touch with your state attorney general's office or with a consumer law attorney. Also, the contract you signed with your original creditor — the creditor who turned your debt over to a collection agency or sold the debt to the agency — may limit the fees that you can be charged. If you do not have a copy of the contract, ask the debt collector for a copy. Get in touch with a consumer law attorney if the debt collector does not respond to your request or says he does not have a copy either.

If you are confused by the debt collector's verification letter — for example, the amount of money the debt collector says you owe is expressed as a lump sum instead of being broken out — contact him again in writing and ask for a clear explanation. If the debt collector does not provide a clear explanation, get in touch with a consumer law attorney.

Paying the debt

If you agree that you owe the amount a debt collector is trying to collect, you may want to go ahead and pay it. However, don't pay it if doing so jeopardizes your ability to pay your high priority debts, such as your car loan, your mortgage, or other secured debts. Also, don't pay it if doing so undermines your ability to cover your basic living expenses, such as food, utilities, and medical insurance. In Chapter 4, we explain how to distinguish between high and low priority debts and expenses.

Do not let a debt collector guilt you into paying a debt that you really can't afford to pay. If you find yourself wanting to give in to the demands of a debt collector because you feel guilty, end the conversation right away so you can collect your emotions and steel your resolve.

Negotiating a settlement

A debt collector may take a *something is better than nothing* attitude and agree to let you clear up your debt by paying less than the total amount you owe. If the collector recognizes that you really can't pay any more than what you are offering, he may settle with you so he can earn at least some money for his efforts. If the debt collector purchased your debt from the original creditor for cents on the dollar, he can still make a profit if he collects at least something from you quickly.

If you are considering filing for bankruptcy, you may want to break our rule about not sharing any personal information with a debt collector. If you mention bankruptcy to a debt collector, the threat of that possibility may motivate him to settle your unsecured debt for less than what you owe. The debt collector knows that after you file for bankruptcy, he will likely get nothing from you.

If you don't feel confident trying to negotiate your own debt settlement agreement, hire a consumer law attorney to do it for you, especially if the debt you owe is substantial.

Debt settlement can cause you to owe more in federal income taxes because the amount that you don't pay is reported to the IRS as income. However, depending on the state of your finances when you settle the debt, the IRS may decide that you are insolvent. If it does, you won't owe any federal taxes.

The fact that you settled a debt shows up as negative information in your credit report because it indicates that you've had financial problems. However, it also indicates that you took responsibility for paying as much as you could on the debt, which may somewhat offset the negatives. Also, your credit report will show that the settled debt is not outstanding anymore, which is a good thing for your credit history.

Sticking to your budget

Before you begin negotiating a settlement with the debt collector, review your budget (see Chapter 4) so you have a clear idea exactly how much you can afford to pay. Do not offer more than you can afford.

When you know how much you can afford, begin your negotiations by offering less. You never know; the debt collector may accept your offer. If he doesn't, you've got room to maneuver, and by agreeing to pay more, you come across as reasonable and accommodating, which may work in your favor.

Before the debt collector agrees to begin negotiating with you, you may be asked to provide information about your assets and your debts, as well as your income and living expenses. Giving this information to the debt collector is a double-edged sword; the debt collector won't negotiate with you unless you provide it, but you are giving the collector valuable information he may use against you to

- ✔ Pressure you into paying more than you feel comfortable paying.

- ✔ Collect from you if you reach a payment plan agreement and later default on it.

- ✔ Collect what you owe if you are unable to reach an agreement with one another.

Any of these potential consequences is a very real danger, so do *not* give any additional information to a debt collector without consulting a consumer law attorney first.

When you negotiate with a debt collector, whether you are negotiating a debt settlement agreement or a payment plan (which we discuss in the upcoming section "Working out a payment plan"), do *not* give him information such as your bank account numbers, place of employment, or references. The debt collector can use that information to help him collect money from you should your negotiations not work out or should you reach an agreement and then not be able to live up to it.

Cleaning up your credit history

As part of your negotiations, ask the debt collector to remove from your credit records all negative information related to the settled debt that has been added to your records since the debt was turned over to him. (The debt collector cannot remove any negative information about your debt that was added to your credit files when the debt was still with the creditor.) The debt collector may scoff at your request, or he may agree to it. As they say, it never hurts to ask.

If the debt collector claims he does not have authorization to get information removed from your credit history and says that only the creditor to whom you originally owed the debt can do so, ask for the name and phone number of the person you should contact. If this person agrees to your request, ask that the agreement be put in writing. That way, if the creditor reneges on its promise, a consumer law attorney may be able to pressure the creditor to make good on your agreement. After reaching this type of agreement, you need to check your credit histories (see Chapter 2) to make sure that the negative information has been removed.

Putting the deal in writing

After you and the debt collector reach an agreement on a debt settlement amount, get the details of the agreement in writing before you give the collector any money. Otherwise, you risk paying the money and then having the debt collector claim that there never was a deal. It's also a good idea to hire a consumer law attorney to review the agreement so you can be certain it protects you and does not have the potential to create problems for you down the road.

If the debt collector won't put your agreement in writing, prepare an agreement yourself, sign it, and send it to the debt collector via certified mail, return receipt requested. That way, if you end up suing the debt collector for failing to live up to the agreement, you have a document that spells out exactly what the debt collector promised to do.

At a minimum, your agreement should clearly state

- How much you have agreed to pay.

- Whether you will pay the settlement amount in a lump sum or over time.

- When the lump sum is due, or when you will make each smaller payment.

- How you will make the payment(s), such as via an electronic bank transfer or with a cashier's check. Avoid giving a debt

> collector a personal check because some unscrupulous debt collectors use the information on consumers' checks to transfer money out of their bank accounts.
>
> ✔ That the debt collector agrees to report to the credit bureaus it works with that your debt has been "paid in full" as soon as the debt collector receives the settlement amount from you.
>
> ✔ Any concessions that the debt collector has agreed to make.
>
> ✔ Under what conditions the agreement will have been breached or broken, and the consequences of the breach. For example, if you do not make your payments by the date they're due or if you don't make them at all, you have breached the agreement and the debt collector may be entitled to cancel the agreement and begin trying to collect from you all over again.

Do not sign the agreement until it reflects everything you agreed to and unless you understand everything in it. After you sign the agreement, make a copy for yourself and file it in a safe place. If problems later develop with your agreement, you can share this document with a consumer law attorney.

It's a good idea to have a consumer law attorney review the debt settlement agreement before you sign it to make sure that your interests are well protected and that you are not creating any potential problems for yourself in the future.

Getting right with the IRS and credit bureaus

When a debt collector agrees to settle a debt that you owe for less than the full amount, the IRS looks at the amount you are not paying as income to you. Therefore, if you settle a debt for at least $600 less than what you owe on it, the debt collector may have to file an IRS 1099-C. If so, the debt collector will send you a completed copy of this form for your taxes. However, depending on your financial situation, you may not have to pay taxes on the income listed on the form. Consult with a tax professional in this situation.

If the debt collector agrees that after you pay the settlement amount he will report to the credit bureaus that your debt has been paid in full, and/or if he agrees to get negative information related to the collection account removed from your credit files, order copies of those files about one month after you pay the settlement amount. Review them to make sure that the debt collector did what he promised to do. If he did not, you or a consumer law attorney should send the debt collector a letter via certified mail, return receipt requested, politely but firmly demanding that he live up to the terms of your agreement. Attach a copy of the agreement to the letter. Also, make a copy of the letter for your files.

Taking your case to the creditor

If the debt collector refuses to negotiate with you, or if the two of you don't see eye to eye on some aspect of the proposed settlement, contact the creditor who turned your debt over to the debt collector. Find out if the creditor may be willing to negotiate or may see things a little more your way.

If you have proof that the debt collector violated your FDCPA rights or that there is something wrong with the original agreement between you and the creditor (the creditor violated your state's usury law by charging you too much interest or did not disclose all the terms of credit associated with your debt, for example), the creditor may want to settle with you in order to minimize the likelihood that you may file a lawsuit. Of course, the creditor can settle with you only if it has not sold your debt to a debt collector.

Working out a payment plan

If you can't negotiate a debt settlement agreement that you can afford, you can ask the debt collector to let you pay the full amount of the debt over time in a series of payments. A reasonable time to ask for will depend on the size of your debt. If it is a very large debt, your payments could stretch out for years. However, most debt collectors are going to want you to pay what you owe as quickly as possible and may even try to pressure you into borrowing money from a friend or relative to pay the debt off fast.

Review your budget first (see Chapter 4) to figure out how much you can afford each month, and make sure that making the payments will not affect your ability to pay your priority debts and your most important living expenses. As with a debt settlement agreement, get all the details of your payment plan in writing before you pay the debt collector any money.

As we mention in the previous section, never send a personal check to a debt collector. Make any payments that you agree to with a cashier's check. That way, you keep your bank account information private.

Disputing the debt

If you do not agree that you owe a debt at all, or if you disagree with the amount of the debt, send the debt collector a letter disputing it. You must send this letter within 30 days of the debt collector's initial contact with you. According to the FDCPA, after the debt collector receives your letter, he must either provide you with written proof of the debt or cease all communication with you. Although the debt collector is not required to respond within a specific period of time, you should expect that the response will be timely. After all, the debt collector wants to collect from you as quickly as possible; he probably won't let a lot of time pass before getting back to you.

As soon as you let a debt collector know that you dispute a debt, the debt collector must report the debt as "in dispute" to the credit bureaus it works with. If the debt collector does not do so, he has broken the FDCPA, and you should contact a consumer law attorney about what to do. The fact that your debt is in dispute will remain in your credit history until the debt collector provides you with proof that you owe it and that the amount of the debt is accurate. It's possible, therefore, that the "in dispute" information could remain in your credit history for a couple months or even longer if you don't accept the debt collector's initial proof.

Saying that you can't pay

If you do not have the money to pay a debt in either a lump sum or through a series of installments, or if you and the debt collector cannot agree on a settlement amount, send the debt collector a letter stating that you cannot afford to pay what you owe and you do not want to be contacted again about it. Although it's never a good idea to not pay a debt that you owe, it may be your only real option if your finances are in very bad shape. (See Chapter 4 for an explanation of the debts you should always try to pay and the ones that are less important when you cannot pay everything.)

The FDCPA says that after the debt collector receives your letter, she must cease all communication with you other than to confirm receipt of your letter or to let you know about an action she is going to take to try to collect the money (such as suing you).

If the amount of the debt is relatively small, you may never hear from the debt collector again. The same is true if the debt collector determines that you are *judgment proof,* meaning you have no assets that the debt collector can take and your state does not permit wage garnishment.

Asking not to be contacted again

Even if you intend to pay a debt, you can send a debt collector a letter stating that you do not want to be contacted again about it. You may want to exercise this option because the debt collector has been very difficult to deal with or simply because you do not want to be contacted anymore about the money you owe.

Again, after the debt collector receives your letter, he cannot contact you except to confirm receipt of your letter and to inform you about any collection actions he intends to take. If the amount of your debt is relatively small, you may never hear from the collector again. If the amount of the debt is substantial, the debt collector may decide to play hardball and sue you for the money.

Feeling Haunted by Old Debt

A dangerous new breed of debt collector is on the scene. These people specialize in the collection of very old debts and often think nothing of flagrantly breaking the law in order to make a buck. For example, these debt collectors are

- ✔ **Contacting consumers about debts that have been charged off as uncollectible.** When a creditor *charges off* a debt, that essentially means, "I am not going to collect on this debt right now, but I may decide to try to collect it later." The creditor may take this step because it thinks the amount of the debt is too small to bother with or because the consumer who owes it is judgment proof.

  The creditor may decide to try to collect the debt later, maybe even years after the consumer has forgotten all about it, or it may sell the debt to a debt collector who specializes in collecting very old debts. Debt collectors who buy old debts are not breaking any laws unless they violate the FDCPA or your state's debt collection laws when they try to collect an old debt.

  When a debt collector purchases a very old debt that you owe, he can find out how to contact you by working with a *skip tracing* company that specializes in finding people, or he can locate you via the Internet. Also, if the debt collector has an account with a national credit bureau, he can obtain your current address from your credit file.

- ✔ **Trying to collect debts for which the statute of limitations has expired.** The *statute of limitations* is the amount of time during which you can be sued for nonpayment of a debt. The statute of limitations begins on the first day you miss a debt payment, and it typically lasts between four and six years. However, depending on your state and the type of debt, it could be as short as 3 years or as long as 15 years. To find out

Take those library fines seriously

In an effort to fill up their dwindling coffers without raising taxes or user fees, a growing number of municipal governments, including county and local governments, are using debt collectors to collect consumers' unpaid library fines, parking tickets, fees for animal services (like rabies tags), ambulance fees, and the like when their own collection efforts have been unsuccessful. If your local or county government hires a debt collector to try to collect a $10 past-due library fine or a $15 past-due parking ticket from you, the impact on your credit record and credit score is the same as if you had defaulted on a loan. In other words, it will be one more negative in your credit history, and it will bring down your credit score.

the statute of limitations on your past-due debts, speak to a consumer law attorney in your state or contact your state attorney general's office. A debt collector is legally entitled to collect a debt after the statute of limitations has run out on it; however, the debt collector is breaking the law if he sues you over the debt or threatens to sue you.

You can unintentionally reactivate the statute of limitations on an old debt by telling a debt collector that you agree to pay some money on the debt, even a very small amount like $5. When the statute of limitations is reactivated, it starts running all over again as though you just defaulted on the debt. Also, in some legal jurisdictions you can restart the statute of limitations on a very old debt simply by acknowledging that the debt is yours.

After the statute of limitations is reactivated, you are at risk for being sued by the debt collector. If he wins, the court may give the debt collector permission to collect the money you owe by seizing assets you own, putting a lien on an asset you own, garnishing your wages, and so on.

✔ **Telling credit bureaus that an old debt in your credit history is a new debt.** Most negative information can remain in your credit history for only seven years and six months. Some debt collectors take this unscrupulous and illegal step in order to put pressure on you to pay the debt, promising that when you do, they will get the new negative information removed.

Review your Equifax, Experian, and TransUnion credit histories every six months so you can spot problems and get them cleared up (see Chapter 2). If you discover an old debt that should no longer be reported in your credit report, dispute the debt with the credit bureau that prepared the report following the directions that should have come with it. If you are not able to resolve the error yourself, get in touch with a consumer law attorney who has specific experience dealing with credit record problems.

If a debt collector violates your legal rights when he contacts you about a debt that has been charged off or for which the statute of limitations has expired, get in touch with a consumer law attorney right away. You should do the same if a debt collector tries to get away with reporting to the credit bureaus that one of your old debts is new. Don't let the debt collector get away with any illegal actions. Stand up for your rights! The last section of this chapter explains how a consumer law attorney can help you and highlights other actions you can take when your debt collection rights are violated.

Taking Action When a Debt Collector Violates Your Rights

Debt collectors who flaunt the law deserve to be punished for their bad behavior. Even if a debt collector violates the law in a relatively minor way, you should take action by filing formal complaints against the debt collector with the appropriate government offices and by scheduling an appointment with a consumer law attorney to discuss your legal options. Unless you let the debt collector know you mean business, the violations will likely continue and escalate. Taking such action doesn't just provide you with a sense of justice; it can help ensure that the debt collector does not harm other consumers.

Complaining to the Federal Trade Commission

The Federal Trade Commission (FTC) has responsibility for enforcing the FDCPA. Whenever a debt collector violates that law, you should file a complaint with the FTC. Although the FTC will not go after the debt collector on the basis of your complaint alone, if it receives enough complaints about debt collectors working for the same company, it will sue the company. Your complaint can help the FTC build its legal case.

You can file your FTC complaint online at www.ftc.gov. You can also register your complaint by calling the FTC at 800-382-4357, or you can write to the FTC at Federal Trade Commission, Consumer Response Center, 600 Pennsylvania Avenue, NW, Washington, DC 20580.

Be as specific as possible about how and when the debt collector violated your legal rights. If you have any documentation that helps prove the violation, mail your complaint to the FTC and attach copies of the documentation to the letter.

You should also send a copy of your complaint to the debt collector. Just knowing that you have contacted the FTC may be all it takes to convince the debt collector to stop the illegal behavior.

Contacting your state attorney general's office

If your state has a law that applies to debt collectors, file a complaint about the debt collector with your state attorney general's office. Your attorney general's office won't sue a debt collector on your behalf alone, but your complaint may help the office build a legal case against a debt collection company.

Consulting a consumer law attorney

Do not hesitate to make an appointment with a consumer law attorney as soon as a debt collector violates your federal or state debt collection legal rights. If the lawyer agrees that your rights have been violated, and depending on the severity of the violation, the attorney may suggest sending a letter to the debt collector warning that if the behavior continues, you will file a lawsuit. Sometimes, a sternly worded letter from an attorney is all it takes to make a debt collector obey the law.

If the debt collector's behavior has been especially egregious — telling your employer about the money you owe, harassing you constantly about your debt, showing up at your home to threaten you with dire consequences, and so on — or if the attorney's letter to the debt collector does not accomplish its goal, the lawyer may recommend that you file a lawsuit.

You can sue for both actual and punitive damages under the FDCPA. When you sue for actual damages, you are asking the court to order the debt collector to reimburse you for the harm that he did to you. That harm may include lost wages and out-of-pocket expenses, as well as pain and suffering. If you ask for punitive damages as well, you are asking the court to make the debt collector pay you additional money as a way of discouraging him from breaking the law again.

When you sue a debt collector and win, the FDCPA entitles you to collect attorney's fees and court costs from the debt collector regardless of whether the court awards you actual or punitive damages.

If your state has its own debt collection law, your attorney may decide to sue in state court rather than in federal court. Which court you end up suing in depends on exactly how the debt collector violated your rights and whether the FDCPA or your state law offers you better legal remedies for the harm you suffered.

Part III
Tackling Your
High-Stake Debts

The 5th Wave

By Rich Tennant

"When we bought it 5 years ago the mortgage payments seemed huge. But we got used to it. Please, pull up an orange crate and make yourself comfortable."

In this part . . .

*N*ot all debts are created equal: If you fall behind on certain types of debts, you face especially nasty consequences. We're talking about debts like your home mortgage, car loan, rent, court-ordered child support, federal taxes, and federal student loans, among others. In this part, we lay out the consequences you may face if you default on any of these debts, and we show you how to avoid that fate.

Chapter 10

Managing Your Past-Due Mortgage

● ●

In This Chapter

▶ Understanding the various steps in a foreclosure

▶ Taking action to avoid a foreclosure

▶ Knowing what to do when a foreclosure is inevitable

● ●

*Y*ou know the tune: "Be it ever so humble . . ." Whether you own a tract house in suburbia, an inner city brownstone, or a mansion on a hill, losing it in a foreclosure easily ranks as one of life's worst experiences, financially and emotionally. Financially, you lose what is probably your most valuable asset, not to mention all the money you put into it. You may also forfeit any *equity* you built up in your home (the difference between what your home is worth and the balance on your mortgage). Also, aside from filing for bankruptcy, nothing damages your credit history more than a foreclosure.

Emotionally, losing your home means losing a fundamental piece of your life and an important measure of success. A foreclosure may make you feel like a failure; your self-esteem may take a big hit. You may also feel embarrassed because the foreclosure will be in the public records and may even be listed in your local newspaper (along with other foreclosures in your area). And if you lose your home, your friends and neighbors will want to know why you're moving.

As if that isn't enough, a foreclosure disrupts your family's life, adds stress to your relationships with your spouse and kids, and forces you to pack and move (which is difficult even under the best circumstances).

Okay, enough of the bad news. Now for the good news: You can avoid a foreclosure, assuming you tackle your mortgage problem soon enough and are clear about your options. In this chapter, we explain how the foreclosure process works, including what happens after you fall behind on your mortgage in the weeks and months leading up to the date that your home is sold on the courthouse steps. We then describe various steps you can take to hold on to your home. We also highlight the important role that a consumer law attorney can play before, during, and after a foreclosure.

If you fall behind on your home equity loan or on another loan that you secured with your home, you're also at risk for a foreclosure. Your mortgage lender is referred to as the *first lien holder,* and the other lenders with liens on your home are referred to as the *second lien holder, third lien holder,* and so on. When a lender other than your mortgage lender forecloses on your home, that other lender pays off the mortgage lender and any other lenders with earlier liens, and it becomes the owner of your home. Then the lender tries to sell your home to recoup as much of its money as possible.

Getting Familiar with the Foreclosure Timeline

The foreclosure process varies from state to state (according to each state's law) and even from lender to lender. However, the following timeline provides you with a general idea of what happens when you fall behind on your mortgage:

- ✓ **Your mortgage payment becomes due.** Most mortgages have a 15-day grace period. The *grace period* is the period of time after your mortgage due date during which you can pay the loan without being charged a late fee.

- ✓ **Your mortgage is 16 days past due.** When your loan's grace period is up, you are charged a late fee. Your mortgage lender (or the company that is servicing your mortgage for your lender — sending your payment coupons, processing your payments, and so on) may get in touch to find out when it can expect your payment.

- ✓ **You are 30 days late on your mortgage.** If you still have not paid your mortgage, and if your lender has not yet received your next month's payment either, the lender may turn up the heat by calling you and/or sending you notices urging you to get caught up on your mortgage or get in touch.

As soon as you begin having problems keeping up with your mortgage, contact a HUD-approved housing counseling agency. (*HUD* is the U.S. Department of Housing and Urban Development.) These agencies offer consumers free advice and assistance with a wide variety of housing-related issues, including foreclosures. Among other things, the agency will work directly with your lender to try to find a way for you to keep your home. However, while you are working with this agency, stay aware of your foreclosure date; some mortgage lenders will move your foreclosure forward while working with you at the same time. To find a HUD-approved housing counseling agency in your area, go to www.hud.gov/offices/hsg/sfh/hcc/hcs.cfm.

✔ **Your mortgage is between 45 days and 60 days past due**. If you've not paid the full amount of your mortgage *arrearage* (the amount that is past due), and you've not contacted your lender to work out a way to pay it and to continue paying on your mortgage at the same time, the lender will turn your loan over to an attorney who will handle the foreclosure. The attorney will send you a notice called a "Notice of Default," a "Notice of Delinquency," or something similar. The notice indicates exactly how much you must pay in order to get current on your mortgage and the number of payments that are past due. If you've not yet contacted your lender to discuss your mortgage problem, now's the time.

At about the same time you receive the notice of foreclosure, your mortgage lender will probably return to you any partial payments you may have made on your mortgage. Don't spend that money! You may need it as you try to negotiate with the lender to avoid losing your home.

✔ **Your loan is at least 60 days past due.** In most states, the next notice you receive if you've still not worked out a way to deal with your mortgage loan is a "Notice of Acceleration." (The exact name of the notice in your state may be a little different.) The notice tells you that the entire amount of your outstanding loan balance is now due in full, not just the past-due amount. It also indicates when and where your home will be sold if you do not pay the loan balance. This notice marks the official start of your foreclosure.

✔ **About 90 to 100 days after your loan has become past due.** At this point, you still have time to avoid the loss of your home, but your options are fewer and less attractive. Meanwhile, the foreclosure clock is ticking. Exactly how much time you have before your home is taken from you depends on whether foreclosures in your state are nonjudicial (statutory) or judicial.

Nonjudicial foreclosures tend to happen a lot faster. See the upcoming sidebar "Judicial versus nonjudicial: What's the difference?" for the basic distinctions between the two types.

Until your home is sold to a new buyer, your lender will usually be happy to call off the foreclosure if you can come up with the bucks you need to reinstate your loan, which involves paying your mortgage arrearage in full plus all late fees and all the lender's foreclosure-related expenses. However, if you have a history of missing mortgage payments, your lender may decide that you've been so much trouble it would prefer to foreclose rather than let you reinstate your loan. If you do reinstate it, you must resume making your regular mortgage payments again.

✔ **Assuming the foreclosure process moves forward.** If you have not already consulted with a HUD-approved housing counseling agency, now's the time — don't delay! But if you believe that your lender is about to take back your home, get in touch with a bankruptcy attorney. Filing for bankruptcy stops the foreclosure process and buys you some time to figure out what to do about your mortgage. The upcoming section "Handling a Hopeless Situation" discusses the benefits of filing.

✔ **Sometime after you receive the acceleration notice.** Shortly after, or months after, you get the notice (the timing depends on how foreclosures work in your state), your home is sold in a public auction, possibly on the front steps of your county courthouse. Most home auctions are poorly advertised, so there probably won't be a lot of bidders for your home — maybe just your mortgage lender. Few bidders means that foreclosed homes are typically sold for what is owed on them or for less. If your home is auctioned off for less than your outstanding loan balance, you have to make up the difference, or *deficiency.* If you can't afford to pay it, your lender can sue for the money.

In a few states, you still have a small window of opportunity to reinstate your loan even after your home has been auctioned off. Review your loan paperwork or mortgage document to find out if you have such a window, or talk to a real estate attorney.

✔ **After the foreclosure sale.** After your home has been sold, a local sheriff, constable, or marshal shows up with an eviction notice that indicates the date by which you and all your belongings must be out of the house. You may also be told who purchased your home and for how much.

Judicial versus nonjudicial.
What's the difference?

When your lender initiates a foreclosure, the process will involve the court, be purely administrative, or be some combination of both. A foreclosure that involves the court is referred to as a *judicial* foreclosure, and one that does not is called a *nonjudicial* or *statutory* foreclosure. Which process you go through when your house is foreclosed on depends on the state where your home is located.

In a *judicial* foreclosure state, your lender must sue you in order to get the court's permission to take your home. You receive an official notice, or *summons,* from the court, informing you of the lawsuit. You have to attend at least one court hearing. If you're not already working with a consumer law attorney, hire one as soon as you receive this notice!

Judicial foreclosures are relatively time consuming. From start to finish, they may take as long as a year. You can delay or stop a foreclosure at any time up until the sale of your home.

If foreclosures in your state are *nonjudicial* (statutory), there is no lawsuit and no court hearing, so the process is much faster than a judicial foreclosure. In fact, after the process begins, your home may be sold in just a few months. The mortgage lender probably has to file paperwork with the court, advertise your debt in your local newspaper, send you the appropriate notice(s), and give you one more opportunity to either pay the full amount that you owe or work out a way to avoid a foreclosure. Failing both, your home is sold, and you must move out.

Even though there is no court involvement in a nonjudicial foreclosure, hire an attorney to help you anyway. The attorney may be able to stop or slow down the foreclosure process.

For a summary of the foreclosure process in your particular state, go to `www.foreclosures.com/pages/state_laws.asp` or talk to a consumer law attorney.

If your mortgage lender bought your home, it hires a realtor to sell your home for as much as possible.

If your home sold for less than the outstanding balance on your mortgage, you receive a notice from your lender asking you to pay the deficiency. If your lender writes off the difference between what you owed on your mortgage and what your home sells for, it sends a 1099 form to the IRS, and that difference is counted as income for you. As a result, you could owe more in federal income taxes when April 15 rolls around.

However, depending on your financial situation, the IRS may decide that you are insolvent, which means that you would not have to pay any federal taxes that year. Talk to a CPA about whether you are insolvent by IRS standards. If you are, the CPA can file the appropriate paperwork with the IRS to prove your insolvency.

Keeping a Foreclosure at Bay

As soon as you know that you're going to have problems keeping up your mortgage, or as soon as you've missed a payment, get in touch with your mortgage lender to discuss your options. Contact its *workouts* or *loss mitigation* department. Also, get in touch with a HUD-approved housing counseling agency, especially if you are intimidated by the idea of talking with your mortgage lender or don't feel confident about dealing with financial matters.

If you obtained your mortgage through a national lender, you probably have to contact the mortgage servicing company that your lender hired to manage your loan, rather than your actual lender. National lenders don't administer the mortgages they make. Throughout the rest of this chapter, when we refer to your *lender* or *mortgage lender,* know that we're referring to either the mortgage servicing company or your actual mortgage lender.

If you've already missed a payment or two, read each and every notice you receive about your mortgage. The notices inform you of your rights, alert you to important deadlines associated with your past-due mortgage, and provide you with opportunities to try to resolve your mortgage arrearage. Also, if you receive a voice mail message about your mortgage, return the call right away.

Don't assume that if you do not pick up a certified letter related to your past-due mortgage, the foreclosure process won't move forward. It will.

Taking immediate steps

If your finances are not in extremely bad shape, you may be able to resolve your mortgage problem on your own, assuming you act right away. Here are some options for continuing to pay on your mortgage and for getting caught up on any mortgage arrearage:

✔ **Develop a realistic household budget, and stick to it.** In Chapter 4, we explain how to prepare a budget.

✔ **Review your existing budget for expenses you can reduce or eliminate.** In Chapter 5, we offer lots of budget-cutting ideas.

When you can't afford to pay all your debts, always pay your high priority debts first, including your mortgage (see Chapter 4).

✔ **Negotiate reduced payments with your other creditors and put the money you save toward your mortgage.** If you need help negotiating, schedule an appointment with a federally approved credit counseling agency. In Chapter 6, we show you how to negotiate.

✔ **Lower your monthly debt payments by consolidating your debts.** In Chapter 7, we tell you how debt consolidation works and provide consolidation advice.

✔ **Borrow money.** This may be a good option if you are sure that your financial problems are temporary. For example, maybe you fell behind on your mortgage because you lost your job, but you're going to begin a new job next month. Possible sources of short-term cash include

- A loan from a friend or relative

- A cash advance from a credit card

- Money borrowed from your retirement account

- Money borrowed from a cash value (whole life) insurance policy you may own

In Chapter 7, we detail the risks of borrowing from your retirement account or your life insurance policy.

Do *not* borrow money from any of these sources unless you are 100 percent sure that your financial problems are behind you and you'll be able to repay the loan. You only add to your problems otherwise.

If you're having problems paying a mortgage that is federally insured, you may be able to get help from a plan or program that other homeowners are not eligible for. To find out, get in touch with the agency that insured your loan, such as the U.S. Department of Housing and Urban Development (HUD), the U.S. Farmers Home Administration (FmHA), or the U.S. Department of Veterans Affairs (VA). If you obtained your loan through a state or local housing program, contact the agency that administers the loan. The agency may also have special plans or programs for homeowners who are having mortgage problems. You may also want to talk with a HUD-approved housing counseling agency.

Negotiating with your lender

If you can't figure out a way to deal with your mortgage on your own, get in touch with your mortgage lender right away to find out if it will help you. For example,

- ✔ The lender may agree to let you pay any arrearage you owe in a lump sum in a couple of months. This may be a good arrangement if you fell behind on your mortgage because of a temporary financial setback.

- ✔ If a lump sum payment is not realistic, the lender may let you add a portion of the arrearage to each of your regular mortgage payments over a set period of time, or it may agree to add the arrearage to the end of your mortgage so you can pay it off in installments then.

If your lender proposes an arrangement that you don't think you can afford, let the lender know, and propose an alternative.

While you are paying off your mortgage arrearage, you must make all your regular mortgage payments. Negotiating a way to deal with your past-due mortgage does not affect your obligation to continue paying your loan.

Before you approach your lender about your arrearage, pull together relevant financial information: a copy of your loan agreement; your current household budget; proof of your current household income; your most recent federal tax return; and a list of your assets, including their market values. The lender may also want proof of some of your expenses, like your utility bills, car payments, and home mainte-nance costs. Be sure to review the negotiating tips we supply in Chapter 6.

You may read in other books or on Web sites that your mortgage lender may agree to a permanent or temporary change in the terms of your mortgage loan, such as changing the interest rate or lowering your monthly payments. Don't get your hopes up! Such a change is highly unlikely, especially if you got your loan through a national mortgage lender. Most national lenders sell their mortgage loans to investor pools, so the loans are not theirs to change. Your best shot at a temporary or permanent change in the terms of your mortgage is if you obtained your loan through a local lender.

If you are considering renting out your home and living somewhere cheaper so you can better afford to pay your mortgage arrearage and keep up with future mortgage payments, don't move out until you and the lender have reached an agreement. Lenders will negotiate with homeowners in your situation only if the homeowners are still living in their homes. The section "Considering more drastic options" later in this chapter discusses renting out your home.

If you and your lender work out a way for you to pay your arrearage, make sure the plan is communicated to the department handling your foreclosure. Otherwise, the foreclosure will continue moving forward. Also, ask the lender to put the terms of your agreement in writing. If the lender refuses, prepare your own agreement. The agreement should include your loan number and all the agreement terms. Make copies, and send one copy to the person with whom you negotiated the agreement and another to the lender's foreclosure department. Keep the original for your files.

Refinancing your loan

You may want to consider refinancing your existing loan, especially if you have a lot of equity in your home, to pay off your current loan and any arrearage. Your goal is to get a new mortgage with more affordable monthly payments. Your current lender probably won't agree to refinance your loan given the problems you've had with your current loan, but you may find another lender ready to bargain with you. After all, loan officers make money according to the number of new loans they write!

Generally, refinancing isn't a good idea if you don't have a lot of equity in your home. In fact, you may not be able to find a lender who will give you a new loan if you don't have much equity.

If you do refinance and you're retired or close to retirement, try to avoid getting a new 15- or 30-year loan. Having to make mortgage payments for so many years may strain your budget; it could even force you to delay retirement or begin working again if you've already retired. If you don't owe a large amount on your home, a better option is to refinance with a short-term (maybe five-year) loan, if you can afford the payments.

When you think about refinancing, be very careful about the terms you agree to. Read all the fine print in the loan agreement. Watch out for interest rates that start out low and then increase. Also, beware of interest-only mortgages; payments that are affordable during the interest-only period can skyrocket when you begin paying interest *and* principal. At that point, you have to make up for those first years when you paid nothing on the principal.

If your finances are in such bad shape that you can't find a traditional lender to refinance your mortgage, you may want to consider working with a *hard money investor.* This is a legitimate investor who makes loans that traditional lenders consider too risky. A hard money loan comes with high fees and a high interest rate, so it is usually not a permanent solution to your problem. But it could be a good way to buy yourself time to sell your home or to pursue another option for avoiding a foreclosure. To find a hard money lender, talk to a real estate agent, look under "Real Estate Investor" in your local Yellow Pages, or search for "hard money investors" on the Internet.

Considering more drastic options

If you and your lender can't work out a way to pay your mortgage arrearage, you can't find affordable refinancing, and you continue to have problems paying your mortgage, it's time to take more drastic action. You may need to consider

- ✔ **Renting out your home and renting a less expensive home or apartment for yourself.** If you pursue this option, be sure that the rental income from your home covers not just your monthly mortgage payments, but also the cost of your homeowner's insurance and property taxes if those expenses are not included in your monthly payments, as well as the cost of maintaining your home.

- ✔ **Finding someone to assume your mortgage.** If your loan is assumable (your loan paperwork indicates whether it is or isn't), you can try to find someone to take it over so you won't be responsible for paying on the loan anymore. If your loan is not assumable, but it's an option you'd like to consider, your lender may agree to an assumption. After all, getting money from someone else is preferable to not getting any money from you!

- ✔ **Selling your home.** Yes, it's tough, but it may be necessary. We discuss this possibility in the upcoming section "Handling a Hopeless Situation."

How a Lawyer Can Help

When you have problems keeping up with your mortgage and are worried that you may face a foreclosure, the advice and assistance of a consumer law attorney can be invaluable. The attorney can explain exactly how the foreclosure process works in your state, advise you of your legal rights, and talk with you about your alternatives for avoiding a foreclosure.

If you want to negotiate with your lender regarding your mortgage arrearage, but you don't feel comfortable doing so yourself, you may want to hire your attorney to do it for you. In fact, turning the negotiations over to an attorney is wise even if you feel comfortable with negotiating; the attorney knows what you can ask from a lender, is prepared to respond to your lender when it makes an offer, and will understand the lender's (sometimes confusing) lingo.

Here are some other things an attorney may be able to do:

- ✔ Identify problems in your loan paperwork or in your loan closing that can help you stop a foreclosure or slow down the foreclosure process

- ✔ Leverage more negotiating bargaining power with your lender

- ✔ Reduce the total amount that you owe on your mortgage

For example, the attorney may determine that your lender does not have an enforceable lien on your home; has been charging you too much interest; did not accurately disclose all the terms of your mortgage loan according to the requirements of the Truth in Lending Act (TILA); violated the terms of the federal Real Estate Settlement Procedures Act (RESPA); and so on.

If you don't meet with an attorney until after your foreclosure has begun, the attorney may be able to help you gain some control over the process if it turns out that all the required procedures leading up to the foreclosure were not followed or your rights were violated after the foreclosure began. For example, you may not have been given an opportunity to *cure your default* (get caught up on your past-due mortgage), assuming you have that right under your contract or according to your state's law. Or you may not have received certain notices by the required deadlines.

The attorney can also tell if you should consider filing for bankruptcy in order to stop the foreclosure and can refer you to a good bankruptcy attorney. (Some consumer law attorneys are also bankruptcy attorneys.) We discuss bankruptcy in the next section.

For affordable legal help, contact the Legal Aid office in your area or get in touch with your state or local bar association to find out if they have a list of housing attorneys who will help you for little or no money. An alternative to an attorney may be a nonprofit foreclosure prevention organization, if there is one in your area.

Handling a Hopeless Situation

Say your mortgage is 90 to 100 days past due and you've not come up with a way to avoid the loss of your home (unless your rich uncle Harry dies — quick — and leaves you a bundle of cash). Tough action is now required. Your goal should be to minimize further damage to your finances. Here's what you may need to do:

- ✔ **Hire a lawyer.** If you receive a notice that the foreclosure has officially begun and you're not already working with a consumer law attorney, schedule an appointment with one pronto! After a foreclosure begins, the attorney may be able to slow or stop the process, but that becomes more unlikely with each passing day.

- ✔ **Sell your home.** You may be wise to cut your losses and sell. Selling your home is a good idea if you have a lot of equity in it and the real estate market in your area is strong. If you sell it, you'll probably get more for it than if your home is sold on the auction block. Therefore, you're more likely to get the money you need to pay off your lender, and you may even be able to put some money in your own pocket. Selling your home also damages your credit history less than losing it in a foreclosure.

   Don't dillydally around trying to sell your home yourself unless you already know someone who wants to buy it. Work with a real estate agent. You don't have time to waste because the foreclosure clock is ticking away.

- ✔ **Short-sell your home.** If the real estate agent you hire doesn't think you can sell your home for enough to pay your lender everything you owe before the foreclosure date, ask the lender to agree to a *short sale,* which means you can sell your home for less than what you owe on it. The lender may agree in order to minimize its foreclosure costs.

   If your lender agrees to a short sale, before you finalize the sale, try to get a written agreement from the lender stating that you don't have to pay the loan deficiency. Keep in mind that the lender will report the deficiency amount to the IRS as 1099 income, which could cause you to owe more in income taxes that year. However, if the IRS decides that you are insolvent based on the condition of your finances, you won't owe any federal taxes for the year the deficiency is reported. Consult with a CPA to determine whether you are insolvent. The CPA can also file the appropriate paperwork with the IRS to prove that you are.

Your agent may already know someone who would like to purchase your home. If not, the agent may get in touch with a hard money investor who regularly purchases distressed properties like yours. It's not unusual for real estate agents to have relationships with these kinds of investors because the agents receive a finder's fee every time they bring a distressed property to an investor.

✔ **Deed your home back to the lender in lieu of a foreclosure.** This step simply involves giving your home back to your lender. However, it's not an option if you have a lot of equity built up in your home because you will lose the equity.

Although a deed in lieu of foreclosure keeps a foreclosure off your credit history, the fact that you gave your home back will show up. That information does almost as much damage to your credit history as a foreclosure does.

If you give your home back, the lender will expect you to have your home appraised — usually at your expense — in order to find out how much it's likely to sell for. If the appraisal shows that your home won't sell for enough money to pay off the outstanding balance on your home and cover all your lender's foreclosure costs as well, the lender will look to you to pay the deficiency, or it may refuse to okay a deed in lieu of a foreclosure. Or the lender may agree to a deed in lieu of a foreclosure and let you pay less than the full amount of the deficiency if the lender believes that by doing so it will end up with more money than if it proceeds with a foreclosure. Bottom line: The lender will do whatever is in its best interest financially.

✔ **File for bankruptcy.** If things look bleak, you can file for bankruptcy in order to stop a foreclosure. If you file a Chapter 13 reorganization bankruptcy, you can take three to five years to pay off your mortgage arrearage, all late fees you owe, and the foreclosure-related costs your lender has incurred. Plus, you have to continue making your regular mortgage payments at the same time. If you file a Chapter 7 liquidation bankruptcy, you lose your home, but you don't have to pay your mortgage arrearage, any late fees, or the lender's foreclosure costs.

During the six to eight months that you are in Chapter 7 bankruptcy, it's possible (depending on the state of your finances after you've eliminated most of your other debts through the bankruptcy) that you could catch up on your past-due mortgage payments. In that case, you would be current on your mortgage when you emerged from bankruptcy and could keep your home.

If your lender has done anything to violate your rights, your bankruptcy attorney can sue the lender for these violations as part of the bankruptcy process. As a result of the lawsuits, you may end up owing less. For example, maybe your lender did not comply with the federal Truth in Lending Act (TILA) when it gave you your mortgage, charged you too much interest, violated the Real Estate Settlement Procedures Act (RESPA) when you closed on your home, or did not provide you with the required notifications during the months leading up to the foreclosure.

Steering clear of foreclosure scams

Desperate straits sometimes call for desperate measures. However, be careful what you do to avoid the loss of your home. There are plenty of sleazy scam artists who will pretend they can help you when, in fact, they have their sights set on getting your home. If you are contacted by a company or individual claiming to be able to help you avoid losing your home in a foreclosure, or if you find out about such an offer, don't agree to anything or sign any paperwork until you have had a consumer law attorney or a counselor with a HUD-approved housing counseling agency review all the paperwork related to the offer.

Here are some common foreclosure scams:

✔ A company offers to give you a loan so you can get current on your mortgage and to pay your mortgage for a limited period of time. In return, you must make monthly payments to the company. Unless you read all the details in the paperwork, you assume that by making those payments you are repaying the loan the company made to you. In fact, when you sign the agreement, you actually transfer ownership of your home to the company. In other words, the payments you are making are rent payments because you are now a tenant in your own home. To buy back your home, you must pay the home's current market value or a price indicated in the agreement, and often very expensive fees as well. Furthermore, the agreement probably gives the company the right to evict you from the home, maybe if you are just one day late with a payment.

✔ You are told that in return for giving a company the title to your home, you can continue living there while you buy back your home. However, the terms of the buyback are so impossible that eventually you fall behind on your payments and are forced to move out.

✔ A company offers to help you work things out with your mortgage lender so you can keep your home. In exchange, it charges you an exorbitant amount of money. However, the company does little or nothing to really help you, and eventually you lose your home.

Chapter 11

Keeping Your Wheels on the Road

*H*aving your car repossessed can be disastrous. Most of us need a car to get to work, and using public transportation is not always a realistic alternative. Living without a car makes everything more difficult, and to boot, a repossession adds to the negative information in your credit history. (Like most other negative information, the fact that your car was repossessed lingers in your credit history for seven and a half years.)

In this chapter, we explain how repossession works and when the process is likely to begin. We explain what an auto recovery specialist (a.k.a. *the repo man*) can and can't do to take your car, and we tell you how you can get it back after it's been repossessed. We also review your options for avoiding repossession in the first place. Last but not least, we tell you how a consumer law attorney can help you before, during, and after the loss of your car.

Running through a Repossession

If you fall behind on your car payments, you are playing with fire. The company that financed the purchase of your vehicle is legally entitled to take it back without getting the court's permission first. To make matters worse, most states don't require auto lenders to give consumers any advance notice of their repossession plans. In other words, if you live in one of these states, you could walk out your front door one morning and find that your car is not in your driveway, or you could leave your office one afternoon and discover that your vehicle is gone. The repo man took it!

Knowing the law

For specific information regarding when your car can be taken, exactly how the repossession process works, and your repossession rights, do these two things:

- ✔ Find out about the law in your state by speaking to your state attorney general's office or with a consumer law attorney.
- ✔ Review the details of your car loan agreement.

Your loan agreement may give you the right to avoid repossession by *curing the default,* or getting caught up on your car loan within a certain period of time. If you have already missed a loan payment, meet with a consumer law attorney immediately.

When you are worried about having your vehicle repossessed, a natural response is to try to hide it by storing it at the home of a friend or relative or by moving the vehicle out of state. Don't do so until you have checked with a consumer law attorney or with your state attorney general's office. It may be illegal in your state to try to hide your vehicle from the repo man.

Expecting the repo man

The repo man may arrive to take your car when you are at home, at work, at church — pretty much anytime. If he shows up at your home, he can come onto your property to get the vehicle; he can even go into your garage, but he cannot break into the garage if your car is inside and the garage door is locked.

Exercising your rights

If you are aware that a repo man has come to take your car, you don't have to just hand over the keys. No law requires that you make it easy for him. You can even stop the repo man dead in his tracks by telling him, "Do not take my car," "Leave my car where it is," or something similar. Don't assume, however, that he won't try again. He will, and eventually he'll get your vehicle.

In most states, the repo man cannot threaten, bully, or intimidate you physically or verbally in order to scare you into giving up your vehicle, and he cannot use force against you. If he does, he is *breaching the peace,* and that's illegal. At the same time, don't become physical with the repo man, or you may be charged with assault.

If someone claiming to be a government official arrives with the repo man, ask to see proof of that person's official status. Normally, the only reason a policeman or other law enforcement official is involved in a repossession is to deliver a court order requiring you to give up your vehicle. (If you don't obey a court order, you're breaking the law.)

When there is no court order, the law enforcement official is probably there just to intimidate you, which may be a violation of the federal Fair Debt Collection Practices Act or your state's debt collection law. If the person in uniform is just pretending to be a law enforcement official, he is impersonating a law officer, which is a federal or a state offense. Either way, get in touch with a consumer law attorney immediately.

Ask for copies of any legal documents that you are told relate to the repossession. Assuming you receive them, share the documents with a consumer law attorney. They may contain errors or other problems that the attorney can use to try to get your car back. For example, the lender may have violated the federal Truth in Lending Act (TILA) by not revealing all the terms of your loan, or your loan agreement may charge you a higher rate of interest than your state allows.

Preparing for a lawsuit

Call the police immediately if the repo man violates your rights when he is trying to take your car — for example, he breaches the peace or breaks into your locked garage. After the police help you deal with the emergency, contact a consumer law attorney. You may have a good basis for a lawsuit against the repo man.

If other people see the repo man breaking the law, get their names and contact information. If you decide to file a lawsuit, your attorney may want to talk with the witnesses and may decide to call them to testify if the lawsuit goes to trial.

Maintain a record of every expense you incur related to the repossession of your car, including legal fees and court costs, lost wages, travel expenses, copying, and the cost of any medical care you seek because of sleep or emotional problems resulting from the repossession. If you sue your auto lender and win the lawsuit, the judge will probably order the defendant to reimburse you for expenses you can prove.

Having Your Car Auctioned Off

After your vehicle is repossessed, the lender stores it and arranges to sell it in a public auction. In most states, the lender is required to notify you in writing about the date, time, and location of the auction so you can buy your vehicle back or reinstate your auto loan before the vehicle is sold. The upcoming section "Getting Your Vehicle Back" explains the ins and outs of both options.

When your vehicle is sold, the lender applies the sale proceeds to your outstanding car loan balance; to the late fees you owe; and to the lender's costs of repossessing, storing, and selling it. If the proceeds don't cover everything, the lender is legally entitled to ask you to make up the difference, or *deficiency*.

Although your auto lender is legally obligated to sell your vehicle for a "commercially responsible price," don't count on the vehicle selling for enough money to avoid a deficiency. That rarely happens in a public auction.

Arranging to pay the deficiency

If you cannot afford to pay the full amount of the deficiency in a lump sum, ask the lender if you can pay it over time in installments. The lender may okay an installment plan to avoid the expense of trying to collect the money from you. You and the lender need to reach an agreement about the amount of each installment, the amount of any down payment or final balloon payment you may have to make, the interest rate that will apply to the installment payments, and so on.

If you and the lender come to an agreement about paying the deficiency, get it in writing. Do not begin making payments until you have everything in writing. If the lender won't prepare an agreement, write one yourself and send the lender a copy after you have signed and dated the original.

Anticipating what happens if you can't pay the deficiency

What if the lender refuses to let you pay the deficiency through an installment plan and insists that you pay what you owe in a lump sum? Don't give in to his demands if by doing so you jeopardize your ability to keep up with your priority debts and/or your most important living expenses.

Saving the personal items in your car

If you are concerned that your vehicle is about to be repossessed, don't leave any personal belongings in it. Remove the CD player, radio, TV, or VCR if you installed it after purchasing the vehicle. Take out your dry cleaning, CDs, tools, sporting equipment, child seats, and so on. You're entitled to get these items back if they are in your car when it is taken, but let's be realistic: Personal items can easily "disappear" in a repossession.

Also avoid leaving your loan paperwork in the glove compartment of your vehicle. If you hire a consumer law attorney after the repossession, having that paperwork makes her job easier.

If any personal property is in your vehicle when it is taken, write a polite letter to the lender right away saying that you want the items returned immediately or you want to be reimbursed for them. (If you want to get your loan paperwork returned, you should write a similar letter asking for it.) Include in your letter an itemized list of everything you want back. If you have photos of the items, make copies and send them with the letter. Do the same if you have receipts from when you purchased the items. Keep in mind that your loan agreement may give you only a limited period of time to make your request.

Make a copy of the letter for your files. Then send the original letter with copies of all backup information to the lender via certified mail with a return receipt requested. That way you have a record of when the lender received your correspondence.

Consult with a consumer law attorney if the lender refuses to return everything that you have asked for, claims that the items you want back were not in your vehicle when it was taken, refuses to reimburse you for the items, or wants to reimburse you for less than what you believe the items are worth. If any of your personal property is worth a substantial amount of money, the attorney may advise you to sue the lender and/or the company that employs the repo man.

By not giving in, you leave the lender with three options. The lender can

- ✔ **Turn your deficiency over to a debt collector.** In Chapter 9, we explain how debt collectors work and your rights when they contact you.

- ✔ **Sue you for the right to collect the deficiency.** If the lender wins the lawsuit, it may ask the court for permission to do one of several things:

  - Put a lien on one of your assets so you can't borrow against it or sell it until you pay the deficiency.

- Seize one of your assets, sell it, and apply the proceeds to your debt.

- Garnish your wages, assuming wage garnishment is legal in your state. When your wages are garnished, the lender receives a portion of them for a limited period of time.

Contact a consumer law attorney as soon as you know that your lender is going to sue you to collect the deficiency you owe.

✔ **Write off the deficiency and report it as** *uncollectible* **to the credit bureaus it works with.** The lender is most apt to do this if the amount of the deficiency is relatively small. However, when a creditor writes off a debt, it is legally entitled to resume its collection efforts at any time.

Getting Your Vehicle Back

After your vehicle is taken and before it is auctioned off, you have two options to try to get your vehicle back. One option is to buy it back from the lender. Buying it back may make financial sense if your vehicle is worth more than the outstanding balance on your loan.

Your other option may be to reinstate your car loan. *Reinstating* the loan means that you agree to resume paying on it according to your original agreement with the lender.

Don't consider either option until you have reviewed your budget (see Chapter 4). As angry as you may be about the loss of your vehicle, trying to get it back is a really bad idea if your finances are in no better shape now than they were when your car was repossessed.

Also, before you do anything, talk with a consumer law attorney. The attorney may find problems with your loan paperwork or with the way that your car was repossessed. You may be able to use those problems to your advantage if the lender is worried about the possibility of a lawsuit.

Buying back your car

To buy back your vehicle before it is sold, you must make a lump sum payment to your lender that covers the full amount of the outstanding balance on your car loan, all the late fees you owe, and the costs that your lender incurred seizing and storing your vehicle. When you do, the lender gives you *title* to your vehicle, which means that you own it free and clear.

Considering a personal loan

If you are tempted to borrow money from a friend or family member to buy your car back, make absolutely sure that you can afford to repay it. Otherwise, you may have your car, but you may lose an important relationship. If you are sure that you can repay the loan, treat it as seriously as if you were getting the loan from a bank. Put all the terms in writing, and let your friend or relative put a lien on your vehicle. That way, if you default on the loan, the friend or relative has the option of taking the vehicle as payment.

Even if you give your friend or family member a lien on your car, that person may feel uncomfortable taking the vehicle if you default on the loan. Conversely, you may get upset if that person does take it. More often than not, borrowing money from someone you know is a bad idea.

Before you make the payment or sign any buyback paperwork, get a written, itemized accounting from the lender of exactly how much you owe. Because you are paying the loan off early, the accounting should show that the lender is crediting you for unearned interest on the loan and auto insurance payments. If you have any questions or concerns about the accounting, talk with a consumer law attorney.

Instead of buying your car back before the auction, you may want to wait until the auction itself. The advantage of waiting is that if you are the high bidder, you'll probably end up paying less to get your car back at auction. The disadvantage, of course, is that you may not be the high bidder.

Reinstating your car loan

Reinstating your car loan can be another way to get your car back after it has been repossessed. You need to make certain that your car loan allows it, and your lender must say that a reinstatement is okay.

To reinstate your loan, you must not only pay the amount of the loan that is past due plus late fees; you must also reimburse the lender for all its repossession and storage costs. Then you must resume making your regular car loan payments (on time).

You may think that if you reinstate your car loan, you can turn around and sell your vehicle for enough money to pay the loan off and maybe even make a small profit. Don't bank on it. That's a possibility only if you have very few payments left on the loan and your vehicle is worth a lot more than what you owe on it. Because most vehicles start losing value as soon as they hit the road, your car is probably worth less, not more, than your loan balance.

If your car loan agreement gives you the right to reinstate your loan, and you believe that you can live up to all the terms, ask your lender for a reinstatement. Be aware that the lender likely won't agree to your request, preferring instead to get some money for your vehicle right away by selling it at a public auction. But there is always the possibility that your lender may go along with a reinstatement, especially if your vehicle is not worth much. So go ahead and ask; you've got nothing to lose.

Avoiding a Repossession in the First Place

Repossession may not be inevitable, assuming you act quickly enough. You can take steps to avoid it, including negotiating with your lender, selling your vehicle, and filing for bankruptcy.

If you are not sure whether any of these options are right for you, meet with a consumer law attorney. The attorney can help you evaluate them in light of the state of your finances, the laws of your state, and the terms of your loan agreement.

Negotiating a way to keep your car

Say that your credit history is in relatively good shape and you haven't yet missed a car loan payment, but you are worried about keeping up with those payments. You may want to approach your lender about extending the term of your loan (its *duration*) in order to lower your monthly payments. If the lender agrees, you will pay more in interest over the life of the loan, but that trade-off may help you keep your vehicle.

Having realistic expectations

Review your budget (see Chapter 4) before you begin negotiating with your car lender so you know exactly how much you can afford to pay on your car loan each month. If you agree to more than you can afford and you default on your new loan agreement, the lender will probably initiate repossession.

If you just need some temporary relief from your car payments, maybe because you lost your job and your new one does not start for a month or two, your lender may agree to work with you. For example, the lender may let you make interest-only payments or reduced loan payments for a while. (Usually an auto lender will not extend a temporary relief arrangement past three months.)

Before you ask for such temporary relief, read your loan agreement. It may give your lender the right to *call* your loan, or demand that you pay it in full immediately, even after you get caught up on what is past due. If that's what your loan agreement says, you can ask the lender to waive its right to call the loan, but the lender probably will say no. Even if your lender agrees, don't expect to get the change in writing.

Make sure that you understand exactly how you must make up the difference between what you would have been paying on your loan if you had continued making your regular payments and what you will be paying if your lender agrees to give you temporary relief. Your lender may want you to pay the difference in a lump sum after you begin making your regular loan payments again or at the end of your loan agreement. Or the lender may agree to let you pay the difference in installments at the end of your loan.

If your lender does not seem interested in negotiating, you may be able to sweeten the pot by putting up more collateral. In other words, the lender puts a lien on another asset you own (in addition to the lien it has on your vehicle). If you don't live up to the new loan payment arrangement, the lender can take both assets. This option may interest a bank or credit union. If your loan is with a national car lender, like GMAC or Ford Motor Credit (companies that finance cars on a national basis and do not make any other kinds of loans), this option won't work. National car lenders are not interested in getting additional loan collateral.

If you're not confident about your negotiating ability or you tend to get flustered by numbers and legalese, ask an attorney, CPA, or friend to do the negotiating for you. Some lenders can be very difficult to deal with and have no qualms about taking advantage of your weaknesses.

Protecting yourself

If your lender agrees to any temporary or permanent changes in the terms of your car loan, ask for everything to be put in writing. Don't sign the agreement until you have read it thoroughly and have received clear answers to any questions you have.

If possible, have a consumer law attorney review the agreement before you sign it. The attorney can make certain that you are adequately protected, that the lender is not charging you more than the allowable maximum rate of interest, and that the lender has disclosed all the terms of credit as required by the federal Truth in Lending Act.

When you read the agreement, pay careful attention to these provisions:

- ✔ The amount of your payments
- ✔ The payment due date
- ✔ The interest rate
- ✔ How you must catch up on any past-due loan payments
- ✔ How you must make up the difference between what you would have paid on your car loan and what you will be paying (if the lender agrees to change the terms of your loan for a limited period of time)
- ✔ When you (or the lender) will be considered in default of the agreement
- ✔ The consequences of defaulting

Selling your car

If you fear that you won't be able to keep up your car payments, you can try to sell your car before you miss any loan payments and use the proceeds to pay off your car loan. Your goal is to sell it for more than your outstanding loan balance so you have some cash to buy a used vehicle. However, that rarely happens.

Here's a more realistic situation: You probably owe more on your vehicle than it's worth. Unless you can come up with the difference between what your car sells for and what you still owe on it, the lender won't give you clear title to the vehicle, which means you can't complete the sale.

Another option is to find someone to take over your loan payments, assuming that your loan agreement allows it and the lender okays it. In this situation, the other person takes your car and starts making the loan payments.

 The lender probably won't remove you from the loan paperwork, so even though you no longer have the car, you are still liable for the loan. If the person who assumes your car note loses the vehicle in repossession and does not pay the lender the deficiency that remains after the car is auctioned off, the lender can come after you for the money. Plus, your credit history suffers even though you weren't the one who defaulted. For these reasons, this option works best if you know (and trust) the person who takes over your loan payments.

Selling your vehicle fast (and for a good price)

You end up with more money in your pocket if you sell your car to an individual buyer rather than to a used car dealer. Follow this advice to get your car sold quickly and for top dollar:

✔ **Price your car fairly.** A good resource for determining your car's current national market value is the *Kelley Blue Book*. You can access it at www.kbb.com, or you can find a copy at your local library. Other sites you may want to visit to come up with a realistic asking price include www.edmunds.com, www.nadaguides.com, and www.autosite.com.

After you have determined your vehicle's national market value, review ads for cars similar to yours in your local newspaper and/or in local car buying and selling magazines. In your area, your vehicle may command a higher or lower asking price than the market value indicated by the national resources.

Ask for slightly more than you are willing to take because most buyers expect you to negotiate. If you get no nibbles after you have advertised your car, reduce the price.

Consider the overall condition of your car when you decide on an asking price. Discount the price for dents and dings, old tires, worn upholstery, a radio that gets iffy reception, a CD player that does not work, and so on.

✔ **Take care of inexpensive repairs before you put your car on the market.** Be prepared to share your repair and maintenance records with potential buyers so they know that you have taken good care of the car.

✔ **Clean your car inside and out before you show it to prospective buyers.** First impressions count!

✔ **Let your friends and relatives know that you are selling your car.** Advertising it via word of mouth could save you the cost of an ad.

✔ **Advertise in your local newspaper and/or on the Web.** Web sites to consider include www.craigslist.com or car buying and selling sites like www.autobytel.com, www.autotrader.com, and www.cars.com. If you advertise on the Web, include a photo or two.

When you write your ad, highlight your car's pluses but don't misrepresent its condition. The pluses may include that your car has had just one owner, it's always been kept in a garage, it has low mileage, it's never been in an accident, it's in perfect condition inside and out, and so on.

To be safe when potential buyers want to look at your car, meet them during the day in a public location like a mall parking lot, rather than at your home. Also, have someone else with you when you meet with a prospective buyer to sign the sale paperwork.

Giving your car back voluntarily

When you and the lender can't work out a way for you to keep your car, and when selling it is not a viable option, you can just give it back to the lender. Doing so is called a *voluntary repossession*. The main benefit is that you don't have to reimburse the lender for the costs of repossessing your car. However, you may still have to pay the lender for the costs of storing and selling it.

After you give your car back, the process works pretty much as if you lost your car in repossession. Your car is auctioned off; the lender applies the sale proceeds to your loan's outstanding balance, all unpaid late fees, and the costs of storing and selling the vehicle; and you must pay any deficiency.

Don't voluntarily give up your car or sign any paperwork related to it without trying to get your lender to give you some concessions. After all, you'll be saving the lender the cost of repossessing the vehicle. For example, you may want to ask the lender to let you off the hook for any deficiency you may owe and to agree not to report the voluntary repossession to the credit bureau(s) it works with. Your lender probably won't agree to most concessions, but it may forgive a very small deficiency if it decides that collecting it would probably take too much time and money, or if it knows that you are *judgment proof* because you own no assets and your state does not permit wage garnishment.

If your lender agrees to some concessions, put them in writing (because the lender probably won't do so). Sign and date the document, and send a copy to your lender via certified mail; request a return receipt for your records. That piece of paper will come in handy if the lender goes back on your agreement.

Most auto lenders are pretty hard nosed and not disposed to making concessions to consumers who have fallen behind on their loan payments. However, it never hurts to ask. Who knows, your lender may just have a heart!

Filing for bankruptcy

Filing for bankruptcy buys you time to figure out what to do about your car loan, and it stops a repossession dead in its tracks because of the *automatic stay*. The automatic stay makes all your creditors cease their efforts to collect from you as long as you are in bankruptcy. However, if you filed for bankruptcy in the past and your case was dismissed because you didn't comply with some aspect of the bankruptcy process, the automatic stay lasts for just 30 days. (A bankruptcy judge may agree to extend it.)

Don't even think about handling your own bankruptcy! It's a complicated process, and you won't fully benefit from it if you try to represent yourself. To locate a good bankruptcy attorney in your area, go to the Web site of the National Association of Consumer Bankruptcy Attorneys (NACBA) at www.nacba.org, or contact your local or state bar association for a referral.

An attorney will help you figure out which type of bankruptcy you must file — a Chapter 7 liquidation or a Chapter 13 reorganization — based on your financial information and the requirements of the federal bankruptcy law. Most consumers file for Chapter 13 bankruptcy. The attorney will also handle all the paperwork that a bankruptcy involves, help you deal with your creditors, and be by your side when you have to go to court.

Before you can file for bankruptcy, federal bankruptcy law requires that you consult with a federally approved consumer credit counseling agency and obtain a *certificate of credit counseling completion* from the agency. The consultation can take place in person, via the Internet, or on the phone, and it must occur no less than 180 days before you file. To find a list of federally approved consumer credit counseling agencies, go to the U.S. Trustee Program's Web site, www.usdoj.gov/ust. Click on "Credit Counseling & Debtor Education" and then on "Approved Credit Counseling Agencies."

However, say that a repossession is imminent and you need to file for bankruptcy right away in order to avoid the loss of your vehicle. Most bankruptcy attorneys allow consumers in this situation to go through the credit counseling by phone or by computer at their offices. It should take only about 10 or 15 minutes to complete the counseling. After you've done so, the credit counseling agency faxes or e-mails the *certificate of credit counseling completion* to the attorney's office, at which point the attorney files your bankruptcy paperwork with the court.

Benefiting from a Chapter 13 debt reorganization plan

By filing a Chapter 13 reorganization bankruptcy, you get up to 60 months to pay the remaining balance on your car loan, including all past-due payments, interest owed, and late fees. At the start of the bankruptcy, your attorney prepares your debt reorganization plan, which details exactly how you intend to deal with each of your outstanding debts, including your car loan. The bankruptcy court must approve the plan.

After you have the court's approval, you must pay all your debts according to the plan. If you don't, you risk having your bankruptcy dismissed, which means that your auto lender could try again to repossess your car.

Using Chapter 7 to hold on to your car

There are two ways that you can try to keep your car when you file a Chapter 7 liquidation bankruptcy:

- ✔ **Reaffirming your car loan:** By reaffirming (if your lender agrees to it), you continue paying on the loan according to your original agreement with the lender. However, as a condition, after you sign the reaffirmation paperwork, you must pay in one lump sum the full amount of your past-due loan payments, all late fees you owe, and possibly the fees the lender had to pay its attorney as a result of your bankruptcy.

  Your lender may agree to let you pay the amount of the loan that is past due in installments rather than in a lump sum.

- ✔ **Redeeming your car:** To redeem your car, first you must reach an agreement with the lender about the vehicle's current value, and then you pay that value immediately in a lump sum. For example, say that you owe $10,000 on your vehicle, and you and the lender agree that it is worth only $5,000. You have to pay $5,000 to the lender. When you do, the lender releases its lien on your vehicle, giving you clear title to it. In other words, you own your car free and clear.

Unlike most other negative credit record information, which stays on your record for seven and a half years, a Chapter 7 bankruptcy lingers in your credit history for ten years.

For detailed information about how bankruptcy works, pick up a copy of *Personal Bankruptcy Laws For Dummies* by James P. Caher and John M. Caher (Wiley). You can also find out more about how bankruptcy works by visiting the Web site of the American Bankruptcy Institute (www.abiworld.org) and clicking on "Consumer Education Center."

Hiring an Attorney

A consumer law attorney can help you avoid a repossession and can help even after a repossession has occurred.

Before you lose your car

Given how quickly a repossession can happen, ideally you want to meet with a consumer law attorney as soon as you know that you are going to have trouble keeping up with your car payments and before you have missed a single payment. (In many states, one missed payment can trigger repossession.) If you have already missed payments, schedule a meeting right away. There may still be time to prevent the loss of your car.

Bring your loan paperwork to the meeting so your attorney can review it for possible problems. The attorney may be able to use those problems to gain some bargaining power with your auto lender (or to recommend that you sue).

What kinds of problems is an attorney looking for? The lender may have

✔ Violated the federal Truth in Lending Act when it gave you the loan by not disclosing all the loan terms of credit.

✔ Not properly *perfected its lien* on your vehicle. If a lien is not perfected, your lender may not be able to properly repossess your vehicle. Your lender may actually be an unsecured creditor, not a secured one, which means that the lender must get the court's permission to take your car back.

✔ Violated your state's Deceptive Trade Practices Act or a similar law in your state by adding hidden charges to your loan.

✔ Charged you a higher interest rate than your state allows.

✔ Breached or broken your loan agreement. For example, the lender may not have respected your loan agreement's *grace period:* a period of time after the payment due date during which you can pay the loan without incurring a late fee and without being considered in default.

The attorney will review your options for dealing with your car loan problem in light of the terms of your loan agreement, the laws of your state, and the details of your financial situation.

If the attorney advises you to file a lawsuit, she will probably agree to represent you on a *contingent fee basis.* That means you won't pay the lawyer a fee regardless of whether you lose or win the lawsuit. Instead, if you win, the attorney takes her fee from the money that the court awards you. Otherwise, the attorney does not get anything.

If you have a different type of agreement with your attorney, you may have to reimburse her for all court costs and expenses associated with your lawsuit no matter what the outcome of your lawsuit.

After repossession

Meet with a consumer law attorney as soon as your vehicle gets taken to discuss your options for getting it back. Bring with you the loan agreement, any records you kept of conversations you had with your lender when you were trying to avoid repossession, all paperwork related to the repossession, and any records you've kept of expenses you incurred related to the repossession.

If the attorney concludes that your rights were violated when your car was repossessed or sold, or that the lender violated some of your other rights, he may be able to help you get your car back, get the lender to agree to lower the amount of the deficiency you pay, or get some other concessions. The attorney may also conclude that you should sue the lender and/or the repo man.

Finding an attorney

Here are two reliable resources for finding a consumer law attorney:

- ✔ National Consumer Law Center in Boston: www.consumerlaw. org or 617-523-8089
- ✔ National Association of Consumer Advocates in the District of Columbia: www.naca.net or 202-452-1989

Your local or state bar association is another resource; most bar associations provide attorney referrals.

Chapter 12

Avoiding an Eviction and the Loss of Your Utilities

In This Chapter

▶ Steering clear of an eviction

▶ Finding out about the eviction process

▶ Understanding the problems you may face post-eviction

▶ Keeping your utilities turned on

▶ Reestablishing utility service

*W*hen you are struggling to make ends meet and you fall behind on rent, probably the worst thing that can happen is to receive an eviction notice. Suddenly, your bad dream is a full-fledged nightmare. Your mind races as you try to figure out how you can possibly come up with the money you need to stay where you are living. If you conclude that it's *Mission Impossible,* you're faced with the challenge of quickly finding somewhere else to live, not to mention getting all your belongings packed up and moved out, pronto. What a disaster!

We know that facing eviction is incredibly tough, especially if you have children. In this chapter, we try to make the going a little easier by explaining your alternatives for avoiding an eviction. We hope you find one that works for you. If not, we help prepare for what's to come by explaining how an eviction works.

We also provide information about how to avoid having your utilities terminated. We illuminate your options for keeping your lights shining, the water running, your heat and air conditioning blowing, and your phone functioning. We provide an overview of the utility termination process, from the initial notice you receive about your past-due bill to the steps you must take to get your service back on after it's been terminated. We also discuss how your state Public Utility Commission fits into the picture.

Keeping a Roof over Your Head

Throughout this chapter, we use the word *apartment* to refer to the place you live, whether it's actually an apartment or it's a duplex, condo, or home. Our advice applies to any rental property.

You probably signed a lease with your landlord before you moved in. The *lease* is a contract that spells out the obligations you have to your landlord and vice versa. It indicates the start and end dates of the rental contract; the amount of rent you must pay each month; the amount of money you must put up as a security deposit; and all the other terms and conditions of your lease, including when you can be evicted.

 Don't assume that your landlord won't evict you because you have a history of paying your rent on time or because you think that your landlord likes you. Ultimately, your relationship with your landlord is a financial one. If you miss rent payments (even one), your landlord will make a dollars-and-cents decision about what to do.

The laws of your state determine the specific details of the eviction process in your area. However, we can safely say that when an eviction begins, the process moves quickly; you won't have a lot of time to find a new place to live unless you can slow the process down or even stop it.

 Keep in mind that being evicted makes it harder for you to find a new place to live. The new landlord will probably run a credit check as part of the application process, and your current landlord has probably reported your late payments and eviction to the national credit bureaus. If you find a landlord who will rent to you despite your credit history, you may have to pay a larger than usual security deposit and/or get another adult to cosign (and be responsible for) your lease.

For these reasons (and others), you want to avoid eviction at all costs. Evaluate your options for dealing with your rent as soon as you realize you can't keep up with it. Act quickly to pursue whichever option you think is best. Your options may include

✔ Paying your past due rent immediately.

✔ Negotiating with your landlord.

✔ Terminating your lease.

✔ Breaking your lease.

✔ Subleasing your apartment or finding someone to assume your lease.

✔ Getting a roommate.

In the following sections, we detail each option so you can consider which may work best for you.

If you are already in jeopardy of being evicted, meet with a landlord–tenant attorney so you can find out about your state's eviction law, review your lease to see what it says about evictions, and talk about your options. If you cannot afford to pay for an attorney, get in touch with your local tenant's council or your local or state bar association. The tenant's council can advise you of your rights and may be able to refer you to a low-cost/no-cost attorney. Another alternative is to contact the Legal Aid Society in your area; a Legal Aid attorney will help you for free.

Paying your past-due rent

Getting caught up on your past-due rent is the most obvious way to avoid being evicted. However, when money is tight, that can be easier said than done.

If you know that your finances are about to take a positive turn (so you'll be able to keep up with your rent), you may want to borrow money from a friend or relative to pay your past-due rent. You may also want a loan if you intend to move out of your apartment but need more time to find a new place to live.

If you do not want to ask someone you know for the money, you may qualify for help from a nonprofit or government agency in your area that provides emergency housing assistance. Contact your local, county, or state housing or welfare agency. Your church may be another option.

Negotiating a way to stay

Maybe you truly believe that your money problems will be short lived; you've looked at your budget (Chapter 4) and your financial prospects, and you know that things will improve in a few months. If you are certain that you won't have trouble paying your rent after your problems are over, talk with your landlord about making reduced rent payments for a while. Your landlord may agree if you can convince him that your financial prognosis is good and if you have had a good rent payment history until now. However, if you've been a problem tenant — paying your rent late, having noisy parties, making unreasonable demands, and so on — don't hold your breath waiting for a "yes." Your landlord may be happy to show you the door.

You may have a more difficult time negotiating a way to remain in your apartment if your landlord is a big bureaucratic company rather than an individual who maintains a direct relationship with his tenants.

If your landlord is willing to let you make smaller rent payments for a limited period of time, get the terms of your agreement in writing. Be sure the agreement addresses all the following:

- ✔ The amount of the reduced payments.

- ✔ The duration of the reduced payments.

- ✔ When you will be in default of the agreement

- ✔ The consequences of a default.

- ✔ How and when you must pay any rent that is already past due. Your landlord may agree to take the money out of your security deposit, but if your security deposit won't cover it all, you need to agree how you'll make up the balance. Many landlords prefer to reserve security deposits to pay for cleaning and repairing an apartment after a tenant moves out, so your landlord may expect you to pay your past-due rent in full.

- ✔ How you'll make up the difference between your normal monthly rent and what you will be paying. Your landlord may want you to pay the difference in a lump sum by a certain date, or he may expect you to pay a little extra each month after you resume making regular rent payments. Some (but not many) landlords will agree to deduct the difference from your security deposit and then look to you to make up whatever money you may still owe.

- ✔ Whether you must pay an additional security deposit.

Terminating your lease

If your lease is month to month (unlike most leases, which last for a year), you can end it at any time for any reason, as long as you do so according to the terms of the lease. After the lease is legally terminated, your landlord cannot hold you responsible for any future rent payments.

Most month-to-month leases require that you give your landlord at least 30 days written notice of your termination plans. However, if you rented the apartment with a longer lease that has become a month-to-month lease, be sure you look at the lease agreement. Some landlords require 60 days notice given at the end of the month. If you give notice at the beginning of a month, it could be three months before you can legally move out without breaking the terms of the lease.

After you give notice, your landlord is entitled to any back rent or late fees you owe, and to be reimbursed for any damage you have done to your apartment. Your landlord deducts the fees and expenses from your security deposit and is required to send you any money left from the deposit within the period of time specified in your lease. (If you break a lease, do not expect to get your deposit back.) If the security deposit does not cover everything you owe, your lease probably entitles your landlord to ask you for the difference. If you do not pay it, your landlord may sue you. See the sidebar "The skinny on security deposits" in this chapter to find out how security deposits work.

Breaking your lease

Sometimes, breaking your lease can be a good way to avoid an eviction. When you break your lease, you move out before the term of the lease is up and before the landlord files an eviction suit.

If your lease is almost up, and depending on its terms and the laws of your state, it may cost you less to finish out the lease than to break it. (This assumes that you can come up with the money to stay there until the lease ends.)

Before you break your lease, read it carefully to see if it spells out a specific break-your-lease process and the consequences of not following that process. Among other things, your lease may require you to give your landlord a certain amount of advance notice about your plans, and it may obligate you to continue paying rent until your landlord finds someone to replace you as a tenant. However, your state requires your landlord to find a new tenant as quickly as possible.

Your lease may also give your landlord the right to be reimbursed for the expenses he incurs trying to find a new tenant: the cost of a newspaper ad, for example. However, in many leases, reletting fees are a set amount.

Breaking your lease won't release you from your obligation to pay your landlord any past-due rent you owe before you move out. Unless you pay that debt, your landlord deducts it from your security deposit together with any late fees and other expenses you owe. If your security deposit is not large enough to cover everything, you must pay the balance (unless your landlord decides to waive it).

Depending on your state, if you break your lease and your landlord can't rent your apartment for as much as you were paying, he can look to you to make up the difference until your lease term is up.

Renting your apartment to someone else

Subleasing your apartment may be another way to avoid an eviction, depending on the terms of your lease. When you sublease to someone, that person (the *sublessee*) moves into your apartment and pays the rent according to the terms of your lease. However, because your lease remains in effect until its term is up, if the sublessee stops paying the rent, your landlord can hold you liable for the missed payments. Also, the landlord can hold you responsible for any other lease violations the sublessee may commit, such as trashing the apartment and refusing to pay for the damage.

Before you begin the sublease process, read your lease to confirm that it allows subleasing and, if it does, whether you must comply with any special requirements or conditions. For example, most leases (and some state laws) require tenants to get upfront approval from their landlords before they sublet their apartments. You risk being evicted if you don't get that approval. Also, your lease may entitle your landlord to meet whomever you are thinking about subleasing to, and it may require the sublessee to pay an additional security deposit.

If your lease does not allow you to sublet your apartment, your landlord may okay such an arrangement anyway. For example, she may agree to it if she is convinced that you cannot afford to continue paying your rent; subleasing may be the quickest and best way for her to guarantee a reliable flow of rental income.

Screening candidates

Obviously, if you are going to sublease your apartment, it's critically important to screen applicants so you can feel confident that the person you choose will be a responsible tenant. This goes for friends, relatives, and casual acquaintances — not just for strangers.

Ask anyone who wants to sublease your apartment to complete a written application. The application should ask for current contact information, including address, phone number, and e-mail address; personal and rental references; occupation; monthly income; and employer name and contact information. Confirm the application information, and check the references. It's also a good idea to run a background check on anyone you are considering seriously. For between about $10 and $35 (depending on the amount of detail you want), the background check will tell you about an applicant's rent payment history, whether the applicant has a criminal history, and more.

Putting a sublease in writing

When you find someone to sublease to, prepare a written agreement. At a minimum, it should state the following:

- ✔ The amount of rent the sublessee must pay each month and the rent due date

- ✔ The amount of any security deposit your landlord may require from the sublessee

- ✔ All other lease obligations of the sublessee

- ✔ The duration of the sublease agreement

- ✔ The process that the sublessee must follow if he wants to stop subleasing before your agreement is up

- ✔ The consequences of breaking the agreement

Considering similar options

Your lease may allow you to let someone *assume* it, which is a better alternative than subleasing because the person who assumes your lease becomes legally liable for it. In other words, you give up all your interest in the lease. If the person who assumes your lease breaks the lease, your former landlord cannot hold you responsible for any money owed. (This presumes that you get a release from the lease when the other person assumes it; check your lease agreement to make sure that's the case.)

Another alternative is for your landlord to give the new renter a totally new lease and allow you to terminate your own lease without having to pay any penalties. If you save the landlord the expense and hassle of finding a good tenant, she may be willing to take this option.

Sharing your space

Finding a roommate to split the cost of your rent and utilities may be the perfect answer to your problem. Before you let someone move in with you, be sure that your lease allows you to have a roommate. If it does, be clear about any rights your landlord may have, such as the right to approve a roommate before he moves in. If you violate the terms of your lease, you may face eviction.

Tips for finding a roommate or sublessee

Sharing your place with a roommate or subleasing it can be a great way to avoid an eviction. But either arrangement can blow up in your face if you are not careful about who you choose. Follow these steps to minimize your risk:

✔ **Ask your friends, family members, and business associates for referrals.** However, assuming that birds of a feather may flock together, don't ask for a referral from anyone who has a bad rental track record, is an overspender, or is unreliable.

✔ **Prepare an ad that plays up the selling points of your apartment.** Focus on features that make it most attractive, such as its size, location, and amenities. The ad should also provide basic information such as the monthly rent, the amount of any security deposit, and when someone can move in.

Advertise your apartment on Web sites like www.craigslist.org and www.sublet.com. You may also want to place an ad in your local daily paper or your community weekly paper (or in your college or university newspaper if you are a student).

✔ **Post notices about your apartment on community bulletin boards.**

✔ **Take digital photos of your apartment.** You can include them in any online ads you post and send them to anyone who expresses interest.

✔ **Clean your apartment thoroughly and get rid of clutter before you show it to anyone.** Your apartment should make a good first impression.

✔ **Schedule appointments so anyone interested can see your apartment and so the two of you can meet.**

✔ **Have applications available for anyone interested.** Verify all the application information, check references, and run a background check on anyone you are seriously considering. Also, if you are looking for a sublessee, have a copy of your lease available for applicants to review so they know what their obligations would be (such as paying the first and last month's rent).

If you get a roommate, your landlord may be entitled to cancel your current lease so the two of you can sign a new lease as legal *co-tenants*. As co-tenants, you share equal responsibility for complying with the lease terms. This means, among other things, that you are equally responsible for the entire amount of your rent even though you are sharing the cost. If one of you cannot come up with his share of the rent or if one of you moves out suddenly, the other is legally obligated to pay the full amount of the rent due.

If your landlord wants you and your roommate to sign a new lease as co-tenants, make sure that she is not going to raise your rent. Such an increase may undermine the very reason you're going to have a roommate — to lower your monthly rent expense.

Your landlord may also expect you to pay an additional security deposit if a second person moves in. If so, try to get your roommate to pay it because you've already put one deposit down.

Finding a compatible roommate

If you need to find a roommate (see the sidebar "Tips for finding a roommate or sublessee"), first make a list of the qualities you do and don't want in a roommate. Going through this exercise can increase the likelihood that you'll end up with someone you're compatible with. For example, if you like peace and quiet at the end of the day, avoid someone who likes to party a lot or is used to having friends over all the time. If you're a neatnik, avoid living with a slob or else you'll feel like you're in an episode of *The Odd Couple*.

Ask anyone who applies to be your roommate to complete a rental application; see the earlier section "Screening candidates" for advice about what the application should contain. Spend some time with each applicant so you can get a sense of whether that person fits the bill. If you get a bad feeling about someone, no matter how good he or she looks on paper, trust your gut and don't room with that person.

Discussing the business of living together

After you find a roommate, discuss how the two of you will manage the practical aspects of living together. For example,

- ✔ How will the rent get paid each month? Will you each write a check for one-half of the rent, or will one of you write a check for the full amount and get reimbursed by the other?
- ✔ Does the roommate have to pay you the first and last month's rent?
- ✔ Who will pay any additional security deposit your landlord may require?
- ✔ How will you share joint expenses like the bills for utilities, cable, and Internet service?
- ✔ How much notice must your roommate give you if she decides to move out before your lease is up, and what does she owe you financially if she does?
- ✔ Under what circumstances can you ask your roommate to leave if you decide that living together isn't working out?

✔ Is your roommate obligated to help you find an acceptable new roommate if she moves out before your lease is up?

✔ How will you share the housework?

✔ If you are going to share a home, how will you divvy up any chores your landlord doesn't handle, such as mowing the yard and shoveling snow?

Talk through these and any other issues you think are important to address, and put answers down on paper. Doing so helps minimize the potential for misunderstandings and conflict and makes it easier to resolve any problems that may arise. Be sure that both of you sign and date the agreement and that you each have a copy.

You may want to have a landlord–tenant attorney review the agreement you draft before you ask your roommate to sign it. That way, you can be sure it protects you adequately from potential problems, especially if there is a lot of money involved.

If you and your roommate sign a new lease with your landlord and then your roommate breaks the lease by moving out early, your landlord may have the right to ask you to leave. If the lease gives your roommate the right to sublease to someone, the agreement between the two of you should require your roommate to find a sublessee before moving out (assuming that the landlord approves the sublease).

Facing Eviction

You've tried everything you can think of to avoid being evicted, but the writing is on the wall. Now you need to get up to speed on how evictions work.

Before we tell you how evictions *generally* work (the process can be a little different depending on the details of your state's eviction law), you need to know that after the process begins, it moves quickly. An eviction may take just a few weeks to complete, and if a court orders you to vacate your apartment, you may have just a few days to move out. If you are concerned about being evicted, begin looking for a new place to live immediately, and be prepared for your housing hunt to take time; most landlords won't rent to you because you're being evicted.

Also, begin planning now for how you'll come up with the money to pay a new security deposit. Being evicted means that you won't get back the security deposit you paid to your current landlord. Plus, your new landlord may require you to put down a larger than usual deposit given your rental history. (He may also require that you have another adult cosign your lease.)

If you need to move out of your apartment right away but can't yet afford to pay a security deposit or monthly rent, start talking to relatives and friends about staying with one of them until you get back on your financial feet.

Receiving a warning

Before an eviction can begin, your landlord sends you either a *notice to pay or vacate* or a *notice to vacate*. If you receive the first type of notice, your landlord is giving you an opportunity to avoid an eviction by paying what you owe. If you receive the second type of notice, your landlord is telling you that he wants you out, period. The first notice will indicate the date by which you must pay or make payment arrangements in order to continue living in your apartment, and the date by which you and all your belongings must be out if you cannot come up with the money. The second notice just tells you when you must be out.

Assuming you receive a notice to pay or vacate, you can respond in one of several ways. Your best response depends on such things as your short- and long-term financial prospects, the terms of your lease, and your relationship with your landlord.

Paying what you owe

Obviously, a good response to an imminent eviction is to pay your landlord what you owe by the due date. Not only do you avoid being evicted, but you also buy yourself some time to either move out on your own terms or pursue one of the options we describe in the earlier section "Keeping a Roof over Your Head." However, if you have not been able to come up with rent money before now, you probably won't come up with it when the notice arrives.

Moving out by the vacate date

Moving out won't let you off the hook for your past-due rent or for any fees your landlord may be entitled to collect, such as late fees and bounced check fees. In addition, you lose your security deposit.

If your security deposit is not large enough to cover everything you owe, your landlord may be entitled to ask you to make up the difference. If so, talk to your landlord about whether you can pay the difference in installments. If not, unless you can figure out a way to come up with the money, your landlord may turn your debt over to a debt collector or even sue you for it, especially if the amount you owe is substantial.

Disputing the amount that your landlord says you owe

If you disagree with the amount of money that the warning notice says you must pay in order to avoid being evicted, talk to your landlord and write her a letter stating how much you think you really owe. Attach to the letter copies of any documentation you have that helps make your argument, such as copies of past rent checks endorsed by your landlord or correspondence from your landlord. Make a copy of your letter for your files, and send the original letter with copies of the documentation to your landlord via certified mail. Request a return receipt so you know when your landlord received the letter.

Getting a summons from the court

If the eviction process moves forward, your landlord files a *complaint* with your local small claims court, housing court, justice of the peace court, or whatever low-level court in your area handles evictions. The complaint states why your landlord thinks you should be evicted.

After the complaint is filed, an eviction hearing is scheduled. The court sends you a *summons* (which is usually served by a constable) officially notifying you that your eviction has begun. The summons also indicates the date of your eviction hearing or trial.

 If you are not already working with a landlord–tenant attorney, contact one immediately. Don't delay: You may have only a few days to respond to the court's notice. If you can't afford to pay an attorney and your income is low enough, contact your local Legal Aid Society.

Depending on the facts of your situation, the attorney may advise you to do one of the following:

✔ **Fight the eviction.** Tell the judge why you should not have to move out or why your landlord should give you more time to catch up on your rent. The judge may sympathize with your situation and ask your landlord to try to work something out so you can stay put or at least have additional time to find a new place to rent. (For example, maybe the school year is almost over, and you need a few extra weeks to keep your children in school. Or maybe the rental market in your area is very tight, and you need more time to find another apartment.)

To fight your eviction, you may have to file an *answer* or *response* to your landlord's lawsuit by the deadline on the summons. However, in some jurisdictions, you can just show up in court on the date of your trial and indicate that you intend to fight the eviction.

✔ **Settle with your landlord.** Your landlord may agree to drop his lawsuit if you agree to do certain things by a set date, such as pay all the past-due rent that you owe and move out. Get the terms and conditions of any agreement in writing.

✔ **Do nothing.** If you do not respond to the court summons and you don't show up in court on the trial date, the court will probably award your landlord a *default judgment* against you. That means that the landlord gets the right to make you move out by the date set by the judge.

If you don't show up for your trial, you forfeit your right to defend yourself against any lies or misleading statements your landlord may make, and you give up the opportunity to ask your landlord questions that may be helpful to you in the lawsuit. Also, you can't ask the court for extra time to move out.

When you do appear in court, dress neatly and conservatively. You don't have to wear a power suit, but you should avoid plunging necklines, short skirts, tight pants, jeans, shorts, and T-shirts.

Being removed from your home

If your landlord wins the lawsuit, you will probably receive a court notice telling you the date by which you must be out of your apartment. The deadline probably won't be very long after the judge issues his decision. If the notice contains anything you don't understand, talk with your attorney; get an explanation from the office of your local constable, sheriff, or marshal (whichever one enforces evictions in your area); or ask the court clerk's office.

If you don't have a place to move to yet, find one immediately. In the meantime, ask your attorney whether she thinks you can get the eviction delayed or cancelled. For example, the attorney may suggest that you formally appeal the court's decision. If you do, a higher court will hear your request for an appeal. If the judge in that court decides that you are entitled to appeal, your eviction is put on hold, and another eviction trial is scheduled. You may not win the second trial either, but at least you get more time to find a new place to live. The downside is that you may have to pay a bond to appeal.

What if your eviction moves forward, and you and your belongings are still in your residence on the date by which you are supposed to be gone? A local constable, sheriff, or marshal comes to your home, asks you to leave, and usually moves all your belongings into storage. Sometimes, depending on your jurisdiction, your belongings are just moved to the curb. At this point, you are breaking the law if you reenter your home without the permission of the landlord or the court, and you could be taken to jail.

When your belongings are in storage, you have to contact the moving and storage company and make arrangements to reimburse it for its moving and storage costs. Do so quickly: After about 30 days, the moving and storage company will begin selling your things.

Remaining on the hook for the money you owe

After you've been evicted, your landlord may sue you for any past-due rent you still owe and for any late fees and other expenses your lease says he is entitled to. Contact a landlord–tenant attorney right away if you are sued. The attorney may be able to convince the landlord to drop the lawsuit in exchange for you paying a substantial portion of the money you owe, or in exchange for you giving the landlord an asset you own as payment.

The skinny on security deposits

Usually, when you sign a lease agreement, you must give your landlord a security deposit. Then when you legally move out of your apartment, you are entitled to any money left in the deposit after all deductions. (Your state or locality may also entitle you to receive interest on the deposit.) Depending on the terms of your lease and your state's law, the deductions may include unpaid past-due rent and fees, plus the cost of any repairs, maintenance, and cleaning that are beyond normal wear and tear.

Your landlord must provide you with a written itemization of all the deductions taken from your security deposit. You are entitled to receive the itemization within a certain amount of time after you move out — usually no less than two weeks and no more than one month.

If you do not receive the security deposit money you believe you are entitled to and/or the itemized accounting by the required deadline, send a polite letter to your landlord requesting it. If your landlord does not respond or refuses to send you the money or to provide you with the itemized accounting, get legal advice. The attorney may recommend sending a demand letter on his letterhead to the landlord, and the landlord may respond with what you are asking for. Otherwise, you may have to sue the landlord. If you sue for a relatively small amount of money, you can file your lawsuit in small claims court and handle the case yourself. However, if you want to sue for the itemized accounting, you must sue in another court because you can sue only for money in small claims court.

If the lawsuit moves forward and your former landlord wins a judgment against you, the landlord can ask the court for permission to collect on the judgment by garnishing your wages, taking one or more of your assets, or putting a lien on one of your assets. However, if wage garnishment is illegal in your state and if you own no assets of any value (or if all your assets are exempt from the landlord's collection actions), your landlord is out of luck because you are judgment proof.

Maintaining Your Essential Utility Services

You rely on utility companies every minute of every day. They light your home and power your appliances. They keep the temperature just right. They let water flow from your faucets and flush waste down your toilets. They keep you connected to the outside world through telephones and computers. Doing without one or more of these services is not just inconvenient; it may be dangerous to your family's health and safety.

Knowing the players

Most companies that provide utility services are investor-owned, for-profit businesses. In most states, they are regulated by state Public Utility Commissions (PUCs), sometimes known as Public Service Commissions. However, in some states, the utilities that provide your gas, water, and wastewater services are regulated by different government agencies. Visit your state PUC Web site or call your PUC to find out about the specific utility services it regulates.

You may receive your electric power, water, and wastewater from a municipal utility. If you live in a rural area, your electric power may be provided by an electric rural cooperative, which is a private, nonprofit utility owned and operated by its members. Most state PUCs have no jurisdiction over municipal utilities or electric rural cooperatives.

Regardless of who provides your utility services, if you are having a tough time paying your utility bills, you may receive a notice from one or more of them threatening you with the loss of your service. (Maybe you've even had your service terminated for nonpayment.) In the sections that follow, we explain your options for avoiding the loss of your utility services, focusing on investor-owned utilities, and we provide a general explanation of how the termination process works, including the appeals process. If your utility is municipally owned or a rural electric cooperative, contact its customer service office to find out how the utility handles terminations.

We don't discuss wireless phone or cellphone companies in this chapter because they are minimally regulated by individual states, which means they are not held to the same standards as traditional phone companies when it comes to service terminations, appeals, and so on. With no tough consumer-oriented regulations that apply to the wireless industry, you are pretty much at the mercy of your wireless company if you can't afford to pay your cell phone bills.

Avoiding a termination

When you fall behind on a utility bill, the utility sends you a series of notices asking you to pay the outstanding balance. The timing and number of the notices is regulated by your state PUC or by some other state regulatory agency. Initially, the notices are part of your monthly statements. If you don't pay what you owe or make payment arrangements with the utility, you'll probably begin receiving separate notices. Eventually, a final termination notice arrives. At about the same time, someone with the utility company may also call to warn you that you're about to lose your service and to advise you of how you can stop the termination.

The final notice indicates the date on which your service will be disconnected and the date by which you can pay the total amount due to avoid the termination. It lists the reason for the termination, the amount of any reconnection fees you have to pay, and a number to call if you want to speak with someone about the money you owe. The notice also either spells out your termination rights and remedies, including your right to appeal a termination before or after you lose your service, or provides a number to call to find out about them.

When you receive a final notice, it's not too late to avoid having your service disconnected, assuming you act immediately. A government program, a local charity, or even your utility company itself may have programs that can help you with your bill.

Asking for help

Resources in your community may be able to help you keep your utilities on. Some provide emergency assistance when you are about to have a utility service terminated. Others provide help paying your utility bills each month for a limited period of time, assuming you qualify.

Each resource has its own criteria regarding whom it will help and under what conditions. For example, some resources help only people with very low incomes, while others offer assistance only when utility bills are the highest — in the summer or winter, for example. If you apply for assistance from one resource and are turned down, apply to another for help.

When you apply for assistance, be prepared to share basic information about your finances, such as your monthly income and expenses, as well as proof of your income (a pay stub will probably do). You may have to provide additional financial information as well, depending on whom you apply to and the kind of help you ask for.

Most government agencies and nonprofit organizations that offer utility bill assistance do not help consumers pay their water and wastewater bills or their phone bills.

Check into the following community resources when you can't keep up with your utility bills:

- **The utility you are having problems paying:** It may have a special fund for helping qualified customers keep up with their utility bills. Call the utility's customer service office to find out if it does and if you qualify for help.

- **Your state PUC:** Some PUCs offer limited financial assistance to qualified consumers who are having problems staying current on their utility bills. They can also refer you to other sources of assistance.

- **Your state, county, or local human services or housing agency:** If these agencies cannot help you, they can refer you to other possible sources of help.

- **Your state or local Low Income Home Energy Assistance Program (LIHEAP):** This program helps income-eligible consumers pay their heating and cooling bills for a limited period of time. The program is funded by the federal government and administered by local and state governments. For more information about LIHEAP and how to apply for program assistance, read the sidebar "Look to LIHEAP."

Most LIHEAPs do not help pay your light or water bills. Also, every year, the federal government allocates a limited amount of money to LIHEAP. So depending on when you apply for help from the program, there may not be any money left.

- **A local charity:** Some community-based nonprofits provide direct services to low-income individuals and families. These services may include food; clothing; and assistance paying for basic needs like food, shelter, and utility service.

- **A church in your area:** Some churches help needy people pay their bills.

Look to LIHEAP

If your income is low enough and you are in jeopardy of losing your ability to heat or cool your home because you have fallen behind on your utility bill, the Low Income Home Energy Assistance Program, or LIHEAP, may be able to help.

The program is funded by the federal government and administered by individual states or local governments. Eligibility criteria for LIHEAP assistance, as well as levels of assistance, vary from state to state and even from community to community. In addition to helping eligible consumers pay their utility bills, some LIHEAPs also help consumers reduce their future bills by helping finance the cost of weatherizing their homes or making energy-related repairs.

To obtain contact information for the government agency that runs the LIHEAP in your area, go to `www.acf.hhs.gov/programs/liheap/grantees/states.html` or call the National Energy Assistance Referral project (NEAR) at 886-674-6327. Another way to obtain the information is to send an e-mail message that includes your name, as well as the name of your city, county, and state, to the National Center for Appropriate Technology at `energyassistance@ncat.org`.

If you meet the eligibility requirements for the LIHEAP in your area and decide to apply for assistance, be prepared to provide program staff with the following:

✔ Copies of your last several utility bills

✔ Proof of your household's *gross income* (income before taxes and other deductions)

✔ Documentation showing how much you receive from other sources of income, such as Social Security, the federal Supplemental Security Income program, unemployment insurance, state assistance programs, a private pension, and so on

✔ A termination notice you may have received from your utility

✔ Proof of your current address

✔ Proof of the number of individuals living in your household and a Social Security card for each of them

✔ Proof that you are a U.S. citizen or permanent resident

If you do not qualify for LIHEAP assistance, or if you qualify but need more assistance as well, ask LIHEAP staff about other possible sources of help in your community.

If you are elderly, you may be eligible to receive help from a local or state government agency or from a community-based organization in your area that focuses on assisting older adults. To locate such assistance, use the **Eldercare Locator** sponsored by the U.S. Administration on Aging. Call 800- 677-1116 between 9 a.m. and 8 p.m. eastern time, Monday through Friday, or go to `www.eldercare.gov`.

Setting up a payment plan

If you can afford to pay something on your past-due bill each month in order to get caught up, review your budget (see Chapter 4) to determine exactly how much you can pay. Then contact your utility's customer service department to discuss a payment plan. If your past-due balance is not substantial and you can afford to pay it off according to the standard formula your utility uses to calculate monthly payment plan amounts, you may be able to set up a plan over the phone.

If the amount the utility wants you to pay based on its standard formula is more than you think you can afford, ask for a more lenient payment plan. To apply for lower monthly payments, you have to fill out an application. When the utility reviews your application, it takes into account such factors as the amount of your past-due bill, how long the money has been past due, your utility bill paying history, your income relative to your expenses, the size of your family, and how much you can afford to pay on your debt each month.

Maintain a written record of every conversation you have related to your request for a payment plan. Note the name and title of each person you speak to, the date of the conversation, and what was said. If you reach an agreement about a payment plan, record the terms of the agreement, and then compare what you wrote down to the terms of the plan agreement that you receive from the utility. If the agreement contains anything that you do not understand or you didn't agree to, or if the agreement does not reflect something that the utility representative promised, get in touch with the person who helped you work out the plan.

If you get nowhere with the first person you speak to about a payment plan, ask to talk to his supervisor. If you strike out with the supervisor too, you can ask the PUC for help. The next section explains how the PUC can help.

If you and your utility cannot work out a payment plan that you can afford and that is acceptable to the utility, you may be out of luck. Although the utility must *try* to come up with a plan that meets your needs, it is not obligated to agree to one that makes your monthly payments too small and that is going to take too long to complete.

If a termination is imminent and you have run out of options, you may want to appeal to your state PUC. Don't dawdle! Most states limit the amount of time you have to file an appeal. In some states, you have only one week to appeal after your utility notifies you of its final decision. Another option for avoiding a termination is to file for bankruptcy, which we discuss later in this chapter.

Before you agree to any installment payment plan, make sure that you understand all its terms and conditions. For example, the utility may require you to make a lump sum payment on your utility debt as a condition of setting up the plan. If you do not have the money to make the payment, one of the resources we list in the previous section may be able to help you.

Depending on your state, if you don't live up to the terms of your payment plan, your utility does not have to agree to give you another one; it can cut off your service unless you pay what you owe. Also, when you default on the plan, the termination process may be accelerated.

A resource of information about your utility rights is your state utility advocate. This person is usually located within the office of your state attorney general.

Appealing to your state PUC

If you do not agree with a decision your utility makes (and your utility refuses to change its stance), or if you believe that your utility has violated your rights (and it denies that it did anything wrong), you can take your case to your state PUC, assuming it regulates the utility company in question.

To appeal a decision that a municipally owned utility makes, get in touch with your local mayor, city council members, and/or city manager. If your problem is with an electric cooperative, contact the cooperative to find out how to appeal.

You may want to contact the PUC if you and your utility are unable to work out an affordable payment plan or if you disagree with the amount of money it says you must pay to avoid a termination, for example. You can file an appeal with the PUC to try to avoid a termination. When you do, your utility must suspend the termination process. (It can reactivate that process if you lose your appeal.) You can also appeal a termination after it happens.

Starting the process

Most PUCs allow you to file an appeal in writing or by phone. Some also allow you to file online. Filing in writing is best because you have a written record of exactly what you said and what you asked for.

After the PUC receives your appeal, a staff person reviews it. She may try to resolve your problem administratively, or she may send you a letter indicating that the PUC cannot help you or that your utility company did nothing wrong.

If you don't like what the PUC decides, you can submit a written request asking to have your complaint reviewed at a higher level. In your letter, explain why an additional review is merited. Your justification must be more than simply, "I don't like the PUC's first decision." You must be able to argue that your utility violated your rights or did not follow the prescribed termination process to the letter, that the PUC did not adequately review your initial complaint, and so on.

If the PUC agrees to the review, you may have to attend a dispute resolution meeting or conference. If your problem does not get resolved, you can request a formal hearing.

Holding a hearing

Most PUC hearings are more informal than trials; a hearing does not occur in a courtroom, and the rules and procedures are more relaxed than in a trial. Usually, an administrative law judge presides over the hearing, and you and a representative of your utility company are given opportunities to present your sides of the issue.

You can represent yourself at the hearing, or you can have a consumer law attorney represent you. If you represent yourself, it is a good idea to meet with an attorney or with a utility counselor. This person can explain the hearing process to you, review the kinds of questions you are likely to be asked, and discuss possible hearing outcomes. Having this information ahead of time can help alleviate any anxiety you feel about the hearing process and make you a more effective advocate for yourself.

Prior to the hearing, gather up any records you have that help support your side of the issue. For example, if you claim that the amount your utility company says is past due is incorrect, bring proof of what you have paid on past utility bills. If you claim that your service should not be terminated because someone in your family is too ill to do without the service even for a day or two, get a letter from your family member's doctor stating that fact. You may also be entitled to have witnesses attend the hearing and give testimony on your behalf.

At the end of the hearing, the judge makes a decision. If you do not like the decision and it means that a termination is imminent, you may want to file for bankruptcy to stop it (assuming you still cannot come up with the money you need).

Filing for bankruptcy

Filing for bankruptcy is an extreme step to prevent the loss of your utility service. However, if you have pursued other options without success, you may be left with no alternative. You can use bankruptcy not just to keep your utility service on but also to get rid of your past-due utility debt, regardless of whether you file a Chapter 13 reorganization bankruptcy or a Chapter 7 liquidation bankruptcy. However, no later than 20 days after the start of your bankruptcy, you must pay the utility a "reasonable" deposit — usually two to three months' worth of payments — to continue your service.

If you are considering bankruptcy, you must go through credit counseling with a federally approved credit counseling agency no more than six months before you file. When you do, you get a certificate to permit the filing of the bankruptcy. However, if you have to file right away and you have not yet gone through the counseling, you can probably get the required counseling at the office of your bankruptcy attorney by phone or online. (If you are in this situation and have not yet hired an attorney, ask the attorney you are considering hiring if completing the counseling in her office is an option. If not, look for a different attorney.) The credit counseling agency will fax or e-mail the certificate you need to your attorney who, in turn, will file your bankruptcy for you. Usually, all of this can be done in the same day.

As soon as you know the writing is on the wall and filing for bankruptcy is inevitable, meet with a bankruptcy attorney to find out how the process works and to figure out whether you can file a Chapter 7 or a Chapter 13. The attorney will also help you complete all the bankruptcy paperwork and guide you through the bankruptcy process. For detailed information about the consumer bankruptcy process, read *Personal Bankruptcy Laws For Dummies* by James P. Caher and John M. Caher (Wiley).

Reestablishing Utility Service

If your utility service is terminated, you must pay the portion of your bill that is past due, as well as all late fees and a reconnection fee, to get your service back. You may also have to pay a deposit. If you don't have the money to pay everything and can't or don't want to borrow what you need from a friend or relative, look for help from one of the resources listed in the "Asking for help" section earlier in this chapter.

If you believe that your service has been wrongfully terminated —
maybe you think that the utility did not follow all the rules leading
up to the termination — file an appeal with the PUC. If you win, the
utility may waive the reconnection fee and deposit requirements,
adjust the amount that it says is past due, work out a payment plan
so you can pay what you owe, and so on. For more information
about how the appeals process works, see the section of this
chapter called "Appealing to your state PUC."

Depending on where you live, your utility may be prohibited from
terminating your heat during the coldest months of the year or
from cutting off your air conditioning during the summer to avoid
endangering the health of anyone in your household. Also, terminations are usually limited or prohibited if someone in your home
is seriously ill or relies on life-support equipment. In addition, most
utilities must jump through extra hoops before they can terminate
service if an elderly person, infant, or young child lives with you.

Chapter 13

Handling Medical Bills and Child Support Obligations

*W*e address two particularly difficult types of debts in this chapter: medical debt and past-due court ordered child support. They are difficult not only because of the potential legal and financial consequences of not paying them, but also because they can create more emotional stress and upheaval in your life than most other debts. Not paying these debts can have serious negative consequences on the people you care about, like a sick child or spouse who needs ongoing care, or the children from your previous marriage or from an unmarried relationship.

If you're struggling to pay these debts, you won't find easy answers in this chapter. However, you will find a discussion of your options, as well as an overview of what happens if you don't pay them and advice for avoiding legal trouble.

Appreciating the Risks of Not Paying Your Medical Bills

Even if you have health insurance, a brief stay in the hospital or an illness or accident that requires outpatient tests and extended treatment can leave you with a mountain of medical debt to pay. If you have no health coverage, your medical bills can easily exceed what you can ever afford to pay. In fact, medical debt has become one of the leading causes of consumer bankruptcy.

Making matters worse, a growing number of doctors and hospitals are responding to their own economic pressures by getting tough on patients who don't (or can't) pay their medical bills. You may find that a doctor or hospital is willing to be quite aggressive about collecting from you. The medical provider may

✔ **Turn your past-due account over to a debt collector.** Some debt collectors blatantly flaunt the requirements of the federal Fair Debt Collection Practices Act (FDCPA). See Chapter 9 for details on this law and how to respond to a debt collector's efforts.

If a medical provider turns your account over to a debt collector, that fact will almost certainly end up in your credit history. It will lower your credit score, even if the debt is relatively small.

✔ **Sue you for the money you owe.** By doing so, the medical provider can get a court's permission to put liens on your property, freeze your bank accounts, seize your assets, and/or garnish your wages (if you live in a state that allows wage garnishment).

✔ **Refuse to treat you (or your family member).** The provider may take this step even if you (or your family member) have a serious and ongoing medical problem and even if you're paying off the debt through an installment plan. Some medical providers require patients who owe them money to pay cash up front in order to obtain additional medical care. These policies may not create insurmountable barriers to care if you live in an urban area, but they create real problems for people in rural areas where there are few (if any) alternative providers.

Taking Action to Reduce Your Medical Debt

If you've got high medical bills and you're worried about how to pay them, first try to reduce the amount of the bills as much as possible:

✔ **Be sure that the bills are accurate.** When you find errors, get them corrected and get your bills adjusted.

Don't assume that medical billing errors don't matter if you have health insurance. They do. These errors can mean higher co-pays and out-of-pocket costs for you and maybe even higher premiums when your policy is renewed.

✔ **Make your insurance company pay for everything it should.** If your bills are the result of an accident that someone else caused, get that person's insurance company to pay as many of the bills as possible.

✔ **Pursue all medical discounts you may be eligible for.**

✔ **Take advantage of medical bill paying assistance if you're eligible.** You may qualify for help if you have a low income or no health insurance.

In the sections that follow, we detail each of these options.

Reviewing bills with a fine-tooth comb

Too many people put doctors and hospitals on a pedestal. They assume that medical bills are always accurate or are afraid to speak up when they find errors. Get over it! Medical professionals are human beings just like you and me, which means that they sometimes make billing mistakes.

Usually, the mistakes are innocent — information gets keyed in wrong, for example. But even innocent errors can be costly. And some billing errors are deliberate. For example, a doctor may use one code to describe the treatment he provided to you but use a different code to charge more for his services. Or a doctor may purposefully charge you for a procedure you never received, or bill for more hours of operating time than were actually required.

 Studies show that the incidence of hospital billing fraud is rising. Protect yourself by reviewing every medical bill you receive line by line. Look for overcharges, double billings, and charges for care and services you didn't get.

 If you have health insurance, make certain that your medical provider does not bill you for charges you are not responsible for. For example, your medical provider may bill you for the difference between the total amount of your bill and the amount that the insurance paid on the bill even though you're responsible only for making a small co-payment. If this happens to you, fight it; contact the medical provider's billing office first, and get the insurance company involved if necessary.

You may be thinking, "Review my medical bills!! Easy for you to say, but have you ever tried to decipher one of those things?" You're right. Most medical bills are full of codes, numbers, and abbreviations that mean nothing to you and me. So if you can't make heads or tails of your bill, call the medical provider's billing office. Start asking questions, and don't be afraid to ask more questions if you don't understand an explanation or if something doesn't seem quite right. Politely but firmly let the person you speak with know that you're not going to pay your bill until you understand exactly what you're being charged for. The bigger the bill, the more important it is for you to conduct a thorough audit.

For help figuring out your medical bills, order the medical billing workbook published by Medical Billing Advocates of America (MBAA). You can purchase the workbook for $22.95 at the organization's Web site, www.billadvocates.com.

Making your health plan pay what it should

If you have health coverage and your health plan refuses to pay one of your medical claims or does not pay as much as you think it should, read your policy to see if you can find a reason for the company's decision. There may be a good explanation. But if there isn't, contact your plan's customer service office and ask for one.

If you're not satisfied with what you find out, get help resolving your claim issue from your insurance agent or broker or from your employer's plan administrator if you receive health coverage through your job. If these people can't help you, send a letter to the insurance company after calling to get the name and title of the person to whom you should write. Be as specific as possible in your letter about why you think your claim should be paid or why you think more of the claim should be paid.

Your next avenue of recourse if your letter doesn't get results is to appeal your plan's decision. The appeals process should be spelled out in your policy or plan booklet. At the same time, you may also want to file a complaint against the insurance company with your state's insurance department. (It may be called an insurance *commission* in your state.) The department may have a complaint resolution process for resolving problems between consumers and their health plans.

If you let your insurance company know in writing that you have filed a formal complaint against it with the insurance department in your state, the insurer may decide to rethink how it handled your claim. Insurance companies don't want problems with state insurance departments.

Finally, if the amount of money at issue is substantial, you may want to hire a consumer law attorney to help you collect on a claim. A letter from the attorney may be all it takes to convince the insurance company to reverse its decision. Or you may have to file a lawsuit to get results. If the attorney feels that you have a strong case, she will probably agree to represent you on a *contingent fee basis:* You won't pay the attorney an upfront fee, but if you win your lawsuit and collect any money that the court awards you as a result, your attorney takes a percentage of what's collected. Exactly how much your attorney takes and all the other terms of your financial arrangement should be put in writing.

Taking advantage of discounts when you're hospitalized

Pursue all rate reductions you may be entitled to when you or someone else in your family is hospitalized. For example,

- ✔ If your income is very low and you own few if any assets of value, you may qualify for the hospital's charity program. To be eligible, you may have to prove that you applied for and were denied Medicaid coverage. Medicaid is a federal/state program for people with limited incomes. Individual states administer the program and set their own eligibility rules, although the federal government sets broad eligibility guidelines. For more information about the Medicaid program and about your state's particular eligibility rules, go to www.cms. hhs.gov/medicaid/whoiseligible.asp.

- ✔ Some states require hospitals to offer discounts to any uninsured patient regardless of the patient's income. However, hospitals may offer this discount only if you ask for it, so speak up if you don't have health insurance. Then make sure that the discount is reflected on your hospital bill.

- ✔ If your state does not require hospitals to offer discounts to uninsured patients and you have no insurance, ask the hospital to charge you the same prices it charges insurance companies. Insurance companies are billed for services at a much lower rate — as much as 60 percent lower — than what uninsured patients are charged. If the first person you talk to in the hospital's billing office says "no," ask to speak to his manager.

Remind the hospital that charging you the same rates it charges insurance companies makes it easier for you to pay your hospital bill and less likely that you'll have to file for bankruptcy. If you file for bankruptcy, the hospital will receive little or nothing on the bill.

If you don't ask for a discount before you are billed by a hospital, ask for it later and request an adjusted bill.

Pursuing other options for reducing your debt

Depending on your income and the total value of your assets, you may have other options for reducing the amount you owe to medical providers. For example,

- ✔ If your medical bills are the result of an auto accident that was not your fault, make sure that the insurance company of the other driver pays as much as possible on the bills.

- ✔ Contact churches and social service organizations in your area to find out if any of them can help you with your medical bills.

- ✔ Apply for Medicaid. In most states, after you are enrolled in the program, Medicaid not only helps you pay future medical bills but also pays bills that are as old as three months, assuming they are for Medicaid-covered services. For information about your state's Medicaid program, go to www.cms.hhs.gov/medicaid/stateplans.

Some hospitals let you whittle down your debt by doing volunteer work. If this option interests you, speak to a hospital financial counselor.

Tackling Your Remaining Debt

When you know exactly how much you owe on your medical bills, you have a few options for paying the debt (assuming you don't have the cash to pay it in full):

- ✔ **Ask the medical provider to set up an installment plan.** Most providers will let you pay this way, assuming you don't owe so much that it will take years before your debt is paid.

  Before you ask a doctor or a hospital for a payment plan, review your monthly household budget (see Chapter 4) so you know how much you can afford to pay each month. Don't pay more. For a more detailed discussion of installment plans, including negotiating tips, see Chapter 6.

Get clear about the terms and conditions of the installment plan before you agree to it. For example,

- Will you be charged interest? If so, what will the interest rate be?

- Are there any fees associated with the agreement?

- When will you be considered in default of the agreement, and what will happen if you are?

Some doctors and hospitals will not provide additional care to patients who have outstanding debt, sometimes even when they're paying off that debt through an installment plan.

✔ **Pay your medical bills with a credit card.** This option may work if you have a relatively low interest, fixed-rate credit card with enough available credit. You must make sure that you can afford the monthly card payments.

Some hospitals encourage uninsured patients or patients with high deductible policies who can't afford to pay the full amount of their bills to apply for a medical credit card. However, the cards are usually not good deals given their interest rates — as high as 23 percent. You're probably better off negotiating a payment plan because you may not have to pay any interest on your medical debt and, if you do, the interest rate will probably be lower than the rate associated with the medical credit card.

✔ **Get a bank loan.** Obviously, you need to find out if you qualify for one, and you must feel comfortable with the terms.

If you owe a lot of money to a healthcare provider and you own a home, the provider may try to pressure you into paying the debt by tapping the equity in the home or refinancing your mortgage and getting cash out. Bad ideas! Sure, you get the healthcare provider off your back, but your home will be at risk if you can't keep up with the loan payments.

Your final option, if none of the others works, may be to file for bankruptcy. If a medical provider is threatening to take legal action against you, filing for bankruptcy is probably your best move. Depending on your overall financial situation, you may be able to get rid of the debt completely by filing a Chapter 7 liquidation bankruptcy.

If you don't qualify for Chapter 7, you can use a Chapter 13 reorganization to reduce what you owe on some of your debts. You can also get up to five years to pay off most of your remaining debts, including medical debts, through monthly installments. For more information about bankruptcy and medical debts, pick up a copy of *Personal Bankruptcy Laws For Dummies* by James P. Caher and John M. Caher (Wiley).

Before you file for bankruptcy, schedule an appointment with a nonprofit credit counseling agency (see Chapter 8). The agency may be able to help you figure out a way to handle your medical bills some other way.

Prioritizing Paying Child Support

Child support is most often an issue when you are divorced and have *minor* children (which means under age 18 in most states) from your former marriage. Depending on the terms of your divorce agreement, a court order may be in place requiring you to pay your ex-spouse a sum of money each month for a set amount of time. The court order may also require that you provide your kids with health insurance, help pay for their college educations, and so on.

If you have minor children from a non-married relationship, you can also owe child support if the other parent obtains a child support court order.

Assuming the child support court order was written (or modified) after December 31, 1993, and assuming you are employed, your child support payments are automatically deducted from your wages. However, if you and the other parent decided not to have the payments automatically deducted, if you are self-employed, or if you are unemployed, you are legally obligated to make your own child support payments regardless of the state of your finances.

Even if you're going through tough financial times, you have a moral (as well as a legal) obligation to help take care of your kids by paying your court ordered child support each month. Making those payments should be one your top priorities. Your kids should not have to pay the price for your money problems, nor should their other parent have to sacrifice or work harder to make up for the child support you don't pay.

Knowing the Consequences of Not Paying

You face serious consequences if you don't keep up with your child support obligation and the other parent takes steps to get the child support court order enforced. Here are some possibilities:

- ✔ The state that ordered you to pay child support will come after you for the money.

- ✔ A child support debt collection agency may try to collect from you.

- ✔ The other parent may hire an attorney to collect from you.

- ✔ A family law judge may put you in jail until you pay your past-due child support.

Starting a new family has no effect on your financial obligations to the minor children you already have. You must continue providing them with support according to the terms of the child support court order. The court will not modify the court order just because you have more kids.

If you fall behind in your child support obligation, eventually, a government office, a private collection agency, or an attorney may contact you. (When and if you are contacted about your past-due child support largely depends on how aggressive the other parent of your children is about collecting the money you owe.) In the following sections, we explain what you may be up against in each case.

Getting the government involved

Every state has a Child Support Enforcement program (CSE), which is funded in part by the U.S. Department of Health and Human Services (HHS). The CSE office has a variety of tools at its disposal for collecting past-due child support from a parent, although the exact tools vary from state to state.

If you fall behind on your child support payments and your child's other parent contacts the CSE office in the state where your court order was issued, the office will contact you about the money you owe and ask you to pay it.

Assuming you can't afford to pay the money in a lump sum, the office may agree to let you get caught up through an installment payment plan. It may put a lien on one or more of your assets to guarantee that you live up to the terms of the plan. If you renege, it may take the assets, sell them, and apply the proceeds to your child support debt.

When you and the CSE office agree on a payment plan, get the agreement in writing, including all terms and conditions. If the office refuses to okay an installment plan that you can afford, you can file an appeal.

If you ignore the CSE's efforts to contact you about your child support debt, or if you can't reach an agreement with one another about how you will get caught up on your payments, the CSE may do one or more of the following to collect what you owe. (Exactly what the office does and how quickly it acts vary from state to state and also depend on how long your debt goes unpaid and how much past-due child support you owe.) The CSE may

- ✔ Put liens on some of your nonexempt assets so you can't borrow against them, transfer them into someone else's name, or sell them without first paying your child support debt.

- ✔ Take some of your nonexempt assets and sell them in order to pay off your past-due child support debt. However, the CSE office won't take your home or the assets you need to earn a living.

- ✔ Put a lien on your bank and/or investment account or levy the funds in those accounts. (*Levy* is legal talk for seizing the funds.)

- ✔ Suspend or cancel your driver's license and/or your professional license, such as a license to practice law or medicine. It may also suspend your hunting or fishing license.

- ✔ Deny or suspend your passport.

- ✔ Try to embarrass you by posting your photo and information about your child support debt on the Internet or on "wanted" posters.

- ✔ Intercept money you may be awarded by an insurance company in the settlement of a claim, including a personal injury or Worker's Compensation claim.

- ✔ Intercept any money you may win in a lottery.

- ✔ Intercept your state and/or federal income tax refund.

✔ Ask the IRS to collect the money you owe. If the IRS gets in touch about your child support debt and you can't afford to pay it in full, the agency may agree to let you pay in installments. If you don't cooperate with the IRS or if you violate the terms of your agreement with the agency, it may take your tax refunds and/or seize some of your assets, sell them, and apply the proceeds to your child support debt.

✔ Take you to court. Remember: You may even be jailed for past-due child support!

If you owe at least $1,000 in past-due child support, HHS requires that the debt be reported to the three national credit reporting agencies so that creditors, employers, landlords, insurance companies, and anyone else who looks at the reports will see that you have fallen behind on your obligation to your children. Obviously, that information reflects badly on you.

Being pursued by a child support collection agency

Instead of dealing with the government, your children's other parent may hire a private child support collection agency to collect the money you owe. She may do that because she wants quicker action than her state's CSE office can provide or because the CSE has been trying to collect from you but has not yet succeeded.

Although private debt collection agencies don't have at their disposal all the collection tools that state CSE offices can use, they are frequently able to get faster results than the government because they don't have as much bureaucratic red tape to deal with. Also, they juggle fewer cases than CSE offices handle, and they are better staffed. Bottom line: They have more time and resources to focus on collecting the child support you owe. Also, they are motivated by money to keep pursuing you because they get paid by taking a substantial portion of the money they collect.

Initially, most private child support collection agencies will contact you directly to discuss how you intend to get caught up on what you owe. If you cannot pay your debt in full, the agency that contacts you tries to get you to agree to an installment payment plan. If you can't afford one or you aren't able to agree on the terms of a plan, the agency may ask the court for permission to do one or more of the following:

✔ Have your wages garnished, if wage garnishment is legal in your state.

✔ Place liens on some of your assets.

✔ Enforce a lien that may already be in place as part of your divorce agreement.

✔ Freeze assets, such as the money in your retirement plan, any settlements you have received from a lawsuit or from an insurance company, or an inheritance. When these assets are *frozen,* you cannot sell, borrow against, or transfer them without clearing up your child support debt first.

The federal Fair Debt Collection Practices Act (FDCPA) does not regulate private child support collection agencies. However, some states have passed laws to govern what these agencies can and can't do. To date, those states are Arkansas, Connecticut, Illinois, Louisiana, Maine, Oklahoma, Oregon, Texas, Washington, and West Virginia.

If you are contacted by a child support debt collection agency and you cannot afford to pay your debt in a lump sum or through an installment plan, discuss your options with a bankruptcy attorney. The attorney may be able to help you figure out what to do about your debt so you can avoid having to file bankruptcy.

Hearing from an attorney

Another way that the other parent of your minor children may try to collect the past-due child support you owe is by hiring a family law attorney. For example, your former spouse may get in touch with the attorney who represented her in your divorce.

The attorney can take all the same steps that a private debt collection agency can to collect what you owe. These steps include putting a lien on one or more of your assets, enforcing an existing lien, taking a portion of your wages up to the amount of your debt, seizing some of your assets, and freezing some of your assets.

If you hear from an attorney about your past-due child support obligation, get in touch with a family law or bankruptcy attorney right away.

Keeping Up with Your Obligation

When money is tight and you wonder if you can keep up with your child support payments, you *must* do everything you can to make them. Your kids' quality of life is at stake, and you may face serious consequences if you fall behind (as we explain in the previous section).

Making tough choices

To avoid missing child support payments, here are some steps you can take:

- Review your budget for each and every spending reduction you can possibly make. If you don't have a budget, it's time to prepare one (see Chapter 4).

- Consider getting another job or doing freelance work. Use the additional income to help pay your child support.

- Contact your creditors about lowering your monthly payments. In Chapter 6, we tell you how to negotiate.

- Consolidate your debts to reduce the amount you have to pay to your creditors each month. We detail the ins and outs of debt consolidation in Chapter 7.

- If you believe your financial problems are temporary, borrow the money you need to keep up with your child support payments (or catch up on payments you've already missed).

- If you believe your financial problems are temporary, use credit card convenience checks to handle your child support obligation in the short term. Although you'll be charged a high rate of interest on the money you borrow, the cost may be worth it if you can avoid falling behind on your payments.

- Sell assets. Are you driving a nice car? Do you have a boat or a motorcycle? What about that rare coin collection you own? Sell what you can, and use the sale money to take care of your kids.

   If you can't keep up with your child support payments and your mortgage or rent payments too, you may even need to consider selling your home. You can buy a less expensive place to live or find a place to rent.

✔ Ask the court that issued the child support court order to modify the order on a temporary or permanent basis. If the court agrees, you are still responsible for paying any child support you may have already missed. We explain how modifications work in the next section.

✔ File for bankruptcy. You can't use bankruptcy to wipe out past-due child support, but you can use it to get rid of other debt, which may make it easier for you to keep up with your child support obligation in the future. Also, if you file for Chapter 13 bankruptcy, you can have up to five years to pay off the full amount of the child support that is past due. However, you must make each of your current child support payments on time while you are in bankruptcy.

The longer you delay paying your past-due child support, the harder it will be for you to get caught up, and the bigger the potential consequences of falling behind.

Asking the court for a modification

You can ask the court to lower how much you have to pay in child support each month if your financial circumstances have changed substantially since the court order was written. For example,

✔ You lost your job and have not found a new one.

✔ After months of looking, you've landed a new job, but it pays far less than what you used to earn.

✔ You're unable to work because of a serious illness or accident.

Depending on your situation, the court may agree to modify the court order on a temporary or permanent basis. But the court won't agree to a modification unless it is satisfied that you have exhausted all options for keeping up with your current obligation.

If the judge agrees to a temporary modification, the court will determine how long the modification will last and how much you must pay while the modification is in effect. The judge may require you to make up the difference between what you would have been paying and what you actually paid during the period of lower payments by increasing the amount of your child support payments for a while after the modification period ends. Alternatively, the judge may require you to make up the difference by giving your children's other parent an asset that you own that is approximately equal in value to the amount of money she won't be receiving during the modification period.

It's best to work with a family law attorney if you want your child support obligation to be modified. The attorney assesses your situation and lets you know whether you have a good shot at a modification. If you decide to file a request for a modification, the attorney represents you at the hearing.

Filing a request for a modification does not change your obligation to pay child support according to the original court order. Therefore, while you are waiting for the modification hearing to take place, continue making your payments. If you can't pay the full amount of the payments, pay as much as you can. Courts don't look kindly upon deadbeat parents! Also, any child support you don't pay can be collected from you. In fact, the judge may require that you pay what you owe by a certain date as a condition of a modification.

You increase your chances of getting a modification if your kids' other parent agrees to your request for the change. Even better is if the two of you can work out all the terms and conditions of the modification before your court hearing.

Chapter 14

Catching Up on Your Federal Taxes

In This Chapter

▶ Filing your return and paying by April 15

▶ Knowing your options if you can't pay on time

▶ Facing the consequences of getting behind

*O*wing past-due taxes to Uncle Sam is serious business. No creditor has greater power than the IRS to collect from you, and the agency can be relentless and ruthless in pursuit of its money. Furthermore, while your taxes are outstanding, the IRS charges you interest and penalties. As a result, if you drag your feet long enough, you may end up owing more in interest and penalties than you owe in taxes!

In this chapter, we explain how to avoid paying interest and penalties to the IRS by meeting your federal tax obligations on April 15. We then give you the rundown on your options for paying your taxes after they are due, including setting up an installment payment plan with the IRS and asking the agency to let you settle your debt for less. And we explain how bankruptcy can help you deal with your unpaid taxes.

We also clue you in on the consequences of ignoring your federal tax obligations. (Did you know the IRS can put a federal tax lien on your assets, take some of your assets — maybe even your home — and have your wages garnished?) Finally, we explain how the appeals process works when you want to formally object to an IRS decision.

Respecting the Sanctity of April 15

April 15 is drawing near, and you're in a panic. You owe income taxes to Uncle Sam, but you don't have enough money in your bank account to pay them. What to do, what to do? Here's what *not* to do: Don't bury your head in the sand! It'll cost you, big time!

At the very least, file your tax return on time, or file IRS Form 4868, "Application for Automatic Extension to File," which gives you until August 15 to get your return to the IRS. You can download the extension request form at www.irs.gov/pub/irs-pdf/f4868. pdf, order it by calling 800-829-3767, or pick it up at your local IRS office.

An extension to file your tax return is *not* an extension to pay your taxes. Taxes are due on April 15, come hell or high water, and the IRS begins charging interest and penalties on your unpaid taxes on April 16 (as we explain in the next section). For this reason, paying some of your taxes on April 15 is better than paying nothing at all. The more you pay, the less your tax debt will grow because of interest and penalties.

If you don't have enough money in your bank account to pay all the taxes you owe by April 15, consider using one of the following options to get them paid. As we point out in this list, each option can be costly. It's a good idea to consult with a CPA or financial advisor about whether any of these options is right for you. That person may suggest that you will be better off asking the IRS to let you pay what you owe in installments or to let you settle your debt for less through an Offer in Compromise. We discuss both of these payment options later in this chapter.

  ✔ **Pay with plastic.** You have to pay a fee of about 2.5 percent on the amount that you charge to the IRS. And, of course, if you don't pay the full amount of your tax debt when you receive your account statement, you pay interest to the credit card company.

Don't assume that you can pay your taxes with a credit card, declare bankruptcy, and make the debt disappear. If you file for bankruptcy before you've paid off your tax-related credit card debt, the bankruptcy court treats the debt exactly the same way it would treat your taxes if they were still outstanding. In other words, if the taxes would be dischargeable in bankruptcy, you'll be able to use bankruptcy to get the credit card debt discharged. However, if the taxes cannot be discharged in bankruptcy, you cannot use bankruptcy to get rid of the credit card debt either.

✔ **Use a credit card convenience check.** This option is relatively expensive because you probably have to pay a fee to the credit card company for the privilege of using the convenience check. Plus, if you can't pay off the amount of the check right away, interest accrues.

✔ **Borrow against your home equity.** The good news is that the interest you pay on the borrowed money is probably tax deductible. The bad news is that if you can't repay the borrowed money, you may lose your home.

Facing the Music on April 16

If you don't pay the full amount of your income taxes on April 15, you can expect your tax bill to increase, and you can expect to hear from the IRS.

Tallying penalties and interest

On April 16, the IRS begins charging you penalties and interest on your unpaid taxes:

✔ **Penalties:** For every month or part of a month that you have an outstanding income tax debt, you're charged a penalty that equals 5 percent of what you owe (including accrued interest and penalties), with a maximum penalty of 25 percent. If 60 days pass and you've still not filed your tax return, the *minimum* penalty becomes $100 or the full amount of money that you still owe to the IRS — whichever is less.

✔ **Interest:** You're charged interest, compounded daily, on your outstanding tax debt (taxes plus accumulated interest and penalties). The interest rate is the federal short-term rate, which is set every three months, plus 3 percent.

The IRS may agree to reduce the amount of penalties you owe if you have a good reason for needing a reduction. For example, maybe there's been a serious illness or death in your family; or maybe a fire, flood, or earthquake destroyed your tax records. Unfortunately, owing too much to your other creditors or mismanaging your money does not warrant a reduction.

Also, if you can prove to the IRS that it miscalculated the amount of interest it says you owe or made some other error affecting the amount of interest being charged, the IRS may agree to reduce the amount of interest it says you owe so far. In reality, however, convincing the IRS that it made a mistake is a very big challenge.

Being pressured to pay

In addition to penalizing you financially for a past-due tax bill, the IRS starts asking you to pay up.

First, you receive a "Notice of Taxes Due and Demand for Payment," which is essentially an IRS bill for the taxes you owe plus interest and penalties. If you disagree with the amount stated on the bill, immediately call the phone number on the notice or talk to someone at your local IRS office.

If you ignore the first notice, you receive a second notice asking for payment. However, this notice comes with an IRS publication explaining that the IRS may put a federal tax lien on all your assets and/or *levy on* (seize) some of them in order to collect your tax debt.

Next, an outside debt collector may get in touch to try to collect your tax debt or to obtain information that the IRS can use to collect what you owe, possibly by setting up an installment plan for you. (The collector gets 25 percent of any money he collects.)

Figuring out how to pay

If you couldn't pay your taxes on April 15, you probably can't pay them in full after that date either, especially since interest and penalties increase the debt. If that's the case, you probably have only three ways to take care of the debt and prevent the IRS from taking steps to collect the money from you:

   ✔ **Set up an installment payment plan.** Depending on how much you owe in income taxes and the overall state of your finances, an IRS payment plan may be the way to go. In the next section, we explain how installment plans work.

   ✔ **Make the IRS an Offer in Compromise (OIC).** Under certain circumstances, the IRS will let you settle your debt for less than the full amount you owe. However, getting the IRS to consider an OIC, much less accept it, can be an uphill battle. In the upcoming section "Using an Offer in Compromise to cut a deal with the IRS," we clue you in on how OICs work.

✓ **File for bankruptcy.** If your finances are in dire shape and you owe a bundle to the IRS, filing for bankruptcy may be your best bet, especially if you file before the agency puts a federal tax lien on your assets. However, filing won't get rid of your tax debt — it will be waiting for you to pay it when you complete your bankruptcy — nor will it stop the collection efforts of the IRS. Read the section "Filing bankruptcy to deal with your tax debt" later in this chapter for more details.

Paying your taxes in installments

When you can't afford to pay your income taxes in full, you may be able to pay them through an IRS installment plan, which requires you to make monthly payments. However, the IRS won't give you an installment plan if any of your tax returns for previous years have not been filed.

The process for setting up an installment payment plan depends on how much you owe to the IRS: less than $10,000; more than $10,000 but less than $25,000; or more than $25,000. (The more money you owe to the IRS, the more paperwork you have to fill out.) But the first step, regardless of how much you owe, is to fill out IRS Form 9465, "Installment Agreement Request." To get this form, go to www.irs.gov/pub/irs-pdf/f9465.pdf, call 800-829-3767, or visit your local IRS office.

When you complete the form, you have to indicate the following:

✓ **How much you want to pay on your tax debt each month:** The faster you pay off your tax debt, the less you end up paying in interest and penalties. Best-case scenario, you can afford to pay the debt before next year's taxes are due.

However, don't agree to pay more than you can afford. If you fall behind on your payments, the IRS will cancel your installment plan, and it may take steps to collect what you owe. See Chapter 4 for help creating a monthly budget so you know what a realistic payment would be.

✓ **How each payment will be made:** The easiest and safest way to ensure that each payment will be made in full and on time is to have payments automatically debited from your bank account or for your employer to treat them as automatic payroll deductions. However, you can tell the IRS that you will make the payments yourself.

After you've filed your request for an installment plan, the IRS contacts you within 30 days to let you know if your request has been approved or rejected. The agency may tell you that it needs more information before it can make a decision. If your plan is approved, you pay a $43 plan setup fee, which the IRS takes out of your first payment.

If the IRS okays your installment plan, it expects you to comply with two specific terms and conditions. You must

- ✔ **Make each installment payment in full and on time.** Here's an excellent reason to be realistic about how much you can afford to pay to the IRS each month.

- ✔ **Pay your income taxes and file your tax returns on time while your plan is in effect.** In lieu of filing a return, you may file an application for an extension to file, as long as you do so by April 15.

If you don't comply with these conditions, the IRS considers you in default, which means it may cancel the plan and try to collect the money you owe. In other words, you could find yourself facing the very consequences you hoped to avoid by setting up an installment plan in the first place.

Paying off less than $10,000

When you owe the IRS less than $10,000, the agency automatically greenlights your installment plan request, assuming the following are true:

- ✔ The IRS is satisfied that you cannot pay what you owe in a lump sum.

- ✔ You (or you and your spouse, if you file jointly) filed each of your tax returns on time over the previous five years or filed extension requests on time.

- ✔ You paid any taxes due on time during the previous five years.

- ✔ The amount of your monthly payments is high enough to get your income tax debt (including all interest and penalties) paid in full within three years.

Paying off more than $10,000 but less than $25,000

If you owe this much, approval of your installment plan won't be automatic. However, the IRS will probably agree to an installment plan, assuming your monthly payments are large enough to wipe out your income tax debt within five years.

If you can't afford to pay your tax debt within five years through an installment plan, you can ask the IRS to allow you to take longer. However, to get the agency's permission to do that, you have to fill out Form 433-A, "Collection Information Statement." We talk about this form in the next section.

Paying off more than $25,000 in taxes

When you owe the IRS more than $25,000 in taxes and you want to pay that debt in installments, you must complete two forms: IRS Form 9465 and IRS Form 433-A, "Collection Information Statement." You may also have to provide the IRS other information about your finances.

The "Collection Information Statement" asks for a lot of detailed information about your finances. Among other things, you have to provide information about your assets, monthly expenses, and sources of monthly income. Filling out the form is time consuming.

When you fill out the "Collection Information Statement," you tell the IRS exactly what it needs to know if it decides later to try to collect your tax debt, maybe because you default on your installment payment plan. Sure, the IRS can find out the information on its own, but that process takes time. So by completing the "Collection Information Statement," you make it a whole lot easier for the IRS to collect from you. However, you have no choice if you need to pay your tax debt in installments.

The IRS uses the information on the "Collection Information Statement" to figure out how much you can afford to pay on your tax debt each month. To help it make this calculation, the IRS compares your total monthly income from all sources to your total monthly living expenses.

When the IRS adds up your expenses to get a monthly total, it includes only those expenses it considers to be *essential,* and its definition of *essential expenses* may be quite different from yours. For example, its total won't include the monthly cost of your cable television or your gym membership. Also, it won't include the monthly payments you may be making on your credit card debts or on other unsecured debts. In other words, the IRS may end up with a monthly expense total that vastly understates what it really costs you to live. (You may be able to get the IRS to change its mind about an expense it considers nonessential if you can prove that the expense is essential to your ability to earn a living.)

Wait, it gets worse! When it comes to expenses that the IRS *does* consider to be essential, like food and clothing, it may not recognize the total amount that you're spending every month. Here's why: The IRS uses standard monthly guideline amounts to budget for essential expenses, which may be less than what you actually spend. For example, if you spend $400 per month on food but the agency's guidelines say you should be spending only $350, the IRS uses $350 when it calculates what you can afford to pay on your income tax debt each month.

In other words, the IRS may conclude that you can afford to pay more each month on your tax debt than you feel is realistic. Unless you can do some drastic budget cutting, paying off your debt through an installment plan is wishful thinking. What are your options? Get the IRS to accept an Offer in Compromise, or file for bankruptcy. (We discuss each of these in upcoming sections.) Or try to get the IRS to change its mind about what you can afford to pay each month. Doing so probably requires that you formally appeal the agency's decision. For an overview of how the appeals process works, read the sidebar "Appealing an IRS decision."

If your knees shake and your mouth gets dry when you think about negotiating with the IRS, ask someone else to do it for you. That someone else can be an attorney, a CPA, or someone who has power of attorney to conduct your financial affairs. Your representative completes IRS Form 2848, "Power of Attorney and Declaration of Representative," which can be downloaded at www.irs.gov/pub/irs-pdf/f2848.pdf. If you want that person to also have access to confidential information and documents relating to your taxes and your finances — information that the IRS would normally share only with you — your representative also needs to complete IRS Form 8821, "Tax Information Authorization," which can be downloaded at www.irs.gov/pub/irs-pdf/f8821.pdf. Both forms can also be obtained by calling 800-829-3767 or by visiting a local IRS office.

Using an Offer in Compromise to cut a deal with the IRS

If your finances are in such dire shape that you cannot afford to pay the full amount of your income tax debt in installments or any other way, the IRS may agree to let you settle the debt for less — maybe for pennies on the dollar — through an Offer in Compromise (OIC). However, OICs are hard to get, and you won't be eligible for one unless all your tax returns for the previous five years have been filed and you're not already in bankruptcy.

Settling your debt for less with the IRS can be tricky business. Although you can try doing it yourself, you increase the odds of success by hiring a pro like a CPA or a tax attorney with experience negotiating OICs.

Beware of companies that advertise on the Internet offering to help you prepare your OIC (for a fee, of course). Many of them have little or no expertise with OICs and, therefore, little chance of getting the IRS to accept yours.

You initiate the OIC process by completing IRS Form 656, "Offer in Compromise," which is actually a package of forms and worksheets, including a "Collection Information Statement for Individuals." You must also pay the IRS a $150 OIC application fee, although you can get the fee waived under certain conditions. Don't pay the application fee until you know whether you qualify for a waiver.

In addition, you must make a nonrefundable, partial payment on your OIC when you submit your request. The amount of the payment depends on how much you are asking to settle your debt for and the terms of your offer, such as how long you want to take to pay it. Usually, the more time you want, the bigger your offer must be. For example, if you agree to pay your settlement amount in one lump sum, the IRS will probably agree to take less money from you than if you want to pay the settlement amount in installments over a year or more.

After you file all the appropriate IRS forms and pay the application fee and the nonrefundable, partial payment on your OIC, the IRS agrees to formally consider your offer if it concludes that one of the following conditions applies to you:

✔ You will probably never be able to pay the full amount you owe to the IRS, and it will probably never collect the money from you — maybe because you have no assets of value and you make very little money relative to the amount of your tax debt.

✔ The amount of taxes that the IRS says you owe is incorrect. You probably have to make this case to the IRS. The agency is unlikely to make it for you.

✔ Your tax debt *shouldn't* be collected because of an economic hardship or some other special circumstances that you face.

If the IRS decides that one of these conditions applies to you, it evaluates your OIC by using the information on your "Collection Information Statement" form. Meanwhile, the agency halts any actions it may already be taking to collect from you, which means no more calls from debt collectors, no more wage garnishment, and no asset seizures. (If the IRS rejects your OIC, its collection efforts can immediately resume.)

While the IRS is reviewing your OIC, the ten-year statute of limitations on collecting your tax debt is suspended. After it makes its decision, the statute of limitations begins running again. If you're unhappy with the agency's decision regarding your OIC and you file an appeal, the statute of limitations is suspended again while your appeal is being considered. The effect of having the statute of limitations suspended is that the period of time during which the IRS can try to collect from you gets pushed farther into the future.

Getting the green light

If the IRS gives your OIC request the go-ahead, and if you agreed to pay the amount in a lump sum, you must make the payment within 90 days. If you agreed to a short-term deferred payment plan, you have up to 24 months to pay what you owe. And if you set up a longer-term plan, you have to pay the settlement amount in equal payments over the period that remains on the statute of limitations for collecting your tax debt.

When you pay the settlement amount in installments, regardless of the term of your payment plan, you must make each payment on time, *and* you must file your tax returns on time and pay any taxes you owe on time while your plan is in effect. If you don't, you will be in default of your agreement with the IRS, and the agency may take action to collect what you still owe to it.

Being rejected

You're notified in writing if the IRS rejects your OIC. The notice you receive explains why your offer was rejected. Most OICs get rejected because the IRS thinks that the amount of the settlement offer is too small. In other words, the IRS believes it can reasonably expect to collect more from you given the value of your real and personal assets and the amount of your future income.

If the IRS rejects your offer for this reason, it tells you what it considers to be an acceptable settlement amount given your finances. If you don't understand the explanation or disagree with the agency's decision, call the number on the IRS notice.

You can submit a new offer to the IRS if it rejects your first one. If you are working with a CPA or attorney, she may call the IRS revenue officer (also called a *field officer*) assigned to your case to discuss what kind of offer the IRS would find acceptable. If you're handling your own OIC, you can make the same call.

You can also appeal the agency's decision about your OIC. The notice explains how to file an appeal. The sidebar "Appealing an IRS decision" in this chapter summarizes the appeals process.

Filing bankruptcy to deal with your tax debt

Filing for bankruptcy is a good way to deal with your tax debt when your finances are in such bad shape that neither an installment plan nor an OIC is a real option. It's also a smart move if you think that the IRS may be about to seize some of your assets or garnish your wages. Exactly how bankruptcy affects your tax debt is a complicated matter determined by a variety of criteria and considerations, including how long you've owed the taxes and whether the IRS has already put a federal tax lien on your assets.

If the IRS has not yet filed a tax lien, and assuming your tax debt is more than three years old and that you filed your tax returns on time during those three years (or filed for an extension), you can do one of the following:

 ✔ File a Chapter 7 liquidation bankruptcy to get rid of your tax debt.

 ✔ File a Chapter 13 reorganization bankruptcy to reduce the total amount that you owe to the IRS and get three to five years to pay your remaining tax debt, including interest and penalties, in full.

If your income tax debt is less than three years old, you *cannot* use Chapter 7 to get rid of the debt. Instead, you must file Chapter 13, which gives you up to five years to pay the full amount of your income tax debt, including all penalties. If the IRS has already filed a tax lien, you must also pay interest on your outstanding tax debt.

If you file for bankruptcy after the IRS has filed a federal tax lien, your tax debt becomes a secured debt. As a result,

 ✔ You can't use Chapter 7 to wipe out the debt. Instead, you have to pay the full amount after your bankruptcy is over. However, paying it should be easier because you won't owe as much to other creditors.

 ✔ You won't be able to reduce your tax debt through Chapter 13, and you have to pay the full amount of the debt while you are in bankruptcy (over a three- to five-year period). In addition, while you are in bankruptcy, the bankruptcy court charges you interest on your unpaid tax balance. The interest rate will be a local rate.

So, what's the lesson in all this? When you can't afford to pay your federal income taxes and you are thinking about bankruptcy, consult with a consumer bankruptcy attorney immediately — before the IRS puts a lien on your assets. For more information about federal income taxes and personal bankruptcy, get a copy of *Personal Bankruptcy Laws For Dummies* by James P. Caher and John M. Caher (Wiley).

Liens and Levies: Collecting Past-Due Taxes

If you ignore your IRS tax debt, or if you and the IRS can't come to an agreement about an installment payment plan or an OIC, the agency may take steps to collect what you owe. Whether it does, how quickly it does, and exactly *what* it does depend in large part on the specific IRS revenue officer handling your case. Some revenue officers are aggressive (a little like pit bulls), but others are more likely to help you figure out a way to pay your tax debt so you can avoid what comes next.

Besides the personality of the revenue officer, other factors help determine whether the IRS tries to collect your debt. They include

- ✔ **How much you owe.** The more you owe, the more likely that the IRS will try to collect its money.

- ✔ **The amount of your income.** The IRS may decide to garnish your wages in order to collect what you owe.

  Law prohibits the IRS from collecting from you if you can prove that your income is less than your living expenses and that, therefore, your tax debt is uncollectible. However, the IRS determines your expenses according to its standard guidelines, which are very low. Proving that your tax debt is uncollectible may be a losing battle, but a tax attorney or a CPA with experience dealing with the IRS may be able to make your case.

- ✔ **Whether you have any assets that the IRS can take.** If you do, the IRS puts a federal tax lien on all of them. The lien also applies to any assets you may acquire in the future. The next section offers a quick lesson on federal tax liens.

  After the liens are in place, the IRS may *levy on,* or take, some of your assets. The levy may happen right away or not for some time. Find out how levies work in the upcoming section "Losing your assets because of a levy."

If you earn next to nothing and all your assets are exempt from the IRS, you're safe — for now, anyway. (The agency will probably let interest and penalties continue to accrue so your tax debt grows larger by the day.) Periodically, the IRS reviews your financial situation to see if it's improved. If it has, and assuming that the ten-year statute of limitations for tax debt has not expired, the IRS will collect as much as it can from you. The sidebar "What the IRS *can't* take from you" in this chapter offers an overview of the assets that are safe from the clutches of the agency.

Knowing how tax liens work

Before the IRS can put a lien on your assets, it must send you a "Notice and Demand for Payment." If you don't pay the full amount of your tax debt within ten days of the notice date, the IRS puts a

What the IRS *can't* take from you

The IRS has the power to take just about any asset of yours that it can get its hands on in order to collect the taxes you owe. However, there are a few exceptions. These exempt assets are specific to the IRS. In other words, they are not the same as the assets that you can keep when you file for bankruptcy.

The IRS must keep its mitts off the following:

✓ Your fuel, food, furniture, and personal items, up to a certain amount

✓ The books and tools you need to earn a living, up to a certain amount

✓ Unemployment payments

✓ Worker's compensation payments

✓ Certain types of public assistance payments

✓ Service-related disability payments

✓ Certain annuity and pension benefits

✓ Court ordered child support payments

federal tax lien on your assets, including those you have only an interest in. The lien also applies to any assets you may acquire or have an interest in some time later. The lien may even get attached if you apply for an installment payment plan within the ten-day period.

The IRS files the tax lien in your county courthouse, making it part of the public record. Therefore, the lien shows up in your credit history and harms your credit score. You cannot sell, borrow against, or transfer any of the assets that the lien is attached to without paying off the tax lien.

There are only a few ways to get a lien released. You can

✓ Pay the full amount you owe to the IRS in a lump sum, including all penalties and interest.

✓ Pay your debt in full through an installment payment plan. Some IRS agents release a tax lien after your installment plan has been set up.

✓ Settle your debt for less through an Offer in Compromise.

✓ Wait for the ten-year statute of limitations on your tax debt to run out. However, the IRS is likely to refile the lien before the ten years are up.

Appealing an IRS decision

You can appeal most IRS decisions related to your outstanding tax debt by using one of two processes: the Collection Appeals Program (CAP) or the Collection Due Process (CDP).

When you appeal a collection action that the IRS may be about to take, the IRS must suspend the action while your appeal is being considered. (Your appeal has no effect on the accrual of interest and penalties on your unpaid taxes.) If the agency rules against you, the IRS can resume whatever it was doing.

✔ **The Collection Appeals Program (CAP):** You can use this process to try to clear up a dispute related to a lien before or after it has been filed, a pending levy, the seizure of one of your assets, or the denial or termination of an installment payment plan. The good news is that the CAP is relatively fast. The bad news is that if you're unhappy with the outcome of your appeal, you can't take the IRS to court.

Here's how the process works: If you are notified of an IRS decision related to an issue covered by the CAP, contact an IRS collections staff person to let him know that you are disputing the agency's action. (The number to call should be on the notice you receive.) If you get no satisfaction, ask to speak to an IRS collections manager. This person should speak with you about your dispute within a day of your request. If you don't like what the manager tells you either, ask to have your dispute forwarded to an appeals officer.

If an IRS revenue agent contacts you about an IRS decision — for example, she tells you how much the IRS has decided you owe — and if you want to appeal the decision, ask to have a conference with a collections manager. If the meeting doesn't resolve your problem, file a request for an appeal with the IRS Office of Appeals right away by completing IRS Form 9423, "Collection Appeal Request." You can download the form at www.irs.gov/pub/irs-pdf/f9423.pdf or get it by calling 800-839-3676. The IRS must receive your request within two days of the meeting. Otherwise, it can resume its efforts to collect from you. If you file your request for an appeal on time, the appeals officer decision is legally binding on you and on the IRS.

✔ **The Collection Due Process (CDP):** You can pursue this kind of appeal if you receive a tax lien notice or a levy notice from the IRS. In most instances, you must file your appeal with the IRS Office of Appeals within 30 days of receiving the notice. Fill out IRS Form 12153, "Request for a Collection Due Process Hearing," which you can obtain at www.irs.gov/pub/irs-pdf/f12153.pdf. During the 30-day period and while your appeal is being considered, the IRS will put its collection actions on hold, as long as it does not think that its ability to collect from you may be in jeopardy. For example, it may not put things on hold if it believes that you are getting ready to transfer or hide an asset that it wants to take from you.

When the hearing is over, the IRS sends you a letter telling you what the Office of Appeals has decided. If you agree with the decision, you and the agency must abide by it. However, if you don't agree, you have 30 days from the date that the decision was issued to request a judicial review in federal tax court or in a U.S. District Court. If the court reviews your case and decides in favor of the IRS, it's the end of the road for you.

After you get the tax lien released, the IRS sends you a "Release of Federal Tax Lien" notice. It also files that notice with your county courthouse so the public records reflect the fact that the agency no longer has a lien on your assets.

 When you receive the IRS notice, contact the three national credit bureaus in writing and ask them to remove the tax lien information from your credit files. Attach a copy of the IRS notice to your letter. A month or two later, check your credit histories to find out if the information has been removed. If you have problems getting the lien information removed, contact a consumer law attorney who has experience resolving problems with credit reporting agencies.

Losing your assets because of a levy

A *levy* is a powerful collection tool that the IRS can use to seize your real or personal assets. For example, it may levy on the money in your bank accounts; your home and other real estate you own; your car, motorcycle, boat, or RV; and so on. It may also take any commissions you earn and any dividends and rental income you receive. It can also take money out of your retirement account, seize the cash value of your life insurance policy, and garnish your wages.

(In some states, you can be fired just because the IRS is garnishing your wages. For example, if you are responsible for a lot of money, your employer may fire you out of concern that your financial problems may cause you to steal from the business.)

 Usually, the IRS won't levy on your assets unless you've ignored all its efforts to get you to pay what you owe, or your efforts to pay your debt through an installment plan or with an OIC have not worked out. The bigger your debt, the more likely that the IRS will try to seize some of your assets.

If you do nothing to stop the levy, the IRS eventually serves you with a "Notice and Demand for Payment," a "Final Notice of Intent to Levy," and a "Notice of Your Right to a Hearing." These papers are served no less than 30 days before a levy is scheduled to occur.

If you're not already working with a bankruptcy attorney, get one pronto. The attorney may be able to stop the levy or at least put it on hold to give you more time to figure out what to do. For example, you may decide to appeal the agency's levy plans. However, you have a limited amount of time to appeal, so don't dillydally. (The sidebar "Appealing an IRS decision" provides a broad explanation of how the appeals process works.)

For the best results, never handle your own appeal. Hire a CPA or a tax attorney who understands the appeals process and the lingo to help you.

If the levy moves forward and the IRS takes one or more of your assets, you can appeal its action, assuming you can make a case that the agency did not follow all the legally required procedures related to a levy.

If the IRS levies on your bank account, the bank cannot give your funds to the IRS for 21 days, which gives you time to figure out how to avoid the loss of your money. As soon as you find out that the IRS is going to levy on your bank account, meet with a bankruptcy attorney because filing for bankruptcy will stop the levy. If you don't file or you don't file in time, the bank sends the money in your account, up to the amount of your tax debt, to the IRS.

The IRS can levy on any bank accounts that have your name on them even if the funds are not for your own use. For example, if your name is on your mother's checking account so you can help manage her financial affairs, that account is in jeopardy as well.

If the IRS takes one of your assets

When the IRS seizes one of your assets, it uses newspaper advertising and fliers to let people know the asset will be sold in a public auction. Then it must wait at least ten days to conduct the sale.

Before the sale, the IRS decides on a minimum bid amount for your property. Usually that amount equals about 80 percent of the forced sale value of your asset less the amount of any liens other creditors may have on it. (For example, the IRS took your car and your bank has a $5,000 lien against it, or the IRS seized your home and your mortgage company has a $100,000 lien on it.) If you think that the minimum bid amount set by the IRS is too low, you can file an appeal to ask the agency to either recompute the amount or use a private appraiser to make the calculation.

After your property is sold, the IRS uses the sale proceeds to reimburse itself for the costs it incurred taking and selling your property. Then it applies any money left over to your tax debt. If there is not enough to pay that debt in full, you have to pay the balance.

You've got a friend at the IRS

The Taxpayer Advocate Service (TAS) is an independent agency within the IRS charged with protecting the rights of taxpayers. Its main office is in Washington, D.C., but it has at least one local office in every state. For contact information for the office nearest you, go to www.irs.gov/advocate and click on "Contact Your Advocate" and then "View Local Taxpayer Advocates By State." Or you can call 877-777-4778. The local offices report directly to the national TAS office, not to the IRS.

You can ask the TAS for help if you're unable to resolve an issue related to your tax debt despite following the appropriate IRS rules and procedures, including those that apply to the IRS appeals process. For example, you believe that an IRS employee didn't follow IRS rules or didn't act in a timely manner and that you were harmed or will be harmed as a result. The TAS will not help you just because you disagree with an IRS decision.

You can also ask the TAS for help if you believe that you will suffer "a significant economic hardship" as a result of an action that the IRS is about to take or has taken — seizing one of your assets, for example, or garnishing your wages. Examples of "a significant economic hardship" include not being able to pay for necessities such as food, shelter, and clothing; not being able to get to work; and possibly putting your job at risk. Medical emergencies usually qualify too. The TAS may respond to a hardship by issuing a Taxpayer Assistance Order (TAO) in order to stop an IRS collection action.

After the TAS office in your area receives your request for help, a case advocate reviews it, listens to your point of view, and determines if you have legitimate cause for complaint. If your problem falls within the purview of the TAS, someone is assigned to help you. While the office is trying to resolve your problem, the IRS must suspend certain kinds of collection actions. For example, it may not put a lien on your assets or levy one of your assets until it knows the outcome of the TAS efforts.

File IRS Form 911, "Application for Taxpayer Assistance Order," to ask the TAS for help. You can download this form at www.irs.gov/pub/irs-pdf/f911.pdf or obtain a copy at your local IRS office. You can also call 800-829-3767 and ask to have a copy of the form mailed to you.

If your property sells for more than enough to reimburse the IRS for the expenses it incurred taking and selling your property and to pay off your tax debt, you're entitled to ask for the IRS to give you whatever money is left. However, if your creditors have liens on your assets and they file claims with the IRS, the IRS will pay their claims with the leftover money before it pays you a dime.

Getting the asset back from the IRS

You may be able to get the asset back from the IRS before it's sold if one of the following is true:

- ✔ You pay the agency the full amount you owe.

- ✔ The agency decides that the cost of selling the asset will exceed what you owe.

- ✔ You can prove to the IRS that having the property back will help you pay your tax bill.

- ✔ The agency's Taxpayer Advocate Service (TAS) determines that returning the property to you is in your best interest and in the best interest of the government. For example, some of your real estate has toxic chemicals on it, and the IRS decides that you should incur the cost of cleaning up the chemicals. The sidebar "You've got a friend at the IRS" explains what the TAS does and doesn't do.

You can also request that the IRS return the property to you — even after it's been sold — if you can prove that the IRS did not do the following:

- ✔ Provide you with all the legally required notices before taking your property, or give you the proper amount of time to respond to one of its notices.

- ✔ Follow established agency procedures. For example, before it took your asset, the IRS did not confirm exactly how much you owed to it; the IRS failed to make certain that you had equity in the asset it took; or the agency did not ensure that it couldn't collect from you in some other way.

- ✔ Abide by the terms of the installment payment plan you nego-tiated with the agency (if the agreement states that the IRS will not levy on your property).

If the IRS sells some of your real estate, you can redeem or buy it from whoever purchases it within 180 days of the sale. However, you must be able to pay the same amount that the buyer paid for your property plus interest at an annual rate of 20 percent.

Chapter 15

Taking Responsibility for Your Federal Student Loan

In This Chapter

▶ Understanding your repayment responsibilities

▶ Taking steps to avoid a loan default

▶ Finding out about loan consolidation and cancellation

*I*t's pretty easy to get federally guaranteed student loans to help pay for your college education, assuming you have the patience to complete all the application paperwork. The hard part, given how much you may owe when you graduate, is repaying those loans. These 2004 statistics from the *Project on Student Debt* help illustrate the problem:

- ✔ More students than ever before are borrowing money to finance their college educations, and the amounts that they are borrowing are larger than ever before. In just seven years, the amounts they borrowed increased a whopping 60 percent.

- ✔ About two-thirds of college graduates now owe on student loans, compared to less than 50 percent in the early 1990s.

- ✔ Over the last two decades, the amount of debt per student has tripled after adjusting for inflation.

- ✔ Since 1993, the number of students graduating with high levels of student loan debt — at least $40,000 — has increased tenfold. According to the *Project on Student Debt,* most recent college graduates would have difficulty repaying this amount over ten years, which is the average student loan repayment period.

- ✔ More than 40 percent of all college graduates who don't pursue a graduate education point to the amount that they owe in student loans as the reason.

Being saddled with a substantial loan debt after graduation is tough, especially if your job pays less than what you hoped for when you borrowed the money. However, when it's time to start paying back what you borrowed, your student loan lender won't care about any of that. Your lender expects you to repay the money according to the terms of your loan agreement. If you don't, you face serious consequences that can affect your ability to pursue your post-graduation plans like buying a new car and becoming a homeowner.

In this chapter, we help you meet your federal student loan obligations. We explain your options for repaying your loan, and we review the various steps you can take to avoid defaulting on the debt if you have problems keeping up with the payments. We also tell you when you may be eligible to have all or part of your student loan debt cancelled, and we explain the pros and cons of consolidating multiple student loans.

Preparing to Pay Back Your Student Loan

If you finance your college education with a federal student loan, you must repay the loan after you graduate, drop out of school, or stop attending school on at least a half-time basis. Depending on your specific type of loan, you have a grace period of six or nine months before your payments must begin. (See the next section for a summary of the different types of federal student loans.)

Use your grace period wisely by making preparations to pay off your student loan debt. Your preparations should include the following:

✔ **Get clear about exactly what kind of student loan you have.** This is important because the type of loan affects not only the length of your loan grace period but also your loan repayment options, the interest rate you're charged, who to contact if you begin having problems repaying the loan, and so on. If you are not sure what kind of loan you have, review your student loan paperwork or go to the U.S. Department of Education's (DOE) National Student Loan Data System (NSLDS) at www.nslds. ed.gov/nslds_SA. You can also use this site to keep track of the outstanding balance on your loan.

✔ **Find a job so you'll have the money you need to make each of your loan payments.** See Chapter 5 for job-finding advice.

✔ **Prepare a monthly budget.** Your budget will help you allocate your dollars to meet your financial obligations. In Chapter 4, we provide a quick and easy lesson on budgeting basics.

✔ **Choose a loan repayment plan.** The upcoming "Choosing a loan repayment plan" section reviews your options.

Depending on what kind of student loan you have, interest may begin to accrue during the grace period. You can pay the loan interest each month, or you can opt to have all the accrued interest added to the loan's outstanding balance so you can repay the interest later.

At the start of your grace period, a financial aid officer from your school explains your responsibilities as a borrower and provides you with information about your student loan, your repayment options, who to send your payments to, when your first payment is due, and what will happen if you ignore your obligation to repay your student loan. Also, sometime during the grace period, your federal student lender or loan servicer contacts you about repaying your student loan. If the end of your grace period draws near and you've not heard from anyone, contact your lender immediately.

Clarifying the kind of federal student loan you have

There are two basic federal student loan programs, each comprised of a number of various low-interest loans. One loan program is administered directly by the U.S. Department of Education (DOE). Individual lending institutions administer the loans within the other program.

✔ **Direct Loan Program:** Loans within this program are made directly by the DOE. They include Direct Subsidized Loans, Direct Unsubsidized Loans, Direct PLUS Loans, and Direct Consolidation Loans. (We discuss PLUS loans in the sidebar "For parents only: Repaying a federal PLUS loan." We cover Direct Consolidation Loans in the section "Consolidating Your Student Loans.") If you have one of these kinds of loans, DOE's Direct Loan Servicing Center collects and processes all your loan payments.

✔ **Federal Family Education Loan Program (FFEL):** Loans under this program include subsidized and unsubsidized Stafford loans, FFEL PLUS Loans, and FFEL Consolidation Loans. Private lending institutions administer all these loans. (We discuss PLUS loans in the sidebar "For parents only: Repaying a federal PLUS loan." You can find out about FFEL Consolidation Loans in the section "Consolidating Your Student Loans.") When it comes time to repay these loans, you either deal directly with the lending institution that gave you the loan or with a *loan servicer* — a company hired by the lending institution to collect and process your loan payments.

There is a third kind of low-interest federal loan called a *Perkins Loan.* If you have one, you got it when you applied directly to the school you attended. When you repay a Perkins Loan, you send your payments directly to the school or to a loan servicer hired by the school.

Choosing a loan repayment plan

During the grace period after you graduate or leave school, you choose one of four plans for repaying your Direct or FFEL student loan. The plan you choose determines the amount of your loan payments, how long it will take you to repay your loan, and so on. If you don't choose a plan, you are automatically put in a standard plan.

After you choose a repayment plan, you can switch to a different one if you decide that your first choice doesn't work for you or if your financial circumstances change. You can switch plans as often as you like if you have a Direct Loan, but if you have a FFEL Loan, you can make a plan change just once a year.

If you have a Perkins Loan, your school determines the amount of your monthly payments. The school makes its decision based on the amount of the loan and the length of your loan repayment period, which will be no more than ten years.

If you have a Direct Loan, your debt repayment plan options are as follows:

- ✔ **Standard plan:** This plan works much like a traditional bank loan. Every month for a set period of time (up to ten years), you make fixed payments of at least $50 until you've repaid the amount of your loan plus interest. Your monthly payments are higher with this plan than with the other plans, but the total amount of interest you pay is less.

- ✔ **Extended plan:** This plan works like the standard plan except you get between 12 and 30 years to repay your loan. Exactly how long you get depends on how much you owe. Your monthly payments with this kind of plan are smaller than with the standard plan, but you pay more in interest over the loan term.

✔ **Graduated plan:** With this kind of plan, your payments start out small and gradually increase up to a certain amount. The assumption is that when you are first out of school, you can't afford to pay much on your loan, but your income will increase over time so you'll be able to handle larger loan payments. Usually, you get 12 to 30 years to repay your loan with this kind of plan; exactly how long you have depends on the total amount of money you owe when it's time to start paying back the money you borrowed.

✔ **Income-contingent plan:** If you opt for this repayment plan, the size of your monthly loan payments is recalculated every year based on the adjusted gross income you reported on your last IRS tax return. Your family size, the total amount of your student loan debt, and the interest rate on the debt are also considered. If your income is extremely low in a particular year, it's possible that you may not have to pay anything at all on your student loan. Meanwhile, however, interest continues accumulating so the total amount of your debt grows larger.

Here are your payment plan options if you have a FFEL Loan:

✔ **Standard plan:** This plan works like the standard plan for a Direct Loan.

✔ **Graduated plan:** This plan works like the graduated plan for a Direct Loan.

✔ **Extended plan:** You can use this plan if you owe more than $30,000 in FFEL Loan debt. You get up to 25 years to repay the debt, and your payments may be fixed or graduated.

✔ **Income-sensitive plan:** This kind of plan works much like the Direct Loan income-contingent repayment plan.

For help making sense of the dollars and cents of each payment plan, use the DOE's interactive calculators at `www.ed.gov/offices/OSFAP/DirectLoan/calc.html`. You can also talk to your lender or to your school's financial aid office.

If you opt for an income-contingent or income-sensitive repayment plan and you have an outstanding loan balance after 25 years of paying on your loan, the balance will be wiped out. For tax purposes, however, the IRS treats the amount of the loan that is forgiven as income, which could create income tax problems for you when April 15 arrives. (In Chapter 14, we explain your options when you can't afford to pay the taxes you owe.) The 25-year period does not include any periods of loan deferment or forbearance. (We discuss deferments and forbearance later in this chapter.)

For parents only: Repaying a federal PLUS loan

If you are the parent of a college student, you may be helping to finance your son or daughter's education with federal Direct or FFEL PLUS loans. These kinds of loans differ from other types of federal student loans in some important ways:

✓ *You*, not your child, are legally obligated to repay them.

✓ You must begin repaying the loans while your child is still in college.

✓ There is no loan grace period.

✓ You cannot repay a Direct PLUS Loan through an income-contingent plan (but an income-sensitive plan is usually an option if you have a FFEL PLUS Loan).

There are also many similarities between PLUS loans and the federal student loans your son or daughter may have. For example,

✓ As long as your PLUS loan is not in default, you may be eligible for a loan deferment or for forbearance if you are having trouble paying the loan.

✓ If you have multiple PLUS loans, you can consolidate them into a single loan.

✓ Under certain conditions, you can get your PLUS loan cancelled.

For more information about repaying a Direct PLUS Loan, contact the Direct Loan Servicing Center at 800-848-0979. For information about repaying a FFEL PLUS Loan, contact the lender who holds your loan.

If your payments are automatically debited from your bank account, you may qualify for a reduced interest rate on your student loan. Also, some lenders will reduce your rate after you've made a certain number of consecutive monthly loan payments on time. To find out if you are eligible for an interest rate reduction, contact your lender if you have a FFEL Loan or call 800-848-0979 if you have a Direct Loan.

Avoiding a Default

When your loan grace period is up, you are responsible for repaying your loan. If you don't make arrangements to pay back the loan, and if you ignore all efforts by the student loan lender or loan servicer to contact you about setting up a payment plan, you're in default.

You can also default on the loan if you don't keep up with your payments. For example, if you have a Direct or FFEL loan and you're obligated to make monthly payments on the loan, you'll be in default after you are 270 days behind on the payments. If you are repaying the loan on a different schedule, you'll be in default after you are 330 days in arrears. With a Perkins Loan, you're in default after you miss just one loan payment!

If the DOE holds your loan, you can avoid a default by using your American Express, MasterCard, or Visa to catch up on what you owe. To do so, call 800-621-3115.

Realizing the consequences

Defaulting on your student loan has serious consequences. For example,

- ✔ The full amount of your outstanding loan balance, not just the past-due amount, may be due immediately.

- ✔ The loan may be turned over to a debt collection agency.

- ✔ You will owe late fees and collection costs.

- ✔ Your credit history will be damaged.

- ✔ Your federal income tax refunds may be seized and applied to the balance on your loan. Your state tax refunds may also be taken, depending on your state.

- ✔ Your lender may sue you for the money you owe.

- ✔ Your wages may be garnished.

- ✔ In some states, you may be denied a professional license.

- ✔ You won't be eligible for a loan deferment or forbearance.

- ✔ You won't be entitled to additional federal financial aid, including any financial aid you may apply for on your children's behalf.

- ✔ You could lose your eligibility for other federal loans, such as loans from the Federal Housing Administration or from the Veteran's Administration. However, you can reinstate your eligibility by paying the loan in full, by consolidating the loan through either the FFEL or Direct loan consolidation programs, or by rehabilitating your loan through DOE's loan rehab program. We explain consolidation and rehabilitation later in this chapter.

Considering your options

The best way to avoid a default (aside from staying current on your payments) is to contact your lender or loan servicer as soon you realize you are going to have problems making your payments. You should also review your budget (see Chapter 4) to see if you can cut spending, and consider getting a second job to help cover your loan payments. Another option may be to switch to a less expensive repayment plan.

If none of these strategies works, you may need to pursue a loan deferment or forbearance, or even file for bankruptcy in order to avoid a default. We discuss all three options in detail in this section.

If you have multiple student loans and you've already defaulted on one or more of them, you may be able to avoid some of the consequences of a default by consolidating the loans. Contact the appropriate lender(s) to find out if you can consolidate. For more information about student loan consolidation, read "Consolidating Your Student Loans" later in this chapter.

Deferring payments

A loan *deferment* suspends your loan payments for a limited period of time — usually for no more than three years. In other words, during the deferment period, you won't have to pay on your loan.

If the loan that you want deferred is an unsubsidized Stafford Loan, interest accrues during the deferment period. As a result, you owe more at the end of the period than you did at the start, unless you arrange to pay the interest each month.

Although the exact process for getting a deferment depends on your lender, it usually involves completing an application and meeting certain eligibility criteria. For example, to be eligible for a deferment, at least one of the following must apply:

- ✔ You're unemployed.
- ✔ You're enrolled at least half-time in an eligible school.
- ✔ You're in a graduate fellowship program or in a rehabilitation training program for the disabled.
- ✔ You're serving in the military.
- ✔ You'll suffer an economic hardship if you have to make your loan payments.

If you're paying on a Stafford Loan that you obtained prior to July 1, 1993, you may be entitled to receive a deferment for other reasons besides the ones on this list. Talk to your lender or loan servicer.

You'll find additional information about the terms and conditions of a loan deferment at the DOE's Federal Student Aid Web site, studentaid.ed.gov. Click on "Publications" on the right side of the page and scroll down until you find the publication entitled "Repaying Your Student Loans." For specific information related to your situation, contact your lender or loan servicer if you want to defer payment on a Stafford Loan. If you want a deferment on a Direct Loan, get in touch with the Direct Loan Servicing Center by calling 800-848-0979. If you have a Perkins Loan, speak with the school that gave you the loan.

While you're waiting to learn if you've been approved for a loan deferment, you must continue making your loan payments. Otherwise, you risk defaulting on the loan. If that happens, you can kiss your chances for a deferment goodbye.

Finding relief with forbearance

If you can't get a loan deferment, you may be able to use forbearance to avoid a loan default. *Forbearance* either postpones your loan payments or reduces them for a specific period of time — typically between one and three years. You have to pay interest on your loan during the forbearance period, but you can have the accrued interest added to your outstanding loan balance so you can pay it off over time.

To obtain forbearance, you must apply to your lender and prove that your situation merits your getting a temporary break on your student loan obligation. Possible reasons for getting forbearance include the following:

- ✔ Your health is poor, or some other personal problem makes it difficult for you to keep up with your loan payments.

- ✔ You have a medical or dental internship or residency.

- ✔ The amount that you must pay on your student loan (or loans) is equal to or greater than 20 percent of your gross monthly income. This reason applies only to certain types of federal student loans.

Your lender may give you forbearance for other reasons. Contact it to find out.

Using bankruptcy to avoid a default

You can't wipe out your outstanding student loan balance by filing for bankruptcy, unless you get a *hardship discharge,* which is tough to do. You have to be totally down and out financially to qualify for a hardship discharge, and you must prove to the court that you made a good faith effort to repay the loan before you filed for bankruptcy. If you apply for a hardship discharge, a hearing is held, and a bankruptcy judge determines whether you qualify. Your lender attends the hearing to object to the hardship discharge.

Assuming that a hardship discharge is unlikely, you can still use bankruptcy to avoid a default. For example, if you file a Chapter 7 liquidation bankruptcy, you won't have to pay on the loan while you are in bankruptcy. You'll be expected to resume making your payments after the bankruptcy is over. Since you can use Chapter 7 to eliminate other types of debts, you may improve your financial situation enough that keeping up with your student loan obligation after bankruptcy won't be a problem.

If you file a Chapter 13 bankruptcy, you have three to five years to pay the amount of your student loan — principal only — that is in arrears. You cannot pay on the past-due interest while you're in bankruptcy; you must pay it afterwards. In addition, while you are in Chapter 13, you must pay all your current loan payments as they come due.

Turning Things Around after a Default

If you do default on your student loan, you can undo the damage through a loan rehabilitation. Assuming you complete the rehabilitation successfully, your loan is no longer in default, the information related to the default is removed from your credit history, your wages are no longer garnished, and you don't have to worry anymore about having your tax refunds seized. Also, your eligibility for future federal student aid and other types of federal loans is reinstated.

To rehabilitate your student loan, you and the lender have to agree on a rehabilitation plan, including

- ✔ How much your loan payments will be during the rehabilitation period.

- ✔ How many payments you have to make. (Typically, you have to make 12 consecutive on-time monthly payments.)

- ✔ When each payment is due.

The details of your rehabilitation plan depend on the type of loan that's in default and on the agreement between you and to the lender.

After you satisfy all the terms of your loan rehabilitation agreement, you have to resume paying on your loan according to the terms of your original loan agreement. Also, if you rehabilitate a FFEL Loan, the DOE makes the loan available for purchase by a lending institution that participates in the FFEL program. In other words, you may end up working with a different lender (and/or loan servicer) than the one you were paying before your loan went into default.

To find out more about how rehabilitation works and specific details about the process for your particular type of loan, contact the DOE's Federal Student Aid Ombudsman at 877-557-2575. The Ombudsman can answer questions about your student loans and help you resolve loan-related disputes. For more information, go to the Web site www.ombudsman.ed.gov.

Consolidating Your Student Loans

If you have multiple federal student loans, consolidating them into a single loan may be a smart step. You and your spouse can even consolidate all your individual federal student loans into a single loan. Here are the potential benefits:

- ✔ You may be able to lower the overall interest rate you are paying on your student loan debt and also lower the total amount you pay on the debt each month.

- ✔ You can lock in a fixed interest rate, which is advantageous if rates are low.

- ✔ Trading one payment for multiple payments means that you are less apt to be late with a payment or miss a payment and be charged fees and penalties as a result.

- ✔ You may be able to increase the amount of time you have to repay your student loan debt and lower the amount of your loan payments as a result. If you can, you get between 10 and 30 years to pay off the new debt; the exact amount of time depends on how much student loan debt you owe and the loan repayment option you choose when you consolidate. The downside of taking longer to pay off the debt is that you could end up paying a lot more in interest over the life of your loan — as much as 50 percent in certain circumstances.

If you've defaulted on a student loan, you may be able to get out of default by consolidating, assuming you and the lender can come to terms and that you meet certain requirements.

With a few exceptions, all the same loan payment plans outlined in the "Choosing a loan repayment plan" section of this chapter are available to you when you consolidate. Contact the DOE if you want to consolidate your Direct Loans. To consolidate FFEL Loans, shop around for the best deal by contacting lenders who participate in the FFEL program. However, if all the FFEL Loans you want to consolidate are with the same lender, you must consolidate through that lender, unless you need to repay your new loan through an income-sensitive plan and that lender doesn't offer that plan.

If you can't get an FFEL Consolidation Loan, or if you can't get one with income-sensitive terms that you can afford, you may be able to consolidate by using a Direct Consolidation Loan.

Talk to your lender about all the downsides related to consolidating your student loans so you can weigh the advantages of making that move against the disadvantages. For example, get clear about the total cost of paying off a consolidated loan versus the total cost of repaying the full amounts of the student loans you have now. Also, take into account the financial benefits you may lose by consolidating, such as interest rate discounts, loan principal rebates, and loan cancellation benefits, among others. Also, review the DOE's "Consolidation Checklist" at studentaid.ed.gov (click on the "Repaying" tab and then on "Loan Consolidation") to make sure you are not overlooking any important considerations related to consolidating your student loans.

You used to be able to consolidate Direct and FFEL student loans while you were still in school. However, the federal Higher Education Reconciliation Act of 2005 eliminated that option unless you're enrolled less than half-time. Now you cannot consolidate the loans until you are out of college.

Canceling Your Student Loan

Under certain circumstances, and assuming your loan is not in default, your lender may agree to cancel all or part of your student loan. In other words, you won't have to repay it. Yeah! Unfortunately, you can't get your loan cancelled just because you're not able to find a job, you didn't complete your course of study (with a few exceptions), or you are unhappy with the quality of the education your loan helped to finance. You must have a much better reason for a loan cancellation. Here are some examples:

✔ You can't earn a living because you are totally and permanently disabled due to an illness or injury, and your disability is expected to last indefinitely or to result in your death.

✔ Your school closed before you were able to complete your course of study or within 90 days of your withdrawal from the school. However, you're not eligible for a loan cancellation if you are now completing a comparable course of study at another school or if you haven't received a diploma from the closed school but you completed all your required coursework.

If you complete a course of study that is comparable to the one you were pursuing at your former school before it closed, and you have already obtained a discharge of your student loan, you may have to pay back the amount of the loan that was cancelled.

✔ You are a full-time teacher working in a low-income area, or you are teaching a subject for which there is a teacher shortage. To find more, go to `studentaid.ed.gov`. Click on the "Repaying" tab and then on "Cancellation and Deferment Options for Teachers."

✔ You are pursuing a career for which there is a shortage of workers.

Also, if you die, your survivors shouldn't have to pay off your student loan; the lender should cancel it.

If you don't qualify for a loan cancellation based on the criteria in the previous list, there may still be hope! You may be able to get all or some of your federal loan cancelled, or you may be able to get loan-paying assistance, if one of the following is true:

✔ You live in a state that rewards students who pursue specific careers. These states either cancel these students' loans or pay off part of their loans. To find out if your state has such a program and whether you qualify for it, get in touch with the agency in your state that is responsible for postsecondary education. To find out how to contact that agency, call 800-433-3243 or move your mouse to `studentaid.ed.gov`, click on "Funding," and then click on "State Aid."

✔ You enlist in the military. Some branches of the armed services use loan repayment programs as recruitment tools. To find out more, visit your local recruitment office.

✔ You become an AmeriCorps volunteer. The AmeriCorps program provides an opportunity for citizens to donate a year of their lives to working with a nonprofit organization, public agency, or community or faith-based organization that is addressing a critical community need. For more information about AmeriCorps, contact the Corporation for National and Community Service at 800-942-2677 or visit its Web site at www.americorps.org.

If you have studied to be a registered nurse, you may qualify for loan repayment assistance through the Nursing Education Loan Repayment Program (NELRP), assuming you agree to work in an area where there is a shortage of nurses. To find out about the program's terms and conditions, call the federal Bureau of Health Professionals at 877-464-4772 or go to http://bhpr.hrsa.gov/nursing/loanrepay.htm.

The process for getting a federal student loan cancelled is long and involved. For more information about how the process works, contact the Direct Loan Servicing Center at 800-848-0979 for a Direct Loan or the lender or agency that holds your FFEL Loan. If you have a Perkins Loan, get in touch with the school that gave you the loan.

Part IV

Avoiding Debt Problems down the Road

The 5th Wave   By Rich Tennant

"...and don't tell me I'm not being frugal enough. I hired a man last week to do nothing but clip coupons!"

In this part . . .

*W*e look toward the future by giving you the information you need to begin rebuilding your credit history. If you follow the advice here, you can qualify for new credit with attractive terms when your money problems are over. We also help you avoid a recurrence of those problems by filling you in on the fundamentals of financial management.

Chapter 16

Getting Good Credit Back

● ●

In This Chapter

▶ Distinguishing good debt from bad

▶ Understanding the different kinds of credit

▶ Knowing how creditors size you up

▶ Going through the credit rebuilding process

▶ Avoiding credit rebuilding rip-offs

● ●

*W*hen problems with debt have ruined your credit history, it's a good idea to begin the credit rebuilding process as soon as possible so you can add new positive information to the record. Eventually, as the amount of positive information in your credit history increases, you become attractive to creditors again, and you qualify for credit with more favorable terms.

New credit? You may be wondering why we would we want you to owe money to creditors ever again. But we have our reasons!

The first reason is that debt is not necessarily a bad thing. What distinguishes good debt from bad is the kind of debt and how much you owe. Debt can actually be a positive force in your life and a valuable money management tool.

The second reason is that having a credit history full of negative information limits your opportunities and makes it difficult, if not impossible, to achieve your financial goals. For example,

> ✔ Insurance companies may not be willing to sell you the amount of life insurance you feel that you need, and/or they may charge you more for your policies.
>
> ✔ A potential employer may be unwilling to give you a job.
>
> ✔ If you're a renter looking for a new place to live, some landlords will refuse to rent to you.

In other words, a bad credit history closes a lot of doors.

The credit rebuilding advice that we provide in this chapter helps you open those doors. We step you through the credit rebuilding process, and we warn you against trying to accelerate the process by working with a credit repair firm.

Before we turn our attention to the ins and outs of credit rebuilding, we give you some basic information about the various types of credit so that in the future, you're better prepared to make smart credit choices. We also explain how creditors evaluate you when you apply for credit.

Separating Good Debt from Bad

Not all debt is bad. Whether your debt is good or bad depends on the type of debt, the reason you owe it, and whether you can afford to repay it. When used the right way, debt can help you manage your finances more effectively, leverage your wealth, buy things you need, and handle emergencies. But if you're not careful, debt can wreak havoc on your finances and destroy your dreams.

Debt can be a positive force in your life when it helps you

- ✔ Build your family's *net worth* — the difference between the current value of your assets and the amount of debt you owe. A mortgage is a perfect example. Good debt is even better debt when the value of the asset you finance increases over time.

- ✔ Buy something that will save your family money for years to come. For example, you get a loan so you can weatherize your home and lower your utility bills.

- ✔ Purchase something important or essential to your life that you could never afford to buy if you had to pay for it with cash. Examples of this kind of debt include a car loan and a mortgage.

- ✔ Invest in yourself in order to increase your earnings potential. For example, you borrow money to return to college or to upgrade your skills so you can make more money in your current field of work or move into a more lucrative career. Student loans are a common example of this kind of debt.

- ✔ Pay for an unexpected emergency when you don't have the cash to cover it. For example, your car breaks down far from home and you need to have it towed; or you have no health insurance and your child needs expensive medicine.

However, debt can be a negative force in your life when you

✔ Go into debt to buy nonessential goods or services that do not increase your wealth and have no lasting value. Examples include restaurant meals, groceries, clothing, personal items, and vacations. The longer you take to repay the debt and the higher the interest rate on the debt, the worse the debt. Credit card debt is the most common example of this kind of debt.

Credit card debt is not bad if you pay it in full as soon as you receive your statement, or if you pay the debt in full within a very few months and you don't charge more on the card until you've paid off the outstanding balance on your account.

✔ Secure the debt with your home or with another asset you don't want to lose when you're not sure that you can afford to repay the debt.

✔ Have a high interest rate and make low monthly payments. By the time you pay off the debt, the amount you pay in interest exceeds the value of the product or service you financed.

✔ Borrow money from dangerous lenders like advance fee lenders, payday lenders, and finance companies.

Distinguishing Between the Different Kinds of Credit

The word *credit* refers to a wide variety of products, each with its own characteristics. To use credit wisely, you need to understand the differences between each type. That way, you can match your credit needs with the appropriate type of credit. Otherwise, you may pay more than you should for the credit you get, which could get you into serious trouble.

Defining secured and unsecured credit

All credit is either *secured* or *unsecured.* Usually, the more money you want to borrow and/or the worse your credit history is, the more likely it is that you'll qualify only for secured credit.

When your credit is secured, the creditor has a lien on one of your assets, which means that it can take the asset if you don't repay your debt according to the terms of the credit agreement. The asset with the lien on it is referred to as your *collateral.*

Here are common examples of secured debts:

- ✔ **Mortgage:** The home you are financing usually secures this kind of loan.

- ✔ **Car loan:** The car itself is the loan collateral.

- ✔ **Home equity loan:** Your home secures this kind of debt.

- ✔ **Secured credit card:** The money in your savings account or a certificate of deposit (CD) collateralizes your secured credit card. (Get the scoop on how secured cards work in the upcoming section "Using a credit card to begin the rebuilding process.")

- ✔ **Line of credit:** Depending on the specific type of credit line, it may be secured by your home, the funds in your bank account, a certificate of deposit, or some other asset you own. Two of the most common credit lines are a home equity line of credit and a credit line associated with your checking account. (The latter allows you to write checks for more than the total amount of money in the account.)

Unsecured credit works quite differently. When a creditor gives you this kind of credit, it simply accepts your word that you'll repay your debt according to the terms of your agreement with one another. You give your word by signing on the dotted line. If you go back on your word and you don't respond to the creditor's demands for payment or to the calls of the debt collector the creditor may hire, the creditor may sue you to try to collect its money.

Following are examples of unsecured debts:

- ✔ **Some bank loans:** Unsecured bank loans are called *signature loans.*

- ✔ **Most MasterCard and Visa cards:** When you are approved for this type of credit, you agree to pay at least a minimum amount each month on your card balance.

- ✔ **American Express cards:** Depending on the type of American Express card you have, you must either pay the card balance in full each month or you can pay it over time like you can with a MasterCard or Visa.

- ✔ **Retail store and gasoline charge cards:** You must repay these kinds of cards the same way that you must repay a MasterCard of Visa, by paying at least the minimum due each month.

Looking at credit another way

Another way to look at credit is according to whether it's *installment, open-end; installment, closed-end;* or *non-installment* credit.

(Another term for installment credit is *revolving credit.*) What do these terms mean?

✔ **Installment, open-end credit:** Most credit cards fall into this category. You are given a fixed amount of credit — your credit limit — that you can use however you want and whenever you want. When you use the credit, you must pay at least a minimum due amount each month, and you can also pay the full amount that you owe right away.

✔ **Installment, closed-end credit:** You are given a fixed amount of credit to be used for a specific purpose. For example, you buy a couch from a local retailer who finances the purchase. In return, you must pay a set amount of money to the retailer each month until you've repaid your debt, including whatever interest you are charged. Other examples of this kind of credit include car loans, mortgages, and student loans.

✔ **Non-installment credit:** This kind of credit often comes with a very high credit limit, but you must pay the full amount of the credit that you use when you receive your bill. The traditional American Express card is a good example of this kind of credit. Also, if your local grocery store allows you to sign for groceries and then expects you to pay for all your purchases at the end of each month, you're feeding your family by using non-installment credit.

Seeing Yourself the Way Creditors See You

Whenever you apply for credit, reputable creditors evaluate your application according to three basic criteria: your character, capacity, and collateral. They decide how you measure up against these three criteria by reviewing your credit history and checking out your credit score. They may also ask you to provide them with detailed information about your assets and debts.

Your credit history (or credit record) is a record of how well or how poorly you've managed your finances over time. The more negative information there is in your credit history, the more difficult it is for you to qualify for credit with attractive terms. In fact, if your credit history is in really bad shape, some creditors may refuse to give you any credit at all. Others may give you credit only if you collateralize it with an asset you own, which means that if you don't own an asset you can use as collateral, you won't qualify for the credit.

When creditors check out your credit score, they probably look at your FICO score. Although other types of credit scores exist, this is the one most creditors use. Your credit score is based in large part on your credit record information, so the better that information is, the higher your score will be. In Chapter 2, we fill you in on what you can do to boost your score.

Here's how the three C's of credit work:

- ✔ **Your character:** To assess your character, creditors review your credit record information to find out if you've failed to pay your credit accounts on time, stopped paying your child support, been sued by any of your creditors, filed for bankruptcy, and so on. Although having this sort of information in your credit history does not necessarily mean that you're a bad person, it's definitely not helpful when you apply for credit.

- ✔ **Your capacity:** Creditors don't want to give you credit unless they think you can afford to repay it. To make that determination and to figure out how much credit to give you, creditors review your income, find out the amount of debt you already have, and perhaps evaluate your assets. Creditors also review your credit history to see if you've applied for a lot of credit recently. If you have, they may decide that you're a big credit risk; they'll either not give you any credit or give you less than you ask for. They may also charge you a higher rate of interest and may require that you secure the debt with an asset.

- ✔ **Your collateral:** If you apply for a lot of credit or if your credit history is not great, creditors want to know if you have assets that you can use to secure the credit you want. If you don't, they will probably turn down your request for credit.

Rebuilding Your Credit History

If your credit history reads like a horror novel, how do you begin to repair it? Get started as soon as your financial situation has stabilized: You're living on a budget, you've resolved all your debt problems, and/or you've completed your bankruptcy, for example.

The credit rebuilding process is not difficult, but it takes time. Your goal is to add positive information to your credit history by obtaining a small amount of new credit from a reputable creditor, paying it off according to the terms of your credit agreement, obtaining additional credit and paying it off on time, and so on.

Don't sabotage your credit rebuilding efforts by applying for a lot of credit right away. Rebuilding your credit should be a gradual, measured process. Easy does it!

At the same time that you are applying for small amounts of credit and paying it off on time, the negative information in your credit history starts to go away because federal law says most of it can be reported for only seven years and six months. (However, a bankruptcy can remain in your credit history for ten years, and if you've defaulted on your student loan or your child support obligation, that information sticks around until you've cleared up the debts. Federal tax liens are reported until you pay what you owe and get the liens released.)

As long as you manage your finances responsibly while you're rebuilding your credit, the amount of positive information in your credit history will gradually increase. Also, as time goes on, creditors will pay more attention to the positive information you're adding than to any bad information that still remains in your credit history. Eventually, you have a credit history you can be proud of!

If there are underlying reasons for your financial problems — you overspend for emotional reasons, or you've got a gambling addiction, for example — rebuilding your credit before you deal with your demons is a dangerous waste of time. That's because after you rebuild your credit, you're likely to ruin it again (and again and again).

Laying the groundwork for credit rebuilding

Before you begin the credit rebuilding process, you need to get some preliminaries out of the way. These preliminaries help you ensure that the process goes smoothly:

✔ **Order a copy of your credit history from each of the three national credit-reporting agencies.** Review each record for errors, and correct any inaccuracies you find. The last thing you need when your credit histories are already full of negative-but-true information is for them to contain negative-but-false information too!

Each year, you're entitled to a free copy of your credit history from each of the three national credit bureaus. In Chapter 2, we explain how to order yours.

Common credit record errors include the following:

  • *Accounts that don't belong to you.* Watch out! These accounts may be a sign that you've been the victim of identity theft, or they may be the result of an error on the part of the credit bureau that is reporting the information.

- *Incorrect information about your accounts.* For example, your credit report wrongly indicates that you defaulted on a loan or that you paid your MasterCard late, or some of your credit account numbers are wrong.

- *Information about some of your accounts is incomplete.* For example, your credit report does not show that you paid off a loan, got a federal tax lien released, or completed your Chapter 13 bankruptcy.

- *Negative account information that is too old to be reported still shows up.*

- *Some of your identifying information (like your Social Security number, name, or address) is wrong.* These kinds of errors can cause your credit information to be confused with someone else's. As a result, that other person's information could end up in your report.

Correcting credit record problems isn't always easy. If you need some tips, check out *The Credit Repair Kit* by John Ventura (Kaplan Publishing) or *Credit Repair Kit For Dummies* by Stephen R. Bucci (Wiley).

After you correct an error in your credit history, order another copy of that record a month or two later to make sure the erroneous information has not returned. Sometimes, credit reporting agencies mistakenly reinsert erroneous information after that information has been corrected.

✔ **Find out your FICO score.** This is the credit score most creditors use to get a quick measure of how your credit compares to other debtors. It's derived from your credit record information. Generally, the higher your credit score, the more attractive you are to creditors; the lower your score, the harder it is to get credit, and the more the credit you get will cost you. A score between 650 and 700 is good; a score above 700 is stellar. Go to www.myfico.com to get your score.

✔ **Start saving.** A savings account is the foundation of most credit rebuilding. In fact, it may be impossible for you to rebuild without having money in savings. If you have not already begun stashing money away on a regular basis, start now. Save as much as you can each month, even if it's not a lot.

For credit rebuilding purposes, you should have at least $1,000 in a savings account. However, don't stop there. You also need money in savings so you can pay for unexpected expenses with cash rather than with a credit card. Ideally, you should have at least six months worth of living expenses in savings so that if you lose your job or you can't work for a while because of an illness or accident, you can still pay your bills.

An easy way to save is to have your employer automatically deduct money from your paychecks and direct deposit the funds into your savings account.

Using a credit card to begin the rebuilding process

After you've taken care of the credit rebuilding preliminaries, apply for a MasterCard or a Visa. Look for one with attractive terms of credit, and don't accept a credit card offer until you've read the card agreement from start to finish. The sidebar "Credit card comparison criteria" explains the terms to consider.

Credit card companies are entitled to change the terms of your credit card whenever they want, as long as they tell you about the change at least 15 days prior to its effective date. They may make a change because a lot of negative information has been added to your credit history since they gave you credit or because your credit score has dropped. Sometimes a creditor makes a change in credit terms that applies to all its cardholders.

You can use your MasterCard or Visa card in one of two ways to rebuild your credit:

✔ Use your card to make small purchases each month, and then pay the card balance in full and on time.

✔ Use your card to buy something relatively expensive, and pay off the card balance over time. (Make sure you're buying something you need; don't make a nonessential purchase just for the sake of rebuilding your credit!) After you've paid off the first balance, charge something else and pay off that balance too. Always try to pay more than the minimum due each month, and avoid charging anything else on the card until you've paid off each balance.

If you have too much negative information in your credit history, you may not qualify for a regular MasterCard or Visa right away. Instead, you may have to apply for a secured card. If you use the secured card responsibly, you'll eventually qualify for an unsecured MasterCard or Visa.

A secured MasterCard or Visa card looks exactly like an unsecured card. The difference is that the bank issuing the secured card requires that you secure your purchases by depositing a certain amount of money in a savings account at the bank or by purchasing a certificate of deposit (CD) for a certain amount of money.

Credit card comparison criteria

Some credit cards are better than others. Generally speaking, credit cards with low interest rates and low fees are more attractive than cards with higher rates and fees.

The federal Truth in Lending Act makes it easy to compare credit card offers because it requires credit card companies to give you specific written information about the terms of the credit card you apply for or the credit card they offer you when they send you a preapproved offer. (Lenders must give you this same information when you apply for a bank loan.) Here are some of the terms of credit that creditors must provide:

- ✔ **Annual percentage rate (APR):** This is the cost of the credit expressed as an annual rate. Pay close attention to a card's *default* APR — the rate you end up paying if you make a payment late (or pay some other creditor late), you exceed your credit limit, or your credit score drops below a certain amount. Your APR could triple depending on the terms of the credit offer!

- ✔ **Balance calculation method:** When you carry a balance on your credit card, the credit card company figures out how much interest to add to that balance by using one of several different methods. Some methods cost you more in interest than others. The least expensive balance calculation methods are *adjusted balance* and *average daily balance excluding new purchases.* The most expensive are *two-cycle average daily balance including new purchases* and *two-cycle average daily balance excluding new purchases.*

- ✔ **Fees:** Credit card fees can be really costly, so look for cards that have few and low fees. Examples of common fees include an annual or membership fee, a late fee, a bounced check fee, a fee for exceeding your credit card limit, and a balance transfer fee. Believe it or not, some cards charge you a fee every time you use them or because you don't use them often enough!

- ✔ **Grace period:** This is the amount of time you have to pay the full amount of your card balance after the end of the last billing cycle before you're charged interest on the balance. The longer the grace period, the better; a 25-day grace period is probably the best you'll do. Some cards have no grace period; avoid them if you expect to carry a balance on your credit card.

- ✔ **Periodic rate:** This is the rate of interest you're charged each day on your card's outstanding balance. If you expect that you may carry a balance on your credit card, get the lowest rate you can. The rate may be fixed or variable, but even a fixed rate isn't truly fixed because a creditor can raise it at any time after it gives you 15 days notice. Also, pay attention to the interest rates that apply to balance transfers, cash advances, and other transactions you may make with a credit card. These rates won't be the same as the periodic rate.

Your credit limit on the card is a percentage of the money in your savings account or the value of the CD. If you don't pay your credit card according to the terms of your credit agreement, the bank that gave you the card is legally entitled to get paid by tapping your collateral up to the amount of your outstanding card balance, including interest and fees. Also, the card issuer may close your account or ask you to put up additional collateral to keep the account open.

You should shop for a secured credit card by evaluating the same terms of credit that you should consider when you're in the market for a regular credit card (see the sidebar "Credit card comparison criteria"). However, you also need to consider some additional criteria for secured cards:

- ✔ How much collateral you must put up to get the card. The less, the better, because you won't have access to that money.

- ✔ Whether you earn interest on your collateral, and at what rate.

- ✔ The size of your credit limit and whether you can increase it. To increase it, you may have to give the credit card company additional funds for collateral, and you need a record of on-time card payments.

- ✔ When the card issuer can tap your collateral.

- ✔ Whether you can covert the card to an unsecured card at some point, the terms of the conversion, and the terms that will apply to the card after it becomes unsecured. For example, will you have to pay a fee to convert? What will the interest rate be on the card after you do convert? Will the rate be fixed or variable? What will your credit limit be?

- ✔ If you cancel your credit card account, how quickly you'll get back your collateral, and under what conditions you can get your collateral back if the credit card company cancels your account.

Some companies other than banks issue secured cards to consumers, but don't deal with them. They won't report your payments to any of the national credit bureaus, so having one of their cards does not help you rebuild your credit history. Also, some of these companies allow you to use your secured credit card only to purchase items from a catalog of products that they provide.

Getting a loan: The next step in the rebuilding process

Applying for a bank loan (or for a loan from a savings and loan in your area or a credit union you belong to) and paying it back on time is the next step in the credit rebuilding process. Set up an appointment with a loan officer at a bank in your area to discuss your borrowing needs. The bank where you have your checking and savings accounts is a good place to start.

When you meet with a loan officer, be upfront about the fact that you've had financial problems. He'll find out about them anyway when he looks at your credit history. Explain what you have done to improve your finances and avoid money troubles in the future. Let him know that you have begun the credit rebuilding process and, as part of the process, you would like a small bank loan.

If the first loan officer you talk to refuses to lend you money, try a different bank. You may have to meet with loan officers at several different banks before you find one willing to work with you.

If a bank turns you down for a loan, before you apply to another bank make sure that you understand exactly why you didn't get the loan. Then address the reasons you got a thumbs down. Keep in mind that sometimes, qualifying for a bank loan after financial difficulties is just a matter of time; only more time can increase the distance between you and your past problems.

If your credit history is full of very negative information — loan defaults, accounts that were closed by your creditors, IRS tax liens, creditor lawsuits, a bankruptcy, and so on — you may not find a lender willing to give you a loan under any circumstances right away. If that's the case, bide your time and manage responsibly any credit you already have. Eventually, you'll be able to get a loan.

At first, you may qualify only for a small, secured loan — maybe just $500 or $1,000. If you qualify for an unsecured loan, it will also be for a relatively small amount of money, and the interest rate may be a little higher than if the loan is secured.

After you are approved for a loan, make all your payments on time and live up to all the other terms of your agreement with the lender. Then after you've repaid the loan, order a copy of your credit history from whichever credit reporting agency or agencies the lender reports to so you can be sure that the loan-related credit record information is accurate. If you find any errors, get them corrected right away. Don't apply for a second loan until you've cleared up any problems in your credit history related to the loan you've just paid off.

Next, apply for a second loan with either the lender that gave you the first loan or with a different lender. If your first loan was secured, this time you may qualify for an unsecured loan. If not, apply for a second secured loan. Eventually, as your credit record information improves, you'll be able to obtain an unsecured loan.

Looking toward your credit future

Your financial life will start looking up as the credit rebuilding process moves forward, assuming that you follow all the advice in this chapter. Gradually, your credit history will become more positive than negative, and your FICO score will go up.

Periodically during the credit rebuilding process, order a copy of your credit history from each of the three national credit reporting agencies (see Chapter 2). Check each report to make sure the new positive information you are adding to it is being reported accurately, and look for other errors. If you find any problems, get them corrected so they don't derail your credit rebuilding efforts.

As you begin looking more attractive to creditors, you'll qualify for credit with lower interest rates and other consumer-friendly terms. Assuming you don't misuse the credit you apply for, it will help you manage your family's finances better, achieve your family's financial goals, and gain financial peace of mind. In Chapter 17, we show you how to keep your financial life on track after you have your credit back.

As your credit history improves, you may be tempted to apply for a lot of credit. Don't! Every time you apply for credit, that fact shows up in your credit history as an *inquiry.* The more inquiries there are, especially within a relatively short period of time, the more your credit history is damaged and the lower your FICO score will be. Also, if you apply for too much credit, you may find yourself drowning in debt all over again.

Steering Clear of Credit Rebuilding Rip-Offs

Some consumers are so eager to obtain new credit after their money troubles are over that they fall for the promises of credit rebuilding organizations that claim they can make the negative information in credit reports disappear, like magic. Steer clear of these companies! They're bad apples. Some use illegal methods to get you a problem-free credit record; if you do what they tell you to do, you'll be breaking the law too, and you may even be prosecuted.

Recognizing unscrupulous methods

Typically, these firms use one of two methods to get you a problem-free credit history:

- The credit repair firm tells you to apply to the federal government for an EIN (employee identification number) and use that number rather than your Social Security number when you apply for credit. Essentially, the firm is telling you to leave your damaged credit history behind by making creditors think you're someone else. The firm is asking you to commit fraud. Don't do it!

- The firm disputes so much of the information in your credit history that the credit reporting agency can't respond to all the disputes within the time frames established by the federal Fair Credit Reporting Act. The law says that if a credit reporting agency does not resolve a dispute related to information in your credit history by the legally required deadline, the disputed information must be removed from your credit report regardless of whether the information is accurate.

  The problem with this credit rebuilding method is that eventually the credit reporting agency will probably determine that the disputed information is accurate. At that point, the agency will put the information back into your credit history. If that happens, not only will you have wasted your money working with the credit repair firm, but you may be charged with fraud. If you are, you'll have a much bigger problem than a damaged credit history to deal with!

Credit-related laws and federal agencies that can protect you

The federal government has passed an array of laws to protect you when you apply for and use credit. Those laws include

- **The Equal Credit Opportunity Act:** When you apply for credit, this law prohibits creditors from discriminating against you because of your race, country of national origin, gender, age, religion, or marital status. Creditors are also prohibited from discriminating against you because you receive public assistance.

✔ **The Home Equity Loan Consumer Protection Act:** This law requires lenders to give you specific kinds of written information about the terms of a home equity loan or home equity line of credit before you apply for it.

✔ **The Truth in Lending Act:** This law requires creditors to provide you with specific written information about the terms of their credit offers in order to help you understand the cost of the credit and to make it easier for you to compare credit offers.

If you believe that a creditor has violated your rights under one of these laws, you can try to resolve the problem by

✔ Writing a complaint letter to the creditor.

✔ Contacting a consumer law attorney. Depending on the nature of your problem and the amount of money involved, the attorney may recommend filing a lawsuit.

✔ Filing a formal complaint with the Federal Trade Commission (FTC) if your complaint is with a creditor other than a bank, savings and loan, or credit union. You can file a complaint online at www.ftc.gov or by calling 877-382-4357. It's a good idea to complain to the FTC even if you sue the creditor because if it receives a lot of complaints about the creditor or about a particular practice within the creditor's industry, the FTC may file a class action lawsuit on behalf of all consumers who have been harmed by the creditor or practice. Also, sometimes as a result of consumer complaints, Congress passes new legislation or amends existing laws.

If a bank, savings and loan, or credit union has violated your legal rights, register a complaint with the federal agency or office that oversees the lender. Exactly who to contact depends on the kind of lender you want to complain about. Here are your options:

✔ Federally chartered savings and loans and federal savings banks (FSBs): Complain to the U.S. Department of the Treasury, Office of Thrift Supervision, 800-842-6929 or www.ots.treas.gov.

✔ State-chartered banks that are members of the Federal Reserve System: Complain to the Federal Reserve System, Division of Consumer and Community Affairs, 202-452-3693 or www.federalreserve.gov.

✔ State-chartered banks that are insured by the Federal Deposit Insurance Corporation but are not members of the Federal Reserve System: Complain to the Federal Deposit Insurance Corporation, Division of Supervision and Consumer Protection, 877-275-3342 or www.fdic.gov.

✔ Nationally chartered banks (which have the word *national* or the abbreviation *N.A.* in their names): Office of the Comptroller of the Currency, Consumer Affairs Division, 800-722-2678 or www.occ.treas.gov.

✔ Federally chartered credit unions: Complain to the National Credit Union Administration, Consumer Affairs Division, 703-518-6300 or www.ncua.gov.

Some credit rebuilding firms may not ask you to do anything illegal, but they charge you a lot of money for helping you build a new credit history even though they can't do anything that you can't do yourself for little or no money. Also, by sharing your personal and financial information with one of these firms, you make yourself more vulnerable to identify theft because you can't control who at the company sees your information.

Knowing your rights

We know that despite our sage advice, you may decide to hire a credit repair firm anyway. If you do, knowing your rights under the federal Credit Repair Organizations Act (CROA) can help you avoid getting ripped off. Here are some of the law's protections:

- ✔ The credit repair firm must use a written contract to spell out all the services it will provide to you and their total costs.

- ✔ After you sign the contract, the firm must give you three days to change your mind about working with it.

- ✔ Before you sign the contract, the credit repair firm must provide you with a copy of a brochure called "Your Consumer Credit File Rights Under State and Federal Law."

- ✔ The firm cannot take any money from you until it has provided you with all the services that it spelled out in your contract.

If a credit repair firm violates any of the terms of the CROA, your contract with the firm is automatically cancelled, and you do not owe the company one red cent, even if it did everything it specified in its contract. Also, you can sue the credit repair firm for actual and punitive damages. *Actual* damages represent what the firm's CROA violations actually cost you in dollars and cents. *Punitive* damages represent money that the judge may order the credit repair firm to pay you as punishment for breaking the law and to help deter the firm from violating the provisions of the CROA again.

If you want to sue a credit repair firm, don't act as your own lawyer. Hire a consumer law attorney with specific experience handling cases like yours. If you have a strong case, the attorney will take it on *contingency*, which means that the attorney gets paid by sharing in whatever money she may win for you. If you lose your lawsuit, the only money you will probably owe the attorney is reimbursement for her expenses. Also, if you win, the credit repair firm must reimburse you for whatever you pay to the attorney and for your expenses.

Chapter 17

Life after Too Much Debt: Staying on Track

• •

In This Chapter

▶ Using money management fundamentals

▶ Getting advice and assistance from financial pros

• •

You've got your finances under control . . . finally! You're worry-ing less about money now and sleeping easier. Maybe you've even begun to rebuild your credit history with an eye to the future. Congratulations for facing your financial problems head-on and turning your situation around.

Now you face a new challenge: You must continue moving your financial life forward and not get hijacked by too much debt again.

In this chapter, we help you meet that challenge by reviewing key fundamentals of sound money management. We also suggest assembling a team of financial professionals to call on as you move forward, and we explain how each professional can help.

Setting Financial Goals

Now that you are no longer putting every nickel and dime toward your debts and essential expenses, you and your family members have probably begun thinking about how to spend the money you have left over each month, as well as about big-ticket items you would like to finance. Thinking about how to spend your money is fine. But if you start spending without having a plan, you are likely to end up right back in the same financial mess you were in when you first picked up this book. A far smarter approach is to estab-lish your financial goals and then to use your household budget to help achieve them. (See Chapter 4 for a refresher on budgeting.)

Your financial goals should be specific, realistic, time based, and flexible. For example, "By the end of 2007, I will have three creditors paid in full" or "By June 2007, I will have the money I need for a down payment on a car."

When you are setting your financial goals, place each goal into one of three categories:

- **Short-term goals:** These are goals that you believe you can accomplish within the next six months to one year, such as putting a certain amount of money in your savings, paying off a loan, outfitting your kids for the start of school, or having enough money to join a health club.

- **Medium-term goals:** These are goals that you feel you can achieve within the next five years, such as having enough money for a down payment on a home, paying off a car loan, or putting a certain amount of money in your retirement account.

- **Long-term goals:** These are goals that you project will take you longer than five years to achieve. They may include sending your kids to college, having enough money to retire, taking your dream vacation, and so on.

Be realistic about your goals and about how long it will take you to achieve each one. If you are not, you'll be setting yourself up for frustration and disappointment.

A short-term goal for you may be a medium-term or even a long-term goal for someone else. The specific category that a goal belongs in depends on your particular financial situation and on how quickly you want to achieve the goal.

Unless you are lucky enough to come into a financial windfall, you probably can't afford to work toward all your goals at the same time. If you try to do so, you may spread yourself so thin financially that you don't achieve any of them. Instead, prioritize your goals so you know which goals to focus on first. Most likely you will begin working toward short-term goals first because they are probably the most pressing, but you may be able to work on some of your medium- and long-term goals at the same time. For example, maybe you want to pay off your car loan over the next six months, and you also want to start stashing money away for a down payment on a home with the goal of having the money you need in two years.

After you decide which goals to work toward first, decide how you'll achieve each goal and set a realistic time frame for doing what you've set out to do. For example, you may decide to get a second job and put all the money you earn from it toward a certain goal. You may decide to finance another goal through a combination of cash and credit. Revise your budget as necessary.

Building a Financial Safety Net

One of your very first financial goals should be to build up your savings account so you have a financial safety net. Experts advise that you contribute a minimum of 10 percent of your net income to savings every month with the goal of having enough money in the account that you can pay your living expenses for at least six months if you lost your job. That account also allows you to pay cash, not credit, if you are hit with an unexpected big expense.

If you draw down your savings, start building it up again right away. Always be prepared for the next big expense or financial setback.

The easiest way to save is to have a set amount of money automatically deducted from each of your paychecks and deposited directly into your savings account. That way, you never have access to the money so you won't have to worry about spending it before it gets in the bank. Also, you get used to living without it.

Be realistic about the amount of money you can afford to save each month. If you decide to save $100 per paycheck and then you pull out $99 from your savings account to pay for some of your living expenses, you are defeating the purpose of your savings program.

Living with a Budget

In Part I of this book, we advise you to get your spending under control and pay down your debts by living on a budget. We also explain that a budget is a fundamental money management tool (see Chapter 4).

Now that your financial situation has improved, you may be tempted to toss your budget aside and just wing it when it comes to spending your money. Bad idea! Although the numbers in your budget will be different than they were when you had more debt, your budget continues to serve the same purpose as it did before: It helps you allocate your money wisely and know when you need to cut back on your spending. Now you can also use your budget to help you achieve your family's financial goals. Without budgeting for them, those goals may never become realities.

Be sure to review your budget periodically to make sure it continues to reflect your family's values and spending priorities. Also, be sure to revise your budget whenever your financial situation changes.

Managing Your Credit

Throughout this book, we explain a lot about using and abusing credit — as in what *not* to do. The same advice applies when your finances are in better shape. Here are some of the key points:

- ✔ Minimize your use of credit. Pay with cash whenever possible, even it if means that you can't buy something right away because you have to save for it.

- ✔ Avoid letting your credit card balances build. Pay them off as quickly as you can.

- ✔ When you are in the market for credit, shop around for the best terms of credit (see Chapter 16).

- ✔ Check your Equifax, Experian, and TransUnion credit histories every six months, and correct any problems you find. Order your FICO score twice a year as well (see Chapter 2).

- ✔ If you experience a financial setback and begin having problems paying your debts, get in touch with your creditors right away. They are more apt to help you work out a way to avoid a default if you get in touch before you fall behind on your payments.

Most car lenders can take back your car without any advance warning if you miss just one car payment (see Chapter 11).

- ✔ Whenever possible, avoid using your home as loan collateral and borrowing against the equity in your home.

- ✔ Know your credit rights, and don't be reluctant to exercise them. If you need advice about how to handle a money-related legal problem, consult with a consumer law attorney.

- ✔ Remember that credit offers that sound too good to be true are usually bad deals for you or even scams. Steer clear.

Increasing Your Money Management 1Q

All of us can afford to get smarter about money. As students, most of us learned nothing about using credit, managing our money, and making consumer laws work for us. That big hole in your education may be the reason you used to be up to your neck in debt.

In this age of information, there is a wealth of resources for finding out more about money. We recommend that you start your education by using the resources in the following list. Many of them will lead you to other reliable resources that can provide you with more in-depth coverage of the topics you are most interested in:

- ✔ **Bankrate.com (www.bankrate.com):** This Web site gets our vote as one of the best online resources for basic information on a wide variety of financial management topics. It covers credit, debt, home buying, car buying, taxes . . . if you've got a money question, it's an excellent starting point for finding answers.

- ✔ *Bottom Line/Personal* **and** *Bottom Line/Retirement:* These quick-and-easy-to-read monthly newsletters are packed with useful information from the world's leading experts. *Bottom Line/Personal* focuses on a variety of everyday subjects, including money. *Bottom Line/Retirement* is more narrowly focused. Each publication costs $39 per year. To subscribe to either or both, go to www.boardroom.com.

- ✔ *Kiplinger's Personal Finance Magazine:* This is the nation's first personal finance magazine. Every month, it covers a variety of subjects including saving, buying a home or car, using credit cards, investing, and planning for college and retirement. You can find a copy at a newsstand or library, or you can check it out online at www.kiplinger.com/personal finance. An annual subscription costs $23.95.

- ✔ **MSNmoney.com (www.msnmoney.com):** This Web site draws on the talents and knowledge of a wide variety of nationally known financial experts to bring you stories on subjects related to spending, banking, investing, taxes, and financial planning. When you're at the site, sign up for free subscriptions to a variety of money-related newsletters.

Our list would not be complete without noting some other *For Dummies* books (all published by Wiley) that you may want to read in your quest to become a more informed money manager:

- ✔ *Buying a Car For Dummies* by Deanna Sclar

- ✔ *Frugal Living For Dummies* by Deborah Taylor-Hough

- ✔ *Home Buying For Dummies,* 3rd Edition, by Eric Tyson, MBA, and Ray Brown

- ✔ *House Selling For Dummies,* 2nd Edition, by Eric Tyson, MBA, and Ray Brown

✔ *Investing For Dummies,* 4th Edition, by Eric Tyson, MBA

✔ *Managing Your Money Online For Dummies* by Kathleen Sindell

✔ *Personal Finance For Dummies,* 5th Edition, by Eric Tyson, MBA

✔ *Real Estate Investing For Dummies* by Eric Tyson, MBA, and Robert S. Griswold

For more information about these titles, go to www.dummies.com. You can also sign up at the site to receive regular e-tips on making and managing money.

Assembling a Team of Financial Advisors

As your finances improve, you'll have more money to spend and invest, your assets will grow (we hope), and Uncle Sam will want to take a bigger bite out of your income. The more money and other assets you have, the more important it is for you to have a team of financial advisors in place who can answer your questions, help you plan your finances, assist you with your taxes, and help you avoid money-related problems. Depending on your particular situation and on how much of your financial planning and management you want to do yourself, you may want to maintain an ongoing relationship with some of the advisors we list in this section, or you may need their help only periodically.

It can be especially helpful to consult with financial professionals just before or after important life events such as marriage, divorce, the birth or adoption of a child, retirement, the death of a spouse, the receipt of an inheritance, and so on. Each of these events can have important implications for taxes, insurance, investing, and estate planning.

Naming the players

Consider making the advisors on the following list part of your financial team. Although you may not need their help right away, we suggest that you identify the ones you'd like to work with *before* you need their assistance:

✔ **A certified public accountant (CPA):** A CPA can help you manage your money better, fine-tune your savings and investment strategies, and reduce the income tax you owe each year. Some CPAs also prepare tax returns; in fact, some specialize in helping individuals deal with tax-related matters.

The more complicated your taxes — you own rental property, you or your spouse is self-employed, you have a home office, and so on — the more valuable the help of a tax CPA can be. The CPA can help you avoid expensive mistakes that cost you more in taxes and can suggest ways to minimize how much you owe in taxes.

✔ **A financial planner:** A financial planner offers many of the same services as a CPA; some CPAs are also financial planners. A financial planner can help you develop a financial plan to achieve your financial goals and assist you with the implementation of financial planning strategies. The financial planner can also identify financial issues and problems you should address and act as a sounding board when you are getting ready to make a major purchase (like a home) or when you are thinking about making a major life change (such as retiring). She can help you be sure that you have thought through all the issues related to taking that step. Financial planners can also help you decide which investments make the most sense for you.

When you're in the market for a financial planner, steer clear of *commission-based* planners. They make their money by trying to convince consumers to purchase financial products such as insurance, mutual funds, and annuities — products a consumer may or may not need. A better choice is to work with a *fee-based* (or *fee-only*) planner. This sort of planner gets paid by charging a percentage of the dollar value of the assets he manages for you, like stocks, mutual funds, and bonds (but not real estate). A third type of financial planner charges by the hour. This kind of financial planner is most apt to take a big picture look at your finances because he is not trying to sell your products or make money by managing your investments.

✔ **An estate-planning attorney:** This kind of attorney is not just for rich people. If you have assets and you want to be sure that when you die they go to certain people, you need this person's help. He can advise you about various estate-planning tools you may want to use in order to control who ends up with your stuff; these tools include a will, a living trust, an irrevocable trust, and life insurance. He can also help you plan for the management of your finances should you become temporarily or permanently incapacitated and be unable to make your own financial decisions.

✔ **An insurance broker or agent:** Having adequate insurance is an essential aspect of managing your finances and protecting yourself from financial loss. Insurance can also be an important part of your estate plan. An insurance agent or broker advises you about your insurance needs, helps you find the best insurance, and assists you when you're having problems with your insurance company.

An insurance *agent* sells insurance for a specific company, which means that if you work with an agent, your insurance choices are limited. An insurance *broker,* on the other hand, reviews all the insurance products on the market, or those being sold by a wide range of companies, and identifies the products that are best for you.

The assistance of financial advisors can be especially helpful if you receive a substantial inheritance, are nearing retirement, have children and want to begin planning for their college educations, experience a financial setback, begin making substantially more money than you have earned in the past, and so on. Although their advice and assistance cost money, the investment can save you lots of money in the long run.

Finding reliable advisors

The best sources of referrals for the professionals you want on your financial team are the friends, family members, and professional associates whose opinions you respect.

Get the names of several different CPAs, financial planners, and so on. Meet with all of them to find out how they work, how they charge for their services, and if the chemistry between the two of you is right. Go to each meeting armed with a set of questions and a pad of paper for taking notes.

Other sources of referrals to financial professionals include your banker, a financial professional, and the consumer law attorney you may have worked with to clear up your debt problems. Also, organizations such as these can help:

- ✔ Your state or local bar association or the Web site of the American Academy of Estate Planning Attorneys, www. search-attorneys.com

- ✔ The Web site of the Independent Insurance Agents and Brokers of America, www.iiaba.net/agentlocator/ findagent.aspx

- ✔ The Web site of The Financial Planning Association, www.fpanet.org/plannersearch/search.cfm

- ✔ The Web site of the American Institute of Certified Public Accountants, pfp.aicpa.org

Part V
The Part of Tens

The 5th Wave   By Rich Tennant

"Coming out of bankruptcy, I can say I learned my lesson—don't spend what your relatives don't have."

In this part . . .

To end this book, we share some final nuggets of advice and information. First, we focus your attention on additional resources you can turn to for help getting out of debt and managing your future finances. Next, we warn you against trying to manage your debts by taking steps that are likely to backfire.

Chapter 18

Ten Great Resources for Dealing with Debt

· ·

In This Chapter

▶ Finding free financial advice and information

▶ Getting credit and debt information from the federal government

▶ Knowing about organizations you can turn to for help

▶ Discovering newsletters and other resources

▶ Locating a good consumer bankruptcy attorney

· ·

*W*e would like to think that this book is all you need to handle your debts and improve your finances, but we're no dummies! We understand that you may need additional help and information, including one-on-one assistance. So in this chapter we share ten great resources for dealing with your debts and discovering more about how to use credit responsibly.

To write this chapter, we culled our data banks, consulted with our associates, and searched the Web. We feel confident that when you couple the benefits of the resources we highlight here with what you gain from reading our book (not to mention with your own hard work), you'll soon be out of debt and on the road to wealth, enjoying a life free of financial *Sturm und Drang.*

American Bankruptcy Institute (ABI)

If you think that filing for bankruptcy may be in the cards for you, visit the ABI's Web site to gain an overview of how the process works. Go to www.abiworld.org and click on "Consumer Education Center."

While you're there, you can also search for an ABI-certified consumer bankruptcy attorney in your area. Attorneys who are ABI-certified have demonstrated a special interest and expertise in consumer bankruptcy law by passing a comprehensive, daylong written ABI exam and committing to participate in at least 60 hours of legal continuing education over a three-year period. ABI certification is the gold standard in bankruptcy law certification.

Bankrate.com

This ambitious Web site (www.bankrate.com) is first rate. It covers the gamut of financial topics but does an especially good job explaining various issues related to using credit and managing debt. The site is updated daily and is a great place to find reliable information about the latest news related to those subjects. In addition, the site features a variety of online calculators and a free e-mail newsletter.

A Consumer Bankruptcy Attorney

Consulting with a bankruptcy attorney is a smart step to take before your finances are in desperate shape and you have no alternative but to file for bankruptcy. The attorney can provide you with advice about how to avoid bankruptcy, when filing for bankruptcy is a good idea, and what you should and should not do to get the maximum benefit from filing. It's best to work with a board-certified bankruptcy attorney. Some states certify bankruptcy attorneys, and the American Bankruptcy Institute provides qualified bankruptcy attorneys with national certification.

Credit.com

This attractive Web site (www.credit.com) features sound, up-to-date information on the laws that affect you when you use credit; your credit-related rights and responsibilities; and money management checklists, worksheets, and calculators. Sign up for Tidbits, the site's e-mail newsletter that features articles written by personal finance experts.

The Debt-Proof Living Newsletter

Formerly called *Cheapskate Monthly,* this publication provides lots of information and advice to help you make every dollar count when money is tight, or anytime. For more information about the newsletter or to subscribe, go to www.cheapskatemonthly.com.

DebtSmart

This Web site (www.debtsmart.com) is loaded with articles, advice, and online tools to help you manage your debt and make wise credit decisions. You can also sign up for a free subscription to DebtSmart's e-mail newsletter.

The Federal Trade Commission (FTC)

The FTC enforces a wide variety of consumer protection laws related to debt collectors, credit reporting, credit repair, credit applications, and more. It also produces a prodigious number of helpful fact sheets and brochures on credit-related laws, issues related to borrowing money and using credit cards, and a variety of other consumer-oriented topics. Best of all, most of the agency's publications are free! Click your mouse on www.ftc.gov/ftc/consumer.htm to take advantage of the FTC's treasure trove of information.

The National Consumer Law Center

This national nonprofit organization is the nation's leading advocate for low-income consumers. It helps them resolve problems with utility terminations, foreclosures, repossessions, debt collectors, and other debt-related issues. On its Web site (www.consumerlaw.org), it offers free information on some of these topics and sells a number of books on consumer issues, including the *NCLC Guide to Surviving Debt.*

The National Foundation for Credit Counseling (NFCC)

This national nonprofit organization has close to 1,000 offices around the country, many of which are known as Consumer Credit Counseling Service. The offices offer a variety of services by phone or in person, including budget counseling and education, debt management plans, and classes in financial literacy. (Some offices also provide services via the Internet.) All NFCC counselors have been highly trained and certified.

Depending on your income level, NFCC's services may be free; otherwise they will be low cost. For more information about the NFCC and to find an NFCC member nearest you, go to www.nfcc.org or call 800-388-2227.

Suze Orman

Although we think she's just a tad quirky, this nationally known financial personality dispenses consistently sound, down-to-earth advice on her regular Saturday night CNBC television show. She also pens a monthly column for *O: The Oprah Magazine,* and she is the author of numerous books, including *The 9 Steps to Financial Freedom* (Three Rivers Press), *The Laws of Money: 5 Timeless Secrets to Get Out and Stay out of Financial Trouble* (Free Press), and *The Money Book for the Young, Fabulous & Broke* (Riverhead Books).

Chapter 19

Ten Debt Don'ts

*W*hen you are worried about the amount of money you owe to your creditors and confused about how to handle your debts, it's easy to do things that you later regret.

Although there are plenty of ways that you can trip up when you are struggling to keep up with your debts, in this chapter we warn you about the ten most common mistakes we've seen consumers make. We hope that our warnings help you avoid some headaches and hassles.

Ignoring Your Debts

When you feel overwhelmed by your debts, you may be tempted to stuff bills and notices from your creditors in a drawer, and you probably don't return creditors' calls. Bad idea!

Sweeping your debts under the rug just leads to higher bills because interest and late fees keep coming. You end up at greater risk for being sued by your creditors, having your car repossessed, losing your home (or being evicted if you're a renter), and having your utilities shut off. So no matter how much it hurts, open those bills, return your creditors' calls, and put a plan in place for dealing with your debts.

Falling Behind on Car Payments

If you don't stay current on your car loan, you risk having your car repossessed. As we explain in Chapter 11, repossession can happen without any warning after just a single missed payment. One day you have your car, and the next day you don't. If you need your vehicle to earn a living, losing it could spell disaster for your finances. At the very least, it makes life more difficult for you and your family.

Managing Money Without a Budget

It's foolhardy to think that you can get out of debt without using a written household budget to help you reduce your spending and manage what you do with your money. No tool is more fundamental to managing your debts and to ensuring that your limited dollars go toward paying your top priority debts and living expenses.

Review your written budget each pay period to make sure it continues to reflect the state of your finances and so you can decide if you want to revise your budget — allocate more of your income to savings, for example. If you haven't already done so, be sure to read Chapter 4.

Paying Creditors Just Because They're Aggressive

When money is tight and you don't have enough to pay all your debts, never make decisions about which ones you'll pay based on which creditors hound you the most. The ones that bother you the most may be the creditors you should pay last.

Base your decisions instead on the consequences of not keeping up with a particular debt. The bigger and badder the consequences, the more important it is to pay the debt. For example, if you don't pay your mortgage, you could lose your home; if you fall behind on your car loan, your vehicle will be repossessed; and if you don't pay your federal taxes or your child support, you're at risk for a wide range of possible consequences, none of them pleasant.

On the other hand, say that you don't pay your credit card debts. Yes, the credit card companies may eventually sue you to get the court's permission to garnish your wages, seize some of your assets, and so on. But that process takes time — unlike a repossession, for example. And if your debts are not large, a credit card company may decide to write off what you owe as bad debt. Furthermore, you can use bankruptcy to get rid of credit card debt, but filing for bankruptcy won't erase your obligation to pay your mortgage, car loan, federal taxes, or child support.

Making Promises That You Can't Keep

When a creditor contacts you about a past-due debt, or when you contact the creditor to negotiate a way to catch up on past-due payments and stay current on future payments, never agree to pay more than you truly believe you can afford. Base your decision on your household budget.

When you don't have enough money in your checking account to pay what you owe to a creditor, don't give the creditor a postdated check, gambling that by the time the date of the check arrives, the money you need to cover it will be in your account. There is nothing to stop the creditor from depositing the check before its date, which could cause the check to bounce. If that happens, you have to pay an insufficient funds fee to the bank, and you have to pay a fee to the creditor as well. On top of that, if you can't come up with the money you need to make good on the check, you may be prosecuted for passing a bad check.

If you over-promise and then begin having problems living up to the agreement, you lose credibility. That makes it difficult (perhaps impossible) to negotiate any additional concessions. Also, if you default on the agreement you made with a creditor, you may find that the full amount you owe — not just the past-due amount — becomes due immediately.

Continuing To Use Credit Cards

It's a no-brainer! If you're having problems keeping up with your credit card payments, don't rack up more credit card debt. If you can't afford to pay for something with cash, don't buy it.

Help yourself out by leaving your credit cards at home. For even greater protection, put your credit cards in a plastic bag of water and then place the bag in your freezer. If you're tempted to use your cards, by the time the ice has melted, you may think better of it.

Borrowing Against Your Home

When you're having problems making ends meet, don't put your home on the line. You may be tempted to borrow against the equity you've built up or to use your home as collateral to get another type of loan. Don't. If you can't afford to keep up with your loan payments, you could lose what is probably your most valuable asset.

Working with a For-Profit Credit Counseling Agency

Always work with a nonprofit credit counseling agency, not a for-profit agency. A for-profit credit counseling agency is in business to make as much money as possible off your financial woes. Therefore, you cannot trust that its recommendations are in your best interest. Some for-profit agencies may tell you to do things that make them money at your expense and that could get you into legal hot water.

Getting a High-Risk Loan

Some for-profit credit counseling agencies try to loan you money, claiming that the loan is a way out of your financial morass. Other creditors, like finance companies, also claim that their loans will help you deal with your debts. Always beware of loan offers that are made by nontraditional lenders, especially offers that require you to use as collateral your home, car, or some other asset that you don't want to lose.

Although loans from nontraditional lenders may sound tempting, steer clear. If you read the loan paperwork carefully, you find that the loans are a very expensive source of cash and that the terms actually set you up to lose your collateral.

Asking a Friend or Relative to Cosign a Loan

If you cannot qualify for a loan from a traditional lender because of the state of your finances, think twice before you ask a friend or family member to help you get the loan by cosigning for it. If someone you know is the cosigner and then you fall behind on your loan payments, the lender will look to your friend or family member for the money you owe. Not only may paying your loan put your cosigner in a financial bind; it may very well ruin your relationship.

Index

BUSINESS, CAREERS & PERSONAL FINANCE

0-7645-5307-0   0-7645-5331-3 *†

Also available:

✔Accounting For Dummies †
0-7645-5314-3

✔Business Plans Kit For Dummies †
0-7645-5365-8

✔Cover Letters For Dummies
0-7645-5224-4

✔Frugal Living For Dummies
0-7645-5403-4

✔Leadership For Dummies
0-7645-5176-0

✔Managing For Dummies
0-7645-1771-6

✔Marketing For Dummies
0-7645-5600-2

✔Personal Finance For Dummies *
0-7645-2590-5

✔Project Management
For Dummies
0-7645-5283-X

✔Resumes For Dummies †
0-7645-5471-9

✔Selling For Dummies
0-7645-5363-1

✔Small Business Kit For Dummies *†
0-7645-5093-4

HOME & BUSINESS COMPUTER BASICS

0-7645-4074-2   0-7645-3758-X

Also available:

✔ACT! 6 For Dummies
0-7645-2645-6

✔iLife '04 All-in-One Desk Reference
For Dummies
0-7645-7347-0

✔iPAQ For Dummies
0-7645-6769-1

✔Mac OS X Panther Timesaving
Techniques For Dummies
0-7645-5812-9

✔Macs For Dummies
0-7645-5656-8

✔Microsoft Money 2004 For Dummies
0-7645-4195-1

✔Office 2003 All-in-One Desk
Reference For Dummies
0-7645-3883-7

✔Outlook 2003 For Dummies
0-7645-3759-8

✔PCs For Dummies
0-7645-4074-2

✔TiVo For Dummies
0-7645-6923-6

✔Upgrading and Fixing PCs
For Dummies
0-7645-1665-5

✔Windows XP Timesaving
Techniques For Dummies
0-7645-3748-2

FOOD, HOME, GARDEN, HOBBIES, MUSIC & PETS

0-7645-5295-3   0-7645-5232-5

Also available:

✔Bass Guitar For Dummies
0-7645-2487-9

✔Diabetes Cookbook For Dummies
0-7645-5230-9

✔Gardening For Dummies *
0-7645-5130-2

✔Guitar For Dummies
0-7645-5106-X

✔Holiday Decorating For Dummies
0-7645-2570-0

✔Home Improvement All-in-One
For Dummies
0-7645-5680-0

✔Knitting For Dummies
0-7645-5395-X

✔Piano For Dummies
0-7645-5105-1

✔Puppies For Dummies
0-7645-5255-4

✔Scrapbooking For Dummies
0-7645-7208-3

✔Senior Dogs For Dummies
0-7645-5818-8

✔Singing For Dummies
0-7645-2475-5

✔30-Minute Meals For Dummies
0-7645-2589-1

INTERNET & DIGITAL MEDIA

0-7645-1664-7   0-7645-6924-4

Also available:

✔2005 Online Shopping Directory
For Dummies
0-7645-7495-7

✔CD & DVD Recording For Dummies
0-7645-5956-7

✔eBay For Dummies
0-7645-5654-1

✔Fighting Spam For Dummies
0-7645-5965-6

✔Genealogy Online For Dummies
0-7645-5964-8

✔Google For Dummies
0-7645-4420-9

✔Home Recording For Musicians
For Dummies
0-7645-1634-5

✔The Internet For Dummies
0-7645-4173-0

✔iPod & iTunes For Dummies
0-7645-7772-7

✔Preventing Identity Theft
For Dummies
0-7645-7336-5

✔Pro Tools All-in-One Desk
Reference For Dummies
0-7645-5714-9

✔Roxio Easy Media Creator
For Dummies
0-7645-7131-1

* Separate Canadian edition also available
† Separate U.K. edition also available

Available wherever books are sold. For more information or to order direct: U.S. customers
visit www.dummies.com or call 1-877-762-2974.
U.K. customers visit www.wileyeurope.com or call 0800 243407. Canadian customers visit
www.wiley.ca or call 1-800-567-4797.

SPORTS, FITNESS, PARENTING, RELIGION & SPIRITUALITY

0-7645-5146-9   0-7645-5418-2

Also available:
- Adoption For Dummies
  0-7645-5488-3
- Basketball For Dummies
  0-7645-5248-1
- The Bible For Dummies
  0-7645-5296-1
- Buddhism For Dummies
  0-7645-5359-3
- Catholicism For Dummies
  0-7645-5391-7
- Hockey For Dummies
  0-7645-5228-7

- Judaism For Dummies
  0-7645-5299-6
- Martial Arts For Dummies
  0-7645-5358-5
- Pilates For Dummies
  0-7645-5397-6
- Religion For Dummies
  0-7645-5264-3
- Teaching Kids to Read
  For Dummies
  0-7645-4043-2
- Weight Training For Dummies
  0-7645-5168-X
- Yoga For Dummies
  0-7645-5117-5

TRAVEL

0-7645-5438-7   0-7645-5453-0

Also available:
- Alaska For Dummies
  0-7645-1761-9
- Arizona For Dummies
  0-7645-6938-4
- Cancún and the Yucatán
  For Dummies
  0-7645-2437-2
- Cruise Vacations For Dummies
  0-7645-6941-4
- Europe For Dummies
  0-7645-5456-5
- Ireland For Dummies
  0-7645-5455-7

- Las Vegas For Dummies
  0-7645-5448-4
- London For Dummies
  0-7645-4277-X
- New York City For Dummies
  0-7645-6945-7
- Paris For Dummies
  0-7645-5494-8
- RV Vacations For Dummies
  0-7645-5443-3
- Walt Disney World & Orlando
  For Dummies
  0-7645-6943-0

GRAPHICS, DESIGN & WEB DEVELOPMENT

0-7645-4345-8   0-7645-5589-8

Also available:
- Adobe Acrobat 6 PDF
  For Dummies
  0-7645-3760-1
- Building a Web Site For Dummies
  0-7645-7144-3
- Dreamweaver MX 2004
  For Dummies
  0-7645-4342-3
- FrontPage 2003 For Dummies
  0-7645-3882-9
- HTML 4 For Dummies
  0-7645-1995-6
- Illustrator CS For Dummies
  0-7645-4084-X

- Macromedia Flash MX 2004
  For Dummies
  0-7645-4358-X
- Photoshop 7 All-in-One Desk
  Reference For Dummies
  0-7645-1667-1
- Photoshop CS Timesaving
  Techniques For Dummies
  0-7645-6782-9
- PHP 5 For Dummies
  0-7645-4166-8
- PowerPoint 2003 For Dummies
  0-7645-3908-6
- QuarkXPress 6 For Dummies
  0-7645-2593-X

NETWORKING, SECURITY, PROGRAMMING & DATABASES

0-7645-6852-3   0-7645-5784-X

Also available:
- A+ Certification For Dummies
  0-7645-4187-0
- Access 2003 All-in-One Desk
  Reference For Dummies
  0-7645-3988-4
- Beginning Programming
  For Dummies
  0-7645-4997-9
- C For Dummies
  0-7645-7068-4
- Firewalls For Dummies
  0-7645-4048-3
- Home Networking For Dummies
  0-7645-42796

- Network Security For Dummies
  0-7645-1679-5
- Networking For Dummies
  0-7645-1677-9
- TCP/IP For Dummies
  0-7645-1760-0
- VBA For Dummies
  0-7645-3989-2
- Wireless All In-One Desk Reference
  For Dummies
  0-7645-7496-5
- Wireless Home Networking
  For Dummies
  0-7645-3910-8

HEALTH & SELF-HELP

0-7645-6820-5 *†   0-7645-2566-2

Also available:
- Alzheimer's For Dummies
  0-7645-3899-3
- Asthma For Dummies
  0-7645-4233-8
- Controlling Cholesterol For Dummies
  0-7645-5440-9
- Depression For Dummies
  0-7645-3900-0
- Dieting For Dummies
  0-7645-4149-8
- Fertility For Dummies
  0-7645-2549-2

- Fibromyalgia For Dummies
  0-7645-5441-7
- Improving Your Memory For Dummies
  0-7645-5435-2
- Pregnancy For Dummies †
  0-7645-4483-7
- Quitting Smoking For Dummies
  0-7645-2629-4
- Relationships For Dummies
  0-7645-5384-4
- Thyroid For Dummies
  0-7645-5385-2

EDUCATION, HISTORY, REFERENCE & TEST PREPARATION

0-7645-5194-9   0-7645-4186-2

Also available:
- Algebra For Dummies
  0-7645-5325-9
- British History For Dummies
  0-7645-7021-8
- Calculus For Dummies
  0-7645-2498-4
- English Grammar For Dummies
  0-7645-5322-4
- Forensics For Dummies
  0-7645-5580-4
- The GMAT For Dummies
  0-7645-5251-1
- Inglés Para Dummies
  0-7645-5427-1

- Italian For Dummies
  0-7645-5196-5
- Latin For Dummies
  0-7645-5431-X
- Lewis & Clark For Dummies
  0-7645-2545-X
- Research Papers For Dummies
  0-7645-5426-3
- The SAT I For Dummies
  0-7645-7193-1
- Science Fair Projects For Dummies
  0-7645-5460-3
- U.S. History For Dummies
  0-7645-5249-X

Get smart @ dummies.com®

- Find a full list of Dummies titles
- Look into loads of FREE on-site articles
- Sign up for FREE eTips e-mailed to you weekly
- See what other products carry the Dummies name
- Shop directly from the Dummies bookstore
- Enter to win new prizes every month!